How I Found Myself in the Midwest

A Memoir of Reinvention

STEVE GROVE

SIMON & SCHUSTER

New York   Amsterdam/Antwerp   London
Toronto   Sydney/Melbourne   New Delhi

Simon & Schuster
1230 Avenue of the Americas
New York, NY 10020

First Simon & Schuster hardcover edition June 2025

SIMON & SCHUSTER and colophon are registered trademarks of Simon & Schuster, LLC

Simon & Schuster strongly believes in freedom of expression and stands against censorship in all its forms. For more information, visit BooksBelong.com.

For information about special discounts for bulk purchases, please contact Simon & Schuster Special Sales at 1-866-506-1949 or business@simonandschuster.com.

The Simon & Schuster Speakers Bureau can bring authors to your live event. For more information or to book an event, contact the Simon & Schuster Speakers Bureau at 1-866-248-3049 or visit our website at www.simonspeakers.com.

Interior design by Lexy East

Manufactured in the United States of America

10 9 8 7 6 5 4 3 2 1

Library of Congress Control Number: 2025007357

ISBN 978-1-6680-6244-9
ISBN 978-1-6680-6247-0 (ebook)

For Mary, always

Contents

Contents

Author's Note

This book is a story told through my perspective, and I've done my best to tell it as accurately as I can. In some areas, I relied on public documents, news reports, and interviews with colleagues, friends, and family to fill in gaps or enrich my own memory. When quoting people, I've done my best to record their words accurately. In some cases I've used news reports, which are referenced in the notes at the end of the book. Other times, I tried to capture the spirit of conversations.

I received the help of many people to review portions of the book for accuracy. Where the story is imperfect, I'm solely responsible for any errors.

Part I

Landing

Chapter 1

From the Valley to the Prairie

On a windy fall day on the back patio of Eggy's Red Garter in Eveleth, Minnesota, I stood in front of twenty-five angry small business owners. Sitting on folding chairs perfectly spaced six feet apart, they glared at me with a collective grimace.

Proprietors of bars and restaurants of this and a handful of other small towns on Minnesota's Iron Range, they'd gathered for a town hall to discuss the governor's COVID-19 restrictions. It was October 6, 2020.

Margie Koivunen, owner of the Roosevelt Bar next door, took a microphone attached to a portable karaoke machine. Tall and somber, she'd become a leading voice in a local hospitality community that was fed up with pandemic restrictions. She held tightly to the yellow legal pad pages of a handwritten speech that flapped in the wind as she began.

"Your one-size-fits-all restrictions on businesses don't make any sense up here," she said. "We don't have the same COVID cases here like you have down in the Twin Cities."

For the last several months, the state government's business closures and limits on capacity in bars, restaurants, and other businesses had generated no end of controversy. Especially in rural parts of Minnesota. "I've tried to call the governor's office several times and got no answer," she complained.

Then she turned to her fellow small business owners. "Could all of you please stand up?" she asked.

As everyone rose to their feet, the intensity of their disgust felt suddenly stronger. "Now, please sit down when the following statement applies to you: How many of you have taken out a bank loan?"

Several people sat down.

"How many of you have laid off or terminated employees?" Several more sat down.

"How many of you have dealt with stress, anxiety, or depression?" Margie joined the rest of the small business owners as everyone took a seat. "I've long since sat down," she concluded.

The wind was really blowing now, and suddenly the pages of her speech fluttered from her grasp. I jumped forward and grabbed them off the ground before they blew away.

"Nice reflexes," I heard someone mutter. I handed Margie her speech back and hoped the moment provided a bit of levity.

But this was not a crowd in a mood to smile.

I shouldn't have been surprised. For months I'd been hosting roundtables like this one with business owners across Minnesota, sharing the latest pandemic news and hearing their feedback on our efforts to slow the spread of the virus. Most of these conversations happened in my basement, over video conference. But being here in rural Minnesota, in person, felt a lot different. Looking someone straight in the eye who might be losing their business felt a lot different than seeing them on a screen.

Dave Lislegard, the Democratic state representative from this area seated behind me, had invited me to come to his district a few weeks earlier. Getting the commissioner of the state's economic and workforce development agency to come listen to his constituents would make a difference, he said. He didn't have to tell me, but I knew he was also in a tough reelection battle.

Margie handed the microphone to other business owners who expressed their frustration. They talked about having to take second jobs to keep their restaurants afloat. They complained about lack of government assistance. One business owner said his cooks were getting so overheated from wearing masks in the kitchen that they had to cool off in the walk-in freezer.

But mostly, they groaned about the restrictions coming out of the capital, St. Paul. They argued that it was different in Greater Minnesota (what Minnesotans call the parts of the state outside the Twin Cities metropolitan area) and therefore the same restrictions need not apply to them.

Why couldn't we see that?

The pandemic had started seven months earlier, but it felt like seven years. When I joined the governor's cabinet to help grow the economy of my home state the year before, I'd been excited to focus on growth. Success would be measured by the number of startups we could help get off the ground, or the number of small businesses that succeeded under our watch. Our wins would come in the number of innovative businesses we could attract to Minnesota and the jobs we'd create.

But now my job was exactly the opposite. To slow the spread of this deadly new virus, we were shutting down small businesses to keep people safe. I was helping hundreds of thousands of people leave the workplace and get on unemployment insurance. We weren't creating jobs—we were killing them. Minnesota lost over 416,000 jobs in the first month alone.

From the first days of the pandemic, our newly elected governor, Tim Walz—whom I'd known since his upset victory for a congressional seat back in 2006—had asked me to serve as his point person with the business community. Alongside our state's health commissioner, I was tasked with advising him on what our economic approach should be in the crisis, and communicating those decisions to the public.

Like every state government, we were operating without a playbook. Meetings ran around the clock, where we debated our approach to school closures, business restrictions, social-distancing protocols, PPE disbursement, and more.

And every day at 2:00 p.m., we addressed the public in statewide press conferences live on television, sharing the latest information we had and explaining our approach. Under the bright lights of local news media and reporters, my job was to articulate what our business restrictions were, how they worked, and why we were doing what we were doing. I also had to introduce how unemployment insurance worked to thousands of people who never imagined that they'd need it. I myself had only been vaguely aware that the unemployment insurance program was part of the agency I was being asked to lead when I started this job, until my first day, when I had to sign a piece of paper to capture my signature to print on the checks that we issued to people.

Now I was the face of the program to more than 5 million Minnesotans, many desperate for a lifeline. Every customer service complaint mattered, and our system and team were overwhelmed. I heard countless tragic stories of people struggling every day.

How had I found myself here?

My story is a story about coming home. It's a story about taking a very different turn in life, trying something different, and letting it take me somewhere new. It's a story about reinventing myself and investing in community at a time when America often feels unmoored. It's a story that, I hope, offers a fresh perspective to those who are looking for a new way forward in their lives at a time of great upheaval.

Just a few years earlier, I wasn't even living in Minnesota. My wife, Mary, and I were firmly planted in an area of California that's bustling with new ideas and flooded with sunshine. In the heart of Silicon Valley, we lived in Menlo Park—just a few miles from Meta and a few more miles from Google, where we both worked. We'd met at the company, were married in Mary's hometown of San Diego, and had begun a comfortable life together in the Bay Area. We were happy living in the cradle of American innovation.

Every day, I would ride my Vespa scooter fifteen minutes to the Googleplex in the sun, where I led a team that I had started, called the Google News Lab, focused on using Google's resources to help the news industry. Mary was the founder of Google for Startups, a similar outreach effort with a different target—startup companies around the world who would use Google tools to grow faster.

We had incredible colleagues, big budgets; we built global teams and traveled the world. In our living room hung a map with pushpins for every country we'd visited for work, either alone or together. After a while, there were too many pushpins to count.

I loved working in tech, even if I'd stumbled into it. I was a journalist and a teacher who spent much of my twenties doing what I might generously describe as "focused wandering." I taught English in Japan, worked for my dad's small landscaping business, and moved to Boston to do freelance journalism for a few years. Then I went to grad school for public policy, thinking it might make me a sharper journalist. By then, I'd racked up a considerable amount of debt and wasn't sure how I was going to pay it off. Truth was, I didn't really know where I was headed.

And then I discovered YouTube while posting clips for a class project in grad school. I became enthralled with the new phenomenon of online video. Watching people create videos by themselves seen by millions, defining "viral" for the first time in the internet age, I became transfixed. A British senior citizen with the handle Geriatric1927 posted a two-minute video called "First Try," where he shared his "geriatric gripes and grumbles," and quietly racked up over a million views. A pair of high school pranksters calling themselves "Smosh" posted goofy songs and skits and suddenly become stars. It seemed like, overnight, everyone had a broadcast TV truck in their pocket. And the phenomenon instantly started shaping news and politics.

In the 2006 midterm elections, the incumbent senator from

Virginia, George Allen, was caught on video calling his opponent's campaign staffer a "macaca"—a clip that was uploaded to YouTube and became the first viral political video to make national news. The racist quip unearthed deeper issues with Allen's views that commentators claimed swung the election toward his opponent, Jim Webb (though just barely). Not only did that hand the seat to Democrats, but it flipped the entire U.S. Senate.

YouTube Politics was born.

I'd never worked in technology, but was blown away by how this new medium was changing the world around me. With nothing to lose, I sent a one-page letter to info@youtube.com, pitching myself for a position as "news and politics editor," which somehow caught the eye of the right person. The team brought me on board to figure out how, exactly, YouTube should play a role in this new space.

I arrived as one of the first one hundred employees of the company, just as global attention was turning to YouTube and a sudden influx of new cash was coming in from its new owner, Google, to fuel growth.

For the next four years, I built a small team and was shocked when everyone kept answering our calls. I found myself in places I really had no business being. We landed a debate partnership with CNN, the first-ever web-to-TV presidential debates, where YouTubers got to ask questions. Sitting in the front row of the CNN-YouTube presidential primary debate, watching YouTube questions from hospital patients, college professors, schoolkids, and even snowmen (*How will you combat climate change?*) play on the big screen as Barack Obama, Hillary Clinton, and eight other candidates looked on, I pinched myself. Was this really happening?

Sitting next to me were YouTube's founders, Chad Hurley and Steve Chen, and Google's CEO, Eric Schmidt. When the debate was over, Eric turned to Steve and Chad and told them, "Gentlemen, you've arrived."

And that's what it felt like—that technology's moment had arrived on the biggest stage and I was lucky to be a part of it. In those days it all looked like upside. Those already in power now had to answer to those who'd gained power through new platforms. Giving power to the powerless, a voice to the voiceless, felt deeply meaningful.

What could go wrong?

The power of technology in our lives, of course, only increased with each passing year that I was at YouTube, and continued when I moved on to Google. Rising the executive ranks in the world's most innovative company was exhilarating. A sense that anything was possible ran through the company, a feeling that we had the power to do anything. We were moving fast and focused on the upside more than any unintended consequences.

After more than a decade at Google, my view slowly began to change. Being in the cradle of innovation was starting to feel oddly confining. It wasn't just Google, it was Silicon Valley. As a region dominated by one industry, the Valley was starting to feel like a bubble. Yes, tech companies in California were building things that changed the world, but it felt like sometimes we weren't connected to it. Highly affluent and professionally obsessed, the culture of Silicon Valley doesn't look much like the rest of the country, let alone the world that it seeks to change through its groundbreaking innovations.

I worried that I was starting to lose some perspective. Free breakfast, lunch, and dinner at the Googleplex every day is a luxury. So is a campus with everything from a wave pool and climbing gym to a concert hall. But I started to ask myself if the magical kingdom that Google had created was making me smarter about the world or more insulated from it.

I grew up in Northfield, Minnesota, in a family that had to work hard to make ends meet. My dad started a landscaping business with nothing but a wheelbarrow and a shovel, and my summers working for him gave me a front-row seat to what it meant to grind out a living as a small business owner in a small town.

It was hard. I remember my dad bartering landscaping services with our town doctor to pay for the hospital bill that came with my youngest sister's birth. We didn't have health insurance for most of my childhood.

Every day at Google, I felt further and further from my roots.

At the same time, I started seeing how the influences of platforms like YouTube that had drawn me to Silicon Valley in the first place were *not*, in fact, all upside. When the Arab Spring exploded on YouTube in 2010, we scrambled to develop a curation process that could get verified videos of the protests to news organizations to use in their coverage. The mere existence of YouTube gave protesters the confidence to document their struggle to the world and build support for their cause. But those same clips also gave the Egyptian government the ability to identify the protesters and jail them—or worse. YouTube wouldn't create a face-blurring technology to help protesters protect themselves in videos for several more years.

The technology was moving too fast for us to keep up.

And then came "fake news." The Russian attempts at online interference in the 2016 election shocked us at Google, and changed forever our understanding of how technology's power could be manipulated. It also changed how we engaged with the media industry, who had gone from telling us to leave the truth-telling to them, to being outraged that we allowed people to access fake news on our platforms.

Things were shifting under our feet faster than ever. I remained an optimist about technology, but there was something about the changes underway that made me wonder if these new problems, along with other major challenges that seemed to be rushing toward America at breakneck speed, were best solved in Silicon Valley. Maybe other places had perspectives to offer.

Mary was starting to feel similarly. She'd spent the last five years building startup ecosystems around the world and saw innovation happening everywhere. From Milan to Milwaukee, she was building partnerships with local startup incubators, and in some cases building physical coworking spaces for Google to help the next generation of startups get off the ground. Often I'd travel with her and noticed the energy and excitement that existed outside Silicon Valley. Those tech economies felt different from California. More connected to other industries. More focused on solving people's real problems. And free of coastal elitism.

And then, five years into our marriage, our lives changed when Mary became pregnant with twins. We'd struggled for many years to get pregnant, and finally succeeding after multiple rounds of IVF gave us a new perspective. Every parent is changed by their kids, but for those who've struggled to build a family the process takes on a new gravity. We felt lucky. And the process also made us more deliberate people.

What would be the best life for our new little girl and boy? Where did we want to raise them, and what did we want to expose them to? Did we want to live near our extended family?

Answers to questions like these are different for everyone, but the questions got us talking. Mary is the daughter of Thai immigrants— entrepreneurs who found their way to San Diego to start a chiropractic business. Her mother passed away after a long illness a few years into our marriage, and her father still lived in San Diego. Her sister, Annie, was in Chicago and her brother, Joe, in the Bay Area, though he wasn't sure he was there for the long haul.

Meanwhile, my family was all concentrated in the Midwest. I'm the oldest of four kids and have fifteen cousins, most of them in the middle of the country. My sister Kelly lived about one mile from my parents' farm in Northfield, with her husband and five kids.

What if we actually moved to Minnesota? I hadn't lived there in twenty years, and Google didn't have offices there. Mary had been born in Iowa, but hadn't lived in the Midwest since she was two. Nothing was forcing us to move other than our own conversations about what we wanted the next chapter of our life to look like.

We stumbled around that conversation for months. Growing up, I had always wanted to leave Minnesota and seek new horizons. But the more we spoke, coming home was beginning to feel just as exciting.

As I talked with others, I realized we weren't alone in our thoughts. The Bay Area has seen some of the highest out-migration in the country over the past ten years. Minnesotans in particular are famous for moving back home because the quality of life in the state is so high. Minnesota always finds itself on top-five lists of places to live in the country, based on everything from education and infrastructure to amenities and professional opportunity.

Mary was intrigued, too. Her work building startup ecosystems all over the country gave her the sense that there was possibility outside the Valley. As a native San Diegan, though, could she stand the winters? What was it like to live through five months of snow every year?

We both agreed that we loved having twins and raising them with family around to help could be a big, welcome change.

I don't know that there was just one reason we decided to take the leap. Mostly, we felt that reinventing ourselves in a new place would be an adventure. And that maybe, in a moment of so much disruption and pessimism, we'd find purpose in it.

What made it possible wasn't me, but Mary. She'd been offered a new job with a venture capital firm started by AOL's founder, Steve Case, called Rise of the Rest, focused on investing in startups outside the coasts. It was based in D.C., and the assumption was that she would work from Menlo Park. But living in the middle of the country could be a powerful way to live out the mission of her new job.

What if, she suggested, she did the job from Minneapolis?

I could hardly contain my excitement. The momentum of our discussions had grown and this seemed like the perfect path to give Minnesota a shot. Within a month, Mary had taken the job, I'd agreed with Google to work remotely from Minneapolis, and we were searching for a new place to live in Minnesota. It happened fast.

In fact, it happened so fast that part of me wondered if either of us really understood what we were getting into. Especially Mary, who was taking an even bigger leap than me, something that would present us with some challenges in the years that followed.

In April 2018, we moved to a new home in Minneapolis. We planned our arrival to hit in the spring so we could begin our new chapter by enjoying the precious few months of good weather Minnesota has every year.

A week later, an April blizzard dropped a foot of snow on our new front yard.

This is a story of coming home and reinventing my life in my home state. In reflecting on this major personal transition, I hope my journey might offer an opportunity to look at where American life is going. Reinvention has always been at the heart of the American ideal, but it's happening in a more uncertain environment than ever before. So much of what we've taken for granted in this country is shifting. The headlines of America's diminished trust in its core institutions can make the way forward seem less and less clear.

Yet I discovered that the way to a stronger country starts, as it always has, with building stronger local communities. With investing in a physical place and finding purpose in it. For all that technology has done to connect us globally, the deepest purpose we can find comes with investing in our chosen communities and making them feel like home.

Moving home to Minnesota was my first step in that journey, but it wasn't the only one. Eight months after Mary and I moved our young family to Minneapolis, I had the opportunity to leave Google to join Minnesota's state government, becoming the commissioner of the Department of Employment and Economic Development (DEED) under Governor Walz. It was another reboot.

The job was a massive change, for unknown outcomes, with not much assurance of success. Bureaucracies are famously challenging to run, and I would be a complete outsider.

But it also felt like a chance to focus on the very things that inspired Mary and me to move to the heartland in the first place. And when the pandemic hit, that possibility took on a whole new meaning. Leaving the comforts of Google to run a 1,400-person government bureaucracy during a global health crisis gave me more insight into how American life is being transformed than I ever got working in technology. And it gave me a shot at making a real difference in the place I grew up.

I wrote this book to share the insights I discovered to a simple but important question: How can we find purpose in our lives and build community in a modern America that feels increasingly disconnected from its promise?

My journey home taught me many answers to that question. It taught me the power of going local. It taught me that putting yourself in an entirely new situation is often the best way to learn. It taught me that public service is a unique way to make a big impact. It taught me to invest in what makes your chosen community unique. It taught me the benefit of spending time with people who aren't just like you. It taught me about family, faith, and making friends in your forties. It taught me about reconciling old differences, about the kind of father I wanted to be, and about what it really means to have a partner in life.

And it taught me that crises can bring communities closer—when we invest in strengthening the things that bind us together.

I also got something else from moving home to Minnesota. Bringing fresh eyes to my native state gave me a lens into why this place, I came to believe, is uniquely worth watching for insights on where America is headed.

My new community, I discovered, was both exceptional and paradoxical. For example: Minnesota has boasted the lowest unemployment rate in American history, yet it is home to some of the steepest workforce shortages in the nation. It enjoys the moniker "Minnesota Nice," yet has some of the worst racial disparities in the U.S. The state has made decades of outsized investments in education and infrastructure that have helped build the densest Fortune 500 metro area in the entire country, yet tense urban-rural divisions are reshaping the state's political climate—especially since the pandemic. It is consistently named one of the best places to live in the country, despite having some of the coldest temperatures in America. And nestled among a sea of red states in the Midwest, Minnesota has not elected a Republican to statewide office in almost twenty years.

It's a unique place. But most people probably don't give much thought to Minnesota, or to the Midwest in general. "Flyover states" don't get national attention unless they become important in presidential elections. Yet our country ignores the Midwest at its own peril. There is more happening here that has something to say about America's future during a time of great upheaval than you might think.

Just a few months after COVID-19 had arrived, George Floyd, a Black man, was murdered by a white Minneapolis police officer, and caught on video by a bystander, just a few miles from our new home. I heard sirens all night, and walked through burned-out neighborhoods that had been destroyed the next day. As protests unfolded around the world, Minnesota became the center of global attention. The racial disparities that led to George Floyd's murder, and the protests and riots that followed, run deep. They are complex or simple, depending on your view. And they exist everywhere.

Minnesota has had a challenging history of racism, I would discover more deeply in the weeks and months that followed. Tasked with negotiating with legislators for state dollars to rebuild the neighborhoods that were destroyed, I saw up close the challenges and controversy that shape our conversations about race. They served to highlight just what an inflection point we find ourselves at as a state, and as a nation.

And so, in the pages that follow, Minnesota itself is a character in my story, as much as the people and family I connected with in my new community. But I'm not here to cheerlead Minnesota or the Midwest. Rather, I hope my home state's story, like my own, is one worth telling that sheds light on the promise and peril of community renewal.

The story you're about to read is a personal one. It's the story of going from riding my scooter in the sunshine to work at the world's most innovative tech company, to standing on the windy back patio of a bar in northern Minnesota debating the appropriate table size and social-distancing protocols with restaurant owners during the height of the COVID-19 pandemic. And how I learned to find purpose and build community along the way.

My story, like everyone's, is both unique and universal. It's the story of a place and a country that is reinventing itself—through the eyes of a person trying to do the same.

Chapter 2

Exceptionalism

On a balmy July evening in Minneapolis, during the brief and beautiful sliver of perfect weather that lands on the Minnesota calendar every year, when the breeze is warm and the twilight lingers past 10:00 p.m., I walked into the downtown Hilton alongside hundreds of local software engineers.

We were here for a technology conference organized by a local meetup group. As we shuffled into the hotel's large ballroom, I scanned the crowd of mostly white men. There were lots of sci-fi T-shirts, flip-flops, and cargo shorts. It looked more like Silicon Valley than anything I'd seen since Mary, the kids, and I had moved to Minnesota three months earlier in the spring of 2018. Except that I didn't recognize a single face.

The head conference organizer, an energetic engineer named Bridget Kromhout with bright fluorescent pink streaks in her hair, had heard that we had recently moved here. She'd reached out and invited me to give a talk about my work at Google.

"People would be curious to know why you moved to Minnesota from Silicon Valley," she told me.

Eager to impress, I spent hours researching Minnesota's technology sector leading up to the event. I compiled facts about Minnesota's startup success rate, its strong labor market for talent, and its reputation for a high quality of life. I discovered startups were $25 billion of the state's economy, and that more startups survived longer than five years here than in almost any other state in America.

I became a student of my new community, and with every word I wrote, my evangelical zeal grew stronger. The more I learned, the more I found to like—and the more I believed we had made the right decision by uprooting our life to move to Minnesota. By the time I finished, my short talk resembled a sermon more than a speech.

I took my seat in the ballroom alongside hundreds of people who all seemed to know each other. As I scanned the list of other speakers, I started to get nervous. Others were covering topics like API development, microservices, infrastructure, and artificial intelligence. My talk stuck out.

When I was introduced, I took a deep breath and walked onstage. With bright lights in my face, I couldn't see the crowd very well, but I knew the room was packed. Behind me was a giant screen that flashed the slides I'd made about Minnesota's technology strengths: pictures of big success stories like 3M, Medtronic, and Control Data Corporation; statistics about the number of healthcare businesses our "Medical Alley" boasted (15,000); and rankings about our national status (we were ranked a top-five state for female entrepreneurs, for example). In juxtaposition, I'd found a picture online of Silicon Valley sitting underneath a giant bubble, meant to show how isolated it was from the concerns of the rest of the world. I argued that the Minnesota tech economy was worth paying attention to because it was focused on solving real problems. I spoke with the enthusiasm of the converted.

When I finished, people clapped politely as I returned to my seat. I could hear the voices of a few engineers whispering in the row behind me.

"Is he trying to convince us to move to Minnesota?" one man said, sounding a little confused. "I already live here."

I could feel my face turn red, grateful it was too dark for anyone to see. I may have gone a bit overboard in making my case. Deep down, I knew that the audience for the short talk I gave that night was not the hundreds of engineers in the crowd, but the person standing onstage holding the microphone: me.

Consciously or not, I was giving myself a constant pep talk that leaving our lives in California and moving to the middle of the country made all the sense in the world. With each passing statistic I came across, the more I convinced myself of our decision to move here. Things were happening in Minnesota!

Perhaps I shouldn't have felt so out of place in displaying such enthusiasm at the conference. Midwesterners are, after all, some of the most earnest people you'll ever meet. We hold a certain exuberance for where we live, and our aw-shucks optimism is something that's celebrated here, not mocked.

This is especially true in Minnesota. It could come from a deep-rooted pride for having carved out a life in one of the coldest parts of America. Or maybe it comes from living in a state with an economy and culture that have been outliers in the Midwest for decades across dozens of measures, from infrastructure to wages to overall happiness. Whatever the reason, Minnesotans are sincere, heartfelt, and at times delusional about how wonderful their home is.

Though no Minnesotan wants to admit it, the thick-accented depictions of "Minnesota Nice" in the movie *Fargo* hit many of the right notes. Garrison Keillor, the former long-running host of *A Prairie Home Companion* radio show, captured Minnesota optimism well when he spoke of the fictional town of Lake Wobegon as a place "where all the women are strong, all the men are good-looking, and all the children are above average." You could label that optimism as a form of exceptionalism, and of course it can be an Achilles' heel. But as a native son returning home, I leaned into it.

Reinventing your life, at any age, is hard. People find comfort in habits, and making major changes requires a certain belief that the risks will pay off. It's a little easier when you're younger and you have less to lose. I'd moved several times before and found the transition easier. But at forty, I'd already gotten married, had kids, built a career. There was a lot riding on this experiment.

In my first few months back home, I was looking for any kind of momentum I could find. Moments like the conference were a chance to meet new people. While working at Google opened some doors, I wondered what it would be like to work for a company based in my new community. If this experiment in reinvention was going to work, I started to wonder if I should consider looking for a job actually based in Minnesota.

I liked the flexibility of remote work, especially as a parent to young kids, but the trade-off was that I had less time to connect with my new neighbors. Like most people, work was the single biggest time investment in my life. And I was spending it on phone calls or video conferences with people who lived around the world, rather than with people nearby. To give this new life a shot, I didn't just want to be working *from* my new home, but *in* my new home.

I needed to reacquaint myself with my old friend Minnesota. This state I'd grown up in, but hadn't lived in for twenty years, would take some time to get to know again. It was like building a new relationship with a childhood pal after decades apart. I started reading the newspaper every day, and sought out books and articles that chronicled the state's history.

An old 1973 issue of *Time* magazine had Governor Wendell Anderson on the cover, beaming with a freshly caught walleye in his hands next to the headline "The Good Life in Minnesota." The article's lengthy profile was titled "Minnesota: The State That Works." It painted something of a utopian picture:

If the American good life has anywhere survived in some intelligent equilibrium, it may be in Minnesota. It is a state where a residual American secret still seems to operate. Some of the nation's more agreeable qualities are evident there: courtesy and fairness, honesty, a capacity for innovation, hard work, intellectual adventure and responsibility. . . .

Politics is almost unnaturally clean—no patronage, virtually no corruption. The citizens are well educated: the high school dropout rate, 7.6 percent, is the nation's lowest. Minnesotans are remarkably civil: their crime rate is the third lowest in the nation (after Iowa and Maine). By a combination of political and cultural tradition, geography and sheer luck, Minnesota nurtures an extraordinarily successful society.

For Mary and me, our decision went beyond statistics or social indicators. Family was the biggest reason we had sought out Minnesota. Back in California, as new parents of young twins, we were overwhelmed. The day after Luke and Violet were born, it became clear we needed reinforcements. We called my parents and they booked the very next flight from Minnesota and stayed for two weeks. It was a godsend.

My parents are the kind of grandparents everyone dreams of having. They're great with kids, they genuinely enjoy playing with them, and they seem to have a natural instinct about when to get involved and when to step back. Near the end of our parental leave, they moved out to California for a month to look after the kids during the day while we transitioned back to work.

During that stay, we didn't have enough room in our small house for them, so we booked them an Airbnb about three miles away. Every morning they'd come over and take care of the kids while we went off to work. One afternoon, in the pitch-dark of the nursery, my dad was reaching into the crib to pick up Luke and lost his balance, tipping over headfirst into the crib. My parents told us the story that evening through howls of laughter. They were great sports.

When they went back to Minnesota, we didn't know the next time we'd see them. On the drive home from the airport, Mary and I talked about how nice it would be to have them nearby. Being a plane ride away made moments like these a luxury, not the norm.

But since we'd moved back to Minnesota, regular visits became our new routine. The first time we invited the entire family over for a meal in our new home, it just felt right. My siblings and their kids ran around the backyard. I smoked an entire rack of ribs that fed all nineteen of us. My parents helped with the food and the dishes. When everyone got ready to leave, I gave my parents a hug and said, "See you next week."

Another reason we were excited about being in Minnesota was that the community felt more grounded. In California, almost everyone we knew worked in technology, and most held liberal political views. In the 2016 election, 77 percent of Bay Area voters voted for Clinton, the largest percentage of any metro area in the country. At Google, our research team commissioned a study to figure out what we'd missed about the national mood, with researchers traveling to "flyover country" to survey people.

In Minnesota, we only had to walk out our front door and start talking with people to understand the national mood. Clinton had defeated Trump only by two percentage points in the state. The hour-long drive to my parents' house in rural Northfield revealed an equal number of Republican and Democratic lawn signs.

The sheer wealth generated in Silicon Valley was another reason California had felt insular. Every year in the Bay Area, there's a week-long break from school called "ski week," a designated time when families can head to the slopes in Tahoe, or fly to Salt Lake or some other destination, to spend thousands of dollars skiing. For families not swimming in technology cash, the whole concept is comically elitist.

In Minnesota, every week is ski week. Of course, we're talking about cross-country skiing, not downhill skiing at expensive resorts. Cross-country skiing is something that anyone can do in public parks across the state for free, or close to it. As Mary and I settled into Minnesota, I picked up a pair of skis and, while it took a while to learn, I enjoyed it. The people I saw on the trails came from all walks of life.

I was excited about trading Silicon Valley for Minnesota for smaller reasons, too. Less traffic. Cheaper gas. A bigger house for less money. Four major professional sports teams. Cleaner air. Great parks and easy access to nature. Good public schools. And, of course, more than ten thousand lakes.

But maybe the broadest philosophical reason that I was excited about my new home is that, unlike California, Minnesota couldn't lay claim to being the center of the universe. Everyone knows about Silicon Valley, and its innovations have changed the world we live in over the last fifty years. The Midwest is different. While my new home's "Minnesota exceptionalism" comes from a pride about the kind of community the state has created, no one I met here walked around thinking the world revolved around us. That was refreshing. There's a Minnesota saying that captures the humility that people here pride themselves on: "If you do something good and you tell somebody about it, it doesn't count."

These early insights left me feeling optimistic about uprooting from California and landing back home in Minnesota. As I thought about what I might do next, I became less interested in working for another company and instead drawn to do something rooted in my new community. As I searched, I discovered something I'd never thought about while growing up here—that Minnesotans were uniquely committed to civic participation.

The phenomenon was rooted in the state's history. Settled by Yankees with their love for town hall meetings, and later by Scandinavians, who boast the some of the longest-standing democracies in the world, the state had built a reputation for participatory government. Public service was seen as a duty—some even called the state's politics "moralistic." Government was a tool to make life better for your family and your neighbors, and in this cold cradle of the country, looking out for your neighbors was important.

That tradition seemed evident in the Minnesota I was getting to know today. The state consistently boasts the highest voter turnout in the country. It's in the top three for volunteerism and charitable giving per capita. It has the second-highest number of local units of government in the country, despite having only 5.7 million people. It regularly lands near the top of rankings of the most well governed states in the country, no matter which party is in charge. That's a lot of top-five lists.

In fact, this spirit of civic engagement is so strong that there's even a special holiday to encourage generosity, "Give to the Max Day." Started seventeen years ago, in one day Minnesotans raise over $30 million for local nonprofits every year. It's the most earnest thing you've ever seen, like Christmas for a cause.

It wasn't just do-gooder exceptionalism that put Minnesota on the cover of *Time* magazine as a great place to live. The model for success the state built had a distinct approach to it. Keep taxes high enough to build good roads, bridges, and schools. Protect unique natural resources. Invest in education. Use dependable institutions and amenities to attract and keep talented workers. Then let that talented workforce build or work for companies in a state that's great to do business in. Prosperity grows, and with it, tax dollars. Rinse and repeat.

Call it the "Minnesota Model." It has been repeated in various iterations for generations. When Wendell Anderson followed it back in the early seventies, architecting legislative and policy changes that brought a progressive income tax to vastly improve public schools while decreasing reliance on property taxes, it was so successful that people called it something else: the "Minnesota Miracle."

The more I learned about this history for good governance and giving back, the more I thought that maybe the most Minnesotan thing I could do was something in public service.

My curiosity led me to the gubernatorial campaign of Tim Walz, a southern Minnesota Democrat who was basing his bid on a slogan of "One Minnesota." I'd known Walz from a brief stint volunteering for his campaign over twelve years earlier, when he first ran for Congress as a high school geography teacher. I'd been intrigued by his energetic campaign back then, and spent a few weeks following him around his district with a clunky Sony camcorder, filming him at bean feeds, pancake breakfasts, and campaign rallies.

It was a long-shot congressional campaign, but you could feel his momentum growing. Walz was a first-time candidate, but he was a natural. A high school football coach and military veteran, he had a gravelly voice and an incredulous enthusiasm that got people's heads nodding wherever he went. His authenticity was refreshing. Even the national media caught notice, with his dot-matrixed headshot landing on the front page of the *Wall Street Journal.*

My web videos did not exactly go viral. I uploaded them to YouTube, a new site not well known for politics yet, and they got a few hundred views. But it didn't matter. A few months later Walz upset his opponent, and the geography teacher was headed to Washington.

Many years later, now back in Minnesota and living here, I thought volunteering for his new campaign could be a great way to start exploring what public service might look like. I wrote some policy papers for his website that I'm sure no one read. I organized a campaign stop at a job-training center in North Minneapolis. I knocked on doors and handed out flyers. It felt good to do something positive for the campaign in these early months of our lives here.

The national political mood, which felt so polarized and toxic, stood in sharp juxtaposition to the local optimism I felt in the campaign. When the tech community gathered for the Minnesota Cup, the largest startup competition in the state, I organized an informal roundtable with a dozen or so entrepreneurs. As Walz asked them about their ideas, they buzzed with energy about the way the state government might play a role in growing the startup scene.

"Minnesota has a much stronger startup community than people give it credit for," Melissa Kjolsing, a healthcare startup founder, told him. "If the government worked more closely with us to get venture capital flowing into the state, that would really help us grow."

Walz nodded, listening intently. He shared a bit about his vision for "One Minnesota." "It's more than a campaign slogan, it's the way I intend to govern," he explained. "We all do better when we work together."

If that sounded too idealistic, the entrepreneurs clearly didn't think so. They swarmed him afterward, thanking him for coming to hear their ideas.

Walz's campaign continued to pick up speed. More and more Minnesotans were attracted to the promise of "One Minnesota" and seemed to trust he would deliver. All the momentum got me wondering . . . would working in state government be a good next step for me?

When Walz emerged the winner of the 2018 election that November, I was even more intrigued. It seemed crazy to leave the comfort of a great job at Google with two small kids at home. But it felt like exactly what we'd uprooted our lives to do. It appealed directly to the earnestness I felt in rekindling my relationship with this old friend Minnesota, in the new community that Mary and I were hoping to build for ourselves.

As I talked it over with Mary, she liked the idea. When I shared the idea with friends, they were surprised, but just as encouraging. Leaving the private sector for government is not a well-worn path. Government jobs in general get a bad rap, state governments in particular, perhaps because of their reputation for being difficult bureaucracies, or their low salaries.

But who cares if it wasn't common? We'd already changed so much by coming all the way to Minnesota, why not go all in and change everything? This was, of course, deeply naive. But naivete can be your best friend when you're trying to make it in a new place. Getting caught up in all the what-ifs only slows down the momentum you need to find your way. In the following months, I would come to learn that earnestness is actually a secret weapon.

Plus, what I was learning about the unique reputation of Minnesota's government gave me hope that maybe the transition wouldn't be so hard. There were lots of good bureaucrats here—maybe I could be one of them. Maybe I could do something meaningful to help my new state. Maybe putting myself outside my comfort zone would be just what I needed to connect with my new community. And even if none of those things panned out, maybe just trying something new would be fun.

By the time Governor-elect Walz had built a transition team and we began talking, I was ready to figure out how.

The only government department I thought I might be remotely qualified to lead was called the Department of Employment and Economic Development, or DEED, as it is commonly known in Minnesota. The agency included both workforce and economic development departments, and employed about 1,400 people. People knew it as the jobs department. If there was one place where an outsider coming from the private sector might offer something new, being the state's jobs commissioner might be it.

Was I qualified to run a 1,400-person state bureaucracy? No way. But what I'd learned about my old friend Minnesota had inspired some ideas about how to improve the state's standing and increase growth. Luckily the governor thought I might figure it out. A few days after the interview process, he called and asked me to be the commissioner of DEED.

I flew to Silicon Valley and wrapped up my work at Google. I said goodbye to my team and my colleagues, who were a little shocked, but said they were cheering me on. It was easy for everyone I spoke with to admire the idea of what I was going to do, in principle. But how would it actually turn out?

Chapter 3

Government Man

My transition into becoming a government official came with an instruction book. A very thick instruction book. The blue binder with my name on it was sitting on a folding table next to twenty-three others in the lobby of a nonprofit a few miles from the capitol, where the governor's new cabinet had all been asked to come for orientation. I lifted the binder off the table and found a seat in the back of the large conference room. As I flipped through dozens of tabs filled with rules, regulations, and process documents about how to run a government agency, my new colleagues shuffled into the room.

When everyone was gathered, the governor's new chief of staff, Chris Schmitter, welcomed us. Chris had been working with or volunteering for the governor ever since his first congressional campaign over a dozen years ago. He'd just left a job at a top law firm to help lead the governor's new administration. Tall and well spoken, with a neatly combed head of blond hair and an exceedingly likable demeanor, he might have been the only person in the room younger than me.

"Before we get started, why don't we go around the room and get to know each other better," Chris suggested.

The IT commissioner, Tarek Tomes, had two kids at the Air Force Academy and coached high school basketball in his spare time. The transportation commissioner, Margaret Anderson Kelliher, had once been Speaker of the Minnesota House and was an avid quilter. The public safety commissioner, Paul Schnell, had a degree in social work, but had also been a cop, and walked five miles every morning with his dog, Welly, named after the late senator Paul Wellstone.

When it was my turn, I told everyone about our recent move to Minnesota, and about Mary and the twins.

"This is all very new to me," I admitted. Someone asked about my hobbies. I thought about the backyard smoker that Mary had bought me for my fortieth birthday a year earlier. "I've recently taken up smoking," I shared.

There was an awkward silence. "Oh, I mean, I've recently started smoking meat," I corrected myself. The warm laughter in the room made me feel welcome.

After introductions, Chris brought out a series of speakers to teach us about state government. We heard presentations about everything from public sector unions to procedures of procurement. I furiously scribbled notes in the margins of the blue binder, like an eager student. About halfway through the day, the state ethics officer came in front of the room and gave a talk about how to behave as a government official.

Her first slide had a picture of a goldfish swimming in a clear aquarium.

"Everyone's watching what you do, all the time," she warned us. "Never say or do anything you wouldn't be okay with being printed on the front page of a newspaper."

There were a few nervous chuckles. But as the day ended, that image of the sad fish in the aquarium stuck out most in my mind. If that was working in government, then it was a sharp contrast to working in Silicon Valley.

In fact, if you were to extend the analogy, then working at YouTube and Google in the years the internet took off felt more like being a tropical fish swimming in a warm ocean along a pristine coral reef somewhere. The water is warm, and food is plentiful twenty-four hours a day. You're free to pursue your passions, and the only people watching are those who put on snorkeling masks to come down and gawk at how beautiful and important you are.

Working in government, I was about to find out, would feel exactly as the ethics officer forewarned. We were like fish in a cramped aquarium at the city zoo. There's less room to maneuver. Food and other resources are limited, and mostly out of your control. The public can come gawk at you whenever they want, banging on the glass to get your attention, or mocking you if they so choose. After all, they paid for this zoo!

To help me learn how to swim in these new waters, the governor's transition team lined up some people I could get advice from. First was the executive director of a nonprofit that often worked with DEED. He was an expert at navigating government, I was told, and always found ways to win dollars from the state for his nonprofit's programs. He wasted no time launching into a helpful speech on how to do government.

"These people are going to try to tear you down," he warned, pointing outside the room at my soon-to-be colleagues. "They know you're here just for a little while, and they've been here forever."

I'd heard similar warnings before. Strong union protections and a culture of staying in government for a long time were two of the things that made government bureaucracies notoriously slow and hard to move. But I'd never heard someone be so blunt about the challenges someone like me, a new political appointee, would face.

This leader even had a nickname for state government bureaucrats. "I call them the 'weebees,'" he explained, leaning forward. "That's for 'we be here when you arrive, and we be here once you're gone.'"

Since it would be hard to fire "weebees," given government job protections, he told me the best thing to do was to "send the bad ones to Siberia." In other words, assign them to unfavorable jobs that would make them want to leave. I wasn't sure he was joking. His gritty demeanor was full of seasoned implication.

"Stay strong on the inside," he smiled, giving me a fist bump before he left.

I slunk back in my chair, my heart beating a little faster. I appreciated the real talk. But there was something unnerving about viewing my new colleagues as enemies.

Next, I met with Lee Sheehy, a longtime veteran political operator with a big shock of gray hair on his head and an enormous smile. Lee had recently served as Senator Amy Klobuchar's chief of staff.

He told me how hard it was to make change in government, how slow things moved. He was worried I'd get frustrated by the pace compared with Google, and told me to never stop asking for help from those on the outside.

"You can do some really powerful things in government, you've just got to be patient. This isn't the private sector," he advised.

This was feeling more like advice I could manage. But when he got up to shake my hand and leave, Lee added, "Most of us will be surprised if you last more than a year in this job."

I gulped, then straightened up and made a mental note to use that as motivation, which was exactly Lee's intent.

I called many others for advice, drawing from a list of names I was handed by the governor's office with the instructions to "check in with stakeholders," something I'd soon learn was a central exercise of my new job. By the time my first day arrived, my head was dizzy with ideas. One theme that came through often was the importance of setting the right tone in the beginning.

On my first day, I asked the staff to gather for a town hall. There wasn't a room big enough to hold all 1,400 people in the agency, so we found a vacant floor in the building. With low ceilings and almost no natural light, the floor had stains on the ratty gray carpet where cubes used to stand, and it was broken up by large pillars with faded white paint turning yellow. It stood in sharp contrast to the Google campus in California, awash in sunshine and primary colors, with plush carpet, leather furniture, and a snack kitchen every fifty feet.

People trickled in with some trepidation to meet the new guy, feigning smiles in my direction. Once a few hundred people were there, I took the mic and cleared my throat.

"I'm so excited to get to work with you," I offered. "I know this is a room full of talent and I can't wait to learn from all of you."

A few more people mustered smiles. I mumbled through some talking points about why I'd taken the job and the importance of growing the state's innovation economy. Then I shared some lessons about working at Google, followed by a carefully recited disclaimer: "I promise you that I won't bring in the attitude that the government should be run just like Google," I said. "Government is different, and I know it operates differently than the private sector."

I hoped this might comfort people and show that I wasn't naive. When I opened the floor for questions, it was silent. Sweat started pooling underneath the white collar of my dress shirt. I clenched my stomach and resisted the temptation to fill the silence with more chatter.

Finally, a middle-aged woman standing in the front row raised her hand.

"So at Google, you could wear jeans to work, right?" she said.

I nodded.

"Are you going to change the dress code here?" she followed. It sounded reasonable to me, I said. Let's look into it.

An older man holding a walking cane went next. "In my job, I'm on the phone with people all day, something I could do from home. At Google, you could work from wherever you wanted to, right? I mean, you guys invented the internet!"

This elicited a few chuckles. He continued: "Are you going to let us work from home, maybe even just a few days a week?"

It sounded worth exploring. I promised, again, to look into it. More questions flooded in.

"How do you define innovation?" a younger woman asked. "And how can we be more innovative in government?"

A woman with an East African accent asked, "Do you consider yourself a transformational leader?"

I didn't quite know how to answer that one, so I told her I hoped we could all make positive changes through our work. In fact, change was the main theme behind all the questions that came in. No one asked about keeping things the same. If this was a room full of "weebees," they certainly weren't showing their cards early.

Some people in the room were hungry for a different kind of culture in government. Seeing my new team as obstacles wasn't going to make me better at my new job.

But building a stronger community at the agency just might.

———

"The best way to make friends in Minnesota is to go to kindergarten here" is a common saying in Minnesota that I kept hearing when I moved back.

The state has a reputation for having a frozen social environment that can be hard to chisel into. Established social networks are strong, people told me, and despite the state's reputation for "Minnesota Nice," getting someone to invite you over to their house can feel like a monumental achievement.

When I googled "How transplants can make friends in new cities," the top-three results were about Minnesota. I thought Google might be targeting me based on geography, so I logged out of my browser and tried again. Same result—all the top articles were about Minnesota.

Almost 70 percent of people born in Minnesota stay here, one of the highest such rates of any state in the country. People here find their people early and stick with them. Some claim that the state's long, cold winters keep people hibernating for so long that their social muscles atrophy for long stretches of the year.

Of course, I *had* gone to kindergarten here. But I wasn't quite sure how to reenter life in my home state over twenty years after I left. My high school friends had either moved away or built up their lives here, with kids much older than ours and well-established friend groups. I'd grown up in Northfield, a rural farming community and college town, but was now living an hour north in Minneapolis. I was from here, but also different.

Our new home was on a small, quiet street in South Minneapolis. It was newly constructed, though we hadn't built it ourselves. A local developer had knocked down a much smaller house on the lot to build it, and we were the first people to live here.

Mary and I decided not to wait for our new neighbors to invite us over. We packed the kids up in the stroller and went door-to-door, handing out handwritten invitations to our house for a brunch the next weekend. What better way to meet the neighbors than to throw ourselves a welcome party?

That Saturday morning, we set out some bagels and coffee and an egg bake on our dining room table and waited for people to arrive. The kids toddled around on the hardwood floors, oblivious to how nervous Mary and I were feeling.

"What if no one comes?" I joked to Mary.

"Well, at least we'll have enough food for the week ahead," she deadpanned.

Slowly but surely, people started to arrive. Soon there were over a dozen people standing in our dining room, politely introducing themselves and obliging our request to write their names on the sign-up sheet we'd created to get their addresses and phone numbers. People seemed genuinely curious to meet the new family.

A tall, middle-aged woman with long silver hair introduced herself as Pepper. After a cup of coffee and some pleasantries, she shared the story of the neighborhood.

"My house is one of the oldest houses in all of Minneapolis," she claimed proudly, pointing across the street at her two-story yellow home. "It was moved here from the shores of Lake Harriet many years ago."

Our street was a mix of very small homes that looked decades or even a century old, along with a few new homes like ours that were clearly the product of teardowns. Pepper didn't waste time confirming that this was a hot topic on the block.

"The builders of your house were so loud, I had to call the police on them several times," she said. Then, reading the look on my face, she added, "Not that that's *your* fault."

A few others confirmed that some drama had preceded our arrival to the block. Our next-door neighbor was a petite elderly woman named Julia, who had beautiful frizzy hair and an untouched front yard that looked like a small forest, reflecting her view on nature: to do no harm.

"The builders of your house didn't care about wildlife," she shared. "They cut down a beautiful tree in your front yard which was home to so many squirrels." Mary and I saw a look of anguish on her face and instinctively offered an apology for an indiscretion we'd had no part in.

I started to worry that our attempt to be part of our new community might be harder than we thought. Not only did these California transplants stick out, but apparently the house we bought did, too.

We also met a few families, including one a few doors down that had four kids—that seemed promising. A family down the block with a tire swing in their yard seemed friendly.

"Why would you leave California and move *here*?" many of them half joked.

After everyone had left and we'd cleaned the dishes, Mary sat down and dutifully wrote thank-you notes to everyone who'd stopped by. Then we waited to see when the first invitation to someone's house might come back.

A month or so later, an invitation did come through, but not from someone in our neighborhood. A couple named Matt and Ianthe had moved here from Washington, D.C., when he got a job at Target, and they were throwing a barbecue for other transplants in their backyard. We'd met through an acquaintance, and Mary and I jumped at the chance to go.

On a hot sunny day we packed up a salad and went over to their backyard. The twins ran over to a bouncy house on the lawn, and we joined the adults under the shade of a canopy tent standing on the driveway.

Holding paper plates dripping with barbecue and broccoli salad, we began the hard work of looking comfortable and cheery in the face of meeting strangers. We met a doctor named Justin and his wife, Becky, who'd recently moved here from Massachusetts. They both had blond hair and what seemed like permanent smiles on their faces. They were in the same boat as us—new to the state, and still figuring out how they fit in. Becky was from Minnesota like me, which got Justin and Mary joking that every Minnesotan who moves away has a tracking beacon inside them that goes off at some point in their lives, imploring them to move back.

"We're trying to find our way," Justin offered. "The easiest thing has been meeting other parents of kids at our school."

It seemed like a glimmer of a possible friendship. We shared more about our lives in California and why we moved to Minnesota, and they seemed genuinely interested. The fact that we were different from other people felt a little less like a social liability with this crowd.

Our host Matt, who'd been in the state a bit longer, had advice for all of us. "You've got to be assertive. Nobody's going to just reach out to you out of nowhere."

Moving to a new place in your forties is harder, he concurred. His advice was to focus on other transplants. "There's a decent community of transplants here, you've just got to find them."

We left the party feeling hopeful. Trying to chisel into existing social groups in Minnesota seemed like it might be a tough road. But maybe leaning into being different, and finding others who were different, too, would be a good place to start.

Back at the agency, I began to learn that being different wasn't always good—at least with the weebees, who slowly began to reveal themselves.

In a meeting with my new team about an event we were planning, I joked that we should have "someone young pick the opening music" because I'd end up choosing Bruce Springsteen or Fleetwood Mac or some other seventies band. The next day, I got a visit from HR that someone had submitted a complaint that the new commissioner might be "ageist."

A few weeks later, Mary helped me convene a group of startup founders to give me advice on how to build a government program to improve Minnesota's startup scene. Soon after, someone complained to the budgeting department (the Minnesota Department of Management and Budget, or MMB) that I might be mixing my wife's business interests with our government work for financial profit.

Yikes. That hadn't even occurred to me.

I got a call from the commissioner of MMB, a wily veteran of state government named Myron Frans. He'd already served eight years as a commissioner under the previous governor, and having come from the private sector himself, he knew the challenges I would face. He asked me to come by his office for a chat.

We sat down next to a window with a beautiful view of the newly renovated State Capitol building. A large whiteboard hung on the wall next to the window with budget numbers and to-do lists scribbled on it.

As the manager of the stage budget, Myron was a first-among-equals in the cabinet. His small frame and wire-rimmed glasses might give a first impression of a mild number cruncher, but he was a deft operator with a great sense of humor and a reputation for being able to navigate bureaucracy to get things done. That's why the governor had asked him to stay on board after the election to help build and manage his administration.

Myron smiled and told me he wanted to help me be successful.

"Let me show you something," he said, uncapping a blue marker and erasing the contents of the whiteboard. He drew three concentric circles, and pointed to the outside circle.

"This is what's legal," he explained. "Everything we do has to be inside of this circle."

I nodded.

Then he pointed to the middle circle. "This is what's legal *and* ethical. It's not enough just to do things by the books, we have to make sure what we're doing is ethical as well."

I nodded again.

Then he pointed to the innermost circle. "And this is what's *perceived* to be legal and ethical. If people don't think what you're doing is legal or ethical, none of the rest of the circles matter. Everything we do has to be inside of this innermost circle," he concluded.

I nodded a third time. It was valuable advice. Perception was as good as reality in the aquarium. The quick lesson would help me time and again in the weeks ahead.

I was learning quickly that thinking through the effect of every action through the eyes of different stakeholders was a uniquely important skill in government. As time went on, I became convinced this was one of the most important lessons I'd learn in public service. The private sector—especially the industry I'd just left in California—could definitely benefit from this lesson from government.

What helped most with the weebees, however, was simply showing up to work every day and listening.

Remembering the question I'd gotten about wearing jeans at work, I looked at the agency dress code and found it was so old that it included a prohibition against wearing Zubaz, a brand of leisurely sweatpants made popular by Governor Jesse Ventura twenty years earlier. Scratching the dress code and simply asking people to make good choices was an easy early win.

We also made town halls a regular occurrence. I took questions as long as people wanted to ask them. Afterward, I started regularly walking the floor and talking with my new colleagues, and every Friday I sent a "Friday Note" to the whole department sharing what I'd done that week, along with highlights from our work and thoughts on the work ahead. I tried to make the weekly notes personal, though I did get another rebuke when I shared some outside work I was doing with a nonprofit. That, a colleague warned me, could be perceived as soliciting donations.

Building a stronger sense of community at the agency would not only improve our ability to be effective but it could also show my new colleagues I cared. Most political appointees don't take the time to focus on culture because the jobs are temporary, and culture change is hard. But in my first months on the job, I was finding that improving agency culture was a secret weapon to success.

Every time I rolled out a small cultural shift, I was surprised by the feedback.

We launched an annual employee awards system to celebrate our successes. There were tears in the eyes of those who won.

We built a stronger performance measurement system to provide professional development, including the chance to give your manager feedback. People raved about the opportunity to learn how they were doing, and to share feedback with their leaders.

We created a strategic plan for our future, using Google's goal-setting system (OKRs) to track progress. The team felt a sense of direction and focus.

And maybe most important, we started an "Innovation Lab," where people could present new ideas and get help bringing them to life. Investing in a way to solve problems with new ideas gave people an outlet to think differently, in an agency where inertia had long since taken hold.

These were not revolutionary moves. And they were not universally loved. But some basic attention to making the agency a good place to work started building trust, which I hoped would help the team better work together toward the big goals we wanted to achieve.

If I was careful, being different in this new job could be a huge advantage.

I'd come into the agency thinking my background in tech might give me an edge on how to help our state build a stronger technology economy. But I was discovering that the most valuable way an outsider could contribute was by providing a new way of doing things, and to focus on building a strong culture. Mixing some private sector insights with public sector norms just might build the positive energy I needed to get off to a good start.

I still felt like I was learning more than I was contributing. But any momentum I caught early was derived from where I was able to do things differently than they'd been done before. It was a helpful early lesson: sometimes you can make the biggest difference in your community by simply presenting a fresh perspective to a new experience. Being different causes others to treat you differently, which creates space to do things others might struggle to achieve.

DEED's net promoter score (a standard measurement for how likely an employee is to recommend working at an institution) was at negative fifteen when I started. That's not very good. After rolling out some of these changes, we measured again. It had swung all the way to a positive thirteen. We still had a long way to go, but we were moving in the right direction.

At the very least, I started to get more forgiveness for the mistakes I made. On a spring day six months into the job, I stood in a cramped kitchen in our office, pouring a cup of coffee, when our deputy commissioner Kevin McKinnon walked in. A long veteran of state government and a former Canadian hockey star, Kevin had proven a talented colleague and mentor already.

I offhandedly brought up how nice it was that we had free coffee in our office every day. "You know, it's not like I expected free breakfast, lunch, and dinner like we had at Google," I joked. "But the fact that the agency provides free coffee is a nice touch."

Kevin looked at me and smiled, and then broke it to me.

"This isn't free coffee," he shared. "We have an internal coffee club where we all chip in and bring beans in every week to make coffee for the office."

My face turned red. I'd been freeloading coffee for six months and didn't even know it.

We both had a good laugh. I knew that this time, no one would report it to HR.

Chapter 4

Mary

In a crowded airport newsstand at Dulles International Airport in the fall of 2010, I bumped into a colleague from work who was picking up some water and magazines for a long flight ahead. She flashed a perfect smile framed by two dimples, and her voice carried a warmth that instantly put me at ease. Though we barely knew each other, I found myself leaning in to give her a hug before stopping to think if that was an appropriate way to greet someone from the office.

Her name was Mary, and our shared destination was Baghdad, Iraq. We were heading there on a unique business-development trip that she had helped organize with the Pentagon. The U.S. military had built a program to get American companies to invest in markets where our troops were stationed, and Google made their list. Mary was the partnership lead for the company's effort to launch the Iraqi domain of Google.com, and she was asked to bring along someone from YouTube to help develop partnerships with content creators and media companies, too.

I was quick to raise my hand when I heard about the trip. It sounded like a once-in-a-lifetime opportunity.

It was a work trip to a war zone, and neither Mary nor I was looking for romance. But we had a spark between us I couldn't ignore. As our Pentagon handlers drove us around Baghdad to meet internet service providers, media companies, and public officials, I saw the way Mary effortlessly commanded a room and disarmed others with that smile and a genuine interest in them. Her laugh, which came easily and often, kept putting a goofy smile on my face. I had a tendency for introspection, sometimes prone to brooding, so I was amazed at how cheerfully she floated above the fray.

I started wondering how someone this beautiful and intelligent and warm could exist in this world—and how was I only meeting her now? A nickname kept surfacing for her in my head: Sunshine.

In the evenings, back at the apartment complex we were staying at in the Green Zone, we stayed up late into the night with our other colleagues, getting to know each other. Mary was the child of two immigrants from Thailand, both who came to the U.S. separately in their thirties and met in Chicago. Her dad had been studying at the Vatican, but had a change of heart—he moved to America to start over and eventually got a degree in chiropractic care in Davenport, Iowa.

Mary's mom was a nurse who got a visa to help stem America's nursing shortage. They had Mary in Iowa before moving to San Diego to start their chiropractic business, where the climate better resembled Thailand. Together with her older sister and younger brother, Mary was the first generation in a small but tight immigrant family. Her parents never once hired a babysitter, the kids just went where their parents did. They learned America together.

When she graduated, Mary attended Stanford on a full-ride scholarship. In the pictures of her graduation, you can feel the pride beaming from her parents' faces.

In some ways, my background couldn't have been more different—growing up in a small, predominantly white town in Minnesota with dozens of extended family members living in the Midwest. But somehow it felt like we had a lot in common. We both grew up in families that ran small businesses, we both had parents who worked hard and expected the same of us, and we both had stumbled into careers in tech (Mary was a paralegal on the Google IPO: she thought it would be good training for law school, but never left).

A few nights into the Iraq trip, we sat next to each other in the back seat of a military Land Rover on the way to the State Department headquarters for a meeting. I reached over and grabbed her hand, and was relieved when she didn't pull away.

Back in the U.S., we dated for a year and got married soon after. Some couples work because they're a yin and a yang. That wasn't us. We worked because we were similar. From the beginning, it felt like a partnership of equals. We both carried an idealism that was further amplified by working at a global tech company where anything seemed possible. Silicon Valley was still in its utopia phase, and we fed off every bit of it.

We each started new teams at Google: Mary started a global partnerships and outreach effort for entrepreneurs, and I started a similar one for news organizations. After Iraq, we traveled together to Afghanistan, Pakistan, Brazil, Japan, Korea, and various countries in Europe for work. We each built teams and grew partnerships with organizations big and small. Google's influence grew bigger the farther we got from Mountain View. We were young and idealistic and full of energy. It was a special window of time in the history of the internet, where the power of technology was inspiring galloping optimism and the downsides had yet to be seriously recognized.

Though the world felt full of endless possibility, at home we hit our first bump: we were struggling to start a family. We'd both agreed early that we wanted to have at least three, maybe four kids. Like any naive young couple, we thought it would happen as soon as we tried. But negative pregnancy tests piled up for months, and eventually we had to admit that we had a fertility problem. We visited a clinic, where testing showed there were some fertility barriers for both of us. The doctor recommended we begin the process of IVF.

Struggling with fertility is like keeping a dark secret. We felt shame for not being able to do the most basic thing that all life on planet earth was designed to do. It was humbling to have something we wanted so badly to be so outside our control.

Beyond the pain of monthly failure, it was also hard seeing our friends and relatives have kids. It surfaced a darkness and discomfort that felt unfamiliar. We wanted to be happy for others, but each moment was a reminder of our own challenges. It felt like life was passing us by. We had to regularly steel ourselves for the inevitable "When are you starting a family?" question.

The longer we waited, the bigger the gaping hole in our lives felt. About a year into trying IVF, we went on a hike in the Palo Alto Foothills one Saturday morning to clear our heads. As we walked under beautiful California pine trees along a fern-coated ravine, we brainstormed other paths forward if we didn't have children of our own. We discussed adoption, and we thought about getting involved with kids in other ways.

"What if we found a way to help young people find careers in tech?" Mary suggested. The more we chatted, the more excited we became. We'd never had mentors in the technology industry when we were young. And people of color like Mary, who face bigger barriers in a field that is predominantly white, would have a better shot if they had access and exposure to tech careers early in life. The idea instantly felt full of purpose. Plus, we figured, working with young people would be fun.

By the end of the hike, we'd created the idea for an organization that combined aspects of both of our backgrounds into one program. We called it Silicon North Stars: a nonprofit that would bring Minnesota high school students of color and immigrants out to Silicon Valley for a weeklong tech camp once a year to learn from people working in the field, and to test out their startup ideas. Exposure to the industry might help them see themselves in it.

All the bottled-up energy we had for starting our own family we poured into Silicon North Stars. For the next four years, we flew a new class of sixteen students out to California every year and took them around to the major tech company campuses, putting them through a startup boot camp at the end of the week, where they pitched their own ideas in front of dozens of startup founders and venture capitalists.

By the time our fourth class of Silicon North Stars flew out to California for the camp, we'd gone through several more rounds of IVF. We ended up driving to a clinic in Colorado that was considered one of the best in the world. Our three-month-old yellow Lab, Charger, sat in the back seat as we hurtled across the western states, hoping a fresh start with a new doctor might bring us luck.

Nine months later, our twins were born. We were ecstatic, relieved, and terrified. Everything changed at once.

We greeted our fifth class of Silicon North Stars students at the San Francisco airport with Luke and Violet in our arms. The students instantly started playing with the twins, which continued throughout the week as we traipsed around the Valley visiting tech campuses and hearing from Black and brown leaders at companies like Google, Facebook, Uber, Lyft, and GoPro. As our little twins giggled in the arms of these young students, a majority of whom lived below the poverty line and many of whom came from single-parent households, I couldn't help but compare their start in life with the one we hoped to give our own kids.

Our twins would have almost every advantage. Parents who were together, had stable jobs with healthcare, and a broad support network to help when times get tough.

Our Silicon North Stars came from families living with very little money, no meaningful safety net, and highly mobile households with little stability.

Of course it wasn't fair. But that didn't mean there was nothing to be done about it.

Two years later, on the floor of the old Minneapolis Grain Exchange in downtown Minneapolis, we gathered a group of Silicon North Stars for a "Demo Day." Preparing to pitch their startup ideas to a crowd of local supporters, the group of high school students sat nervously on black folding chairs waiting for the program to start.

Mary and I were only a few months into our move to Minnesota, and we'd decided to have the students pitch the startup ideas they created at the Silicon Valley camp back here in Minneapolis, too. The response surprised even Mary and me. Over 150 parents, friends, and members of the local tech community had come out to hear more about the students' ideas.

The setting was symbolic. For decades, Minnesota's original pioneers gathered on the floor of the Grain Exchange to trade farm commodities. A thirty-foot-high mechanical trading board that used to flash the prices of corn, soybeans, and wheat still hung across the wall of what had now become a startup coworking space. Ornate arched doorways lined a balcony, and murals depicting Minnesota's agricultural history hung on the walls.

Sitting below those murals, our students represented a new class of pioneers—immigrants from Somalia, Ethiopia, Vietnam, China, Mexico, and beyond.

One of them was Mary Ghebremeskal, a ninth grader with beautiful curly black hair whose family immigrated from Eritrea just a month before she was born. She lived with her grandmother in South Minneapolis, and had already taught herself to code and built her first website before high school. But she hadn't met anyone who looked like her working in technology.

"Being African American, there's a stereotype that you're not as smart as other people in the tech space," she told us. "I think it's kinda reinforced when you don't see anyone in the field that has your background. I think it's really important for people to say, 'Actually no, this isn't true, no matter who you are and what you look like, you can do whatever you want.'"

The prompt we'd given each team was to create a startup idea that addressed an issue on everyone's mind in the wake of the Parkland, Florida, school shooting just a few months earlier: *How might technology eliminate school shootings in one year, while keeping schools enjoyable and effective environments for learning?*

Mary and her team pitched an idea for an electromagnetic sensor on every school campus that could detect anything shaped like a gun and immediately alert the authorities. Holding a microphone as if she'd been born with one in her hand, Mary walked the crowd through their business plan and marketing strategy.

"In three months' time, we estimate that our device will decrease school shootings by a significant amount," she told the audience. "But if only one life is saved because of this device, that will be a win for everyone."

The crowd gave the students a standing ovation. Mary and her team beamed with pride. Four years later, she earned a full-ride scholarship to Yale.

After the students' pitches, we mingled with the crowd and met those who'd come out to support the students. They shared how inspired they were by the presentations and the students' personal stories. Part of that inspiration came from just how energetic and smart these young people were. But part of it was also from knowing the larger challenges they faced, in particular the hard fact that the gap between Black and brown Minnesotans and their white counterparts was wider here than almost anywhere in the country.

As I learned more about that gap, my reacquaintance with my home state moved beyond Minnesota exceptionalism and into something people call the "Minnesota Paradox." Made more widely known in a 2018 book by Professor Samuel L. Myers Jr. at the University of Minnesota, the paradox is that despite having some of the highest living standards in the country, Minnesota has the widest gap between white people and people of color than almost anywhere in America.

Poverty rates for Black people are four times higher than white people in Minnesota, the third-largest gap in the country. Three-quarters of white Minnesotans own their own homes, while only a fourth of Black Minnesotans do. Myers and other historians chart the source of these disparities back to the earliest settlers to the state, who displaced the Native American population in often brutal fashion. The hanging of thirty-eight Dakota men in the town square of Mankato, Minnesota, in 1862—a tragedy sanctioned by President Lincoln himself—was the largest mass execution in American history.

White settlers continued to instate policies that embedded systemic racism into the development of the state, particularly in housing. Racial covenants in the early 1900s barred Black people from building in certain parts of the city. In the 1950s, the U.S. Department of Transportation built an interstate highway right through the historically Black neighborhood of Rondo in St. Paul, cutting it off from the rest of the city and bringing pollution and displacement to a neighborhood once rich with cultural institutions. They could have chosen to build the road north of the city along abandoned train tracks, but they didn't. Today, the life expectancy in Rondo is sixty-five years, more than two decades less than neighborhoods just a mile away.

Policy decisions that built systemic racism in the state continued into the twenty-first century. Professor Myers coauthored a study in 2015 that showed that between 2008 and 2013, people of color were disproportionately more likely to have their loan applications rejected by banks, a disparity not due to basic variables like credit risk or income.

We saw these inequalities in the lives of almost every student in Silicon North Stars. Now that we were living in the same community as our students, and not two thousand miles away in California, we started to hear from them more often. We'd get calls from kids for help with meals or rides when no one else was available to assist. Others needed books or school supplies, the basics. Often, kids asked us to write recommendation letters for college scholarships so they could afford school. They told us stories of family members ending up in homeless shelters or parents who didn't have cars or couldn't afford gas to transport them to our meetups.

This hadn't been the Minnesota I had experienced as a kid. But, of course, that was naive: no one ever wants to admit there's racism in their community. That's why systemic racism is so insidious—it doesn't require an active public practice of racism; it lets the system do that for us, with the same result: more wealth for white people, and less for people of color.

Yes, Minnesota was exceptional, but for whom?

Seeing my home state through the eyes of kids who were growing up in different circumstances than me, I was even more humbled by the optimism and energy they showed in our program.

When Demo Day was over, Mary and I drove back to our new home with Luke and Violet bundled up in their car seats behind us, and reflected on the evening. We'd started Silicon North Stars to get out of the doom loop that our fertility challenges had dragged us into. Focusing on building our community had given us fresh hope for the world. And working with young people from different backgrounds helped us feel connected to something outside our insular little world in California.

Now back in Minnesota, the nonprofit was also giving us a view into the gaping inequalities in our new community. Our students faced challenges that our kids never would. But they were persistent and smart and knew how to hustle. We were getting more inspiration from them than we'd ever give in return.

Our program wasn't operating at the scale of a tech company—in fact, it was the opposite. But for that reason, it felt deeply meaningful. We were learning the power of small organizations to make a difference in the individual lives of people. There was nothing extraordinary about the program we'd created; it simply took something we felt we could offer and gave it to someone else who needed it. In the process, we had gotten out of our comfort zone in our new community, and not just with other transplants or new neighbors.

While working with our Silicon North Stars was inspiring, back at home we had more elemental concerns: finding childcare for our own kids. It's a struggle for any parent in America today. As a new family in a new community, we were starting from scratch and didn't have much time. Mary made some desperate posts on Facebook, and I started googling "childcare near me."

Dozens of calls and visits later, we found a Russian immigrant named Natalya, who ran a small day care from the first floor of her home, less than a mile from our house. She called it Zen Montessori. Just reading the name somehow gave me hope.

I called her up on the drive home from work, and she told me she had one open slot.

"Is there any way you can make room for one more?" I begged.

"There are regulations that guide how many students I can have," Natalya answered. "But one of my students might be leaving soon; let me get back to you."

I told Mary and we scheduled a visit immediately. We drove to Natalya's house and walked inside. Perhaps our desperation gave us rose-colored glasses, but it seemed magical. A giant reading rug lay on a pristine hardwood floor, with toys, blocks, and games sitting on the shelves that surrounded the room. Five miniature violins hung on the wall, for a music program Natalya had built into her curriculum. Even though ten toddlers were ambling around the room doing various activities, the space looked infinitely cleaner than our own chaotic home.

"You're in luck," Natalya told us. "The student I thought might be leaving is, so I now have two slots."

We put a deposit down that same day and let the relief wash over us.

At first, the kids resisted going to day care. But Natalya was warm and caring. Luke began every day by making macaroni and cheese in a little toaster oven she'd set out. Before long both kids became acclimated and made friends. I found myself wishing that adults could make friends as fast as toddlers.

The more time we spent at Zen, the more I realized just how lucky we were to have found a childcare option for our kids that we liked and was nearby. As I began my job at DEED, I discovered that the agency ran a grant program focused on helping new childcare businesses get started in Minnesota. The reason the program existed is that we were eighty thousand slots short of childcare in the state, a common trend across the country.

The market for childcare is broken just about everywhere in America. There's a massive labor shortage and high turnover in the industry. The wages required to pay and retain workers, along with insurance costs and regulatory burdens for providers, drives the cost up to the point that, for many families, it makes more financial sense for one of the parents to stay at home with the kids rather than work. Economists estimate that the shortage costs the U.S. economy almost $125 billion in lost earnings every year.

It didn't used to be this way.

When I was growing up in Minnesota, my mom started an in-home day-care business to help make ends meet when my dad was getting his landscaping business started. Every day I'd come home after school to find many other people's kids playing in our living room. Because my mom was a registered provider, she was eligible to buy reduced-priced food to feed the kids she looked after, which she picked up from local schools. I remember being thrilled when we got to eat the same rectangular pizza pieces that we got on Pizza Day at school.

For my parents, the part-time business not only provided a financial lifeline, but it connected them with other families in our neighborhood and strengthened their social network in the community. My mom wasn't alone; there were lots of in-home providers back then. But for the last several decades in America, the costs of providing care have flattened the in-home childcare market. In their place, more center-based childcare chains have popped up, because in a business with razor-thin margins, it's easier to operate these at scale.

The feeling of community that people like Natalya and my mom built by looking after kids in their own homes feels like something worth preserving, connecting communities in a way that feels more intimate. You get to know someone when you spend time in their home. I learned about Natalya's family in Russia. Her husband, Keith, taught me about sailing on Lake Harriet. Their son, Leo, became friends with Luke and Violet. When he grew out of his first bike, he gave it to Luke, who learned to ride it on the sidewalk in front of Natalya's house.

As the holidays approached, Natalya invited all the families to a holiday concert. We packed into her living room in our winter coats, crouching into small chairs in front of a makeshift stage the kids had created. After a few holiday songs, Luke and Violet walked onto the stage for a violin duet. Mary and I had no idea it was coming. As they pulled their little violins up to their chins, my heart just about came out of my chest. Their music teacher led them through a rendition of "Twinkle, Twinkle, Little Star," and I felt something I never had before: the pride of seeing your kid learn something new that you had no part in at all. I had to wipe the tears from my eyes before wrapping them both in a hug.

Afterward, Mary and I returned to a conversation we'd visited a couple of times since we'd arrived in Minnesota. Was it time to try for a third kid? Between navigating new jobs and the demands of twins, it was hard to imagine how we'd make it work. But despite the fertility journey we'd been on, we hadn't stopped wanting a bigger family. When it comes to having kids, logic or bandwidth wasn't going to win out over our hearts.

"If we're going to do it, now's the time," Mary said.

A thousand miles away, in a freezer at the IVF clinic we'd been to in Colorado, sat eight frozen embryos we had left from the fertility cycle that had given us Violet and Luke. Just two miles away from our house in Minneapolis, a branch of that same clinic had just opened. It seemed like fate.

Mary called Colorado and they said they could ship the embryos to Minnesota so we could try here. The idea of our potential future offspring flying across the country to Minnesota, just like we had, only added to our sense of possibility.

Chapter 5

Silicon Heartland

P ushing a large, wheeled crate down Pennsylvania Avenue in Washington, D.C., my friends and I could see our nervous laughter freeze in the cold January air. Inside the crate was a TV monitor, a metal stand, a black tablecloth, and a laptop. It was the bare minimum for a low-budget production for a high-flying opportunity: we were interviewing the president of the United States at the White House.

Or, more accurately, YouTube was interviewing the president of the United States at the White House.

It was 2010, a year into President Obama's first term. Just a few months earlier, we had pitched the president's team on the idea of a "YouTube Interview" after his State of the Union address. We'd play him the top-voted questions in the country, allowing him to go straight to the people in his first interview after the major speech. Still fresh off a historic internet-fueled campaign victory, the president and his team agreed to the opportunity to reach younger Americans. It would be the first social media interview Obama did during his time in office.

Inside the White House Library, my team and I cobbled together our makeshift TV set, draping the black cloth over the TV stand with two chairs across from each other. No one at YouTube or Google had asked to see our script for the interview, or reviewed the top questions we'd be asking. We were on our own, in front of millions of viewers who tuned in for the YouTube live stream.

When President Obama walked in, everyone stood. It was like the weather had suddenly changed. Obama cut the tension by turning to a gaggle of White House reporters who were there to watch and quipped, "This kinda makes you guys irrelevant now, huh?"

They laughed and looked down at their notebooks. I don't think they knew quite what to make of the fact that a technology platform was about to interview the leader of the Free World. YouTube had already gained traction globally, but to see a handful of "kids" setting up in the White House to do what they'd trained decades for must have felt surreal.

Our inexperience was clear. In addition to using a homemade TV set, I'd somehow managed to wear brown socks with my black dress shoes, and then proceeded to cross my legs toward the camera during the interview so that my fashion faux pas was clearly visible to the millions of viewers watching.

After the interview, I picked up my phone to several text messages from friends telling me to CROSS YOUR LEGS THE OTHER WAY, hoping I'd see the message and fix my mistake. The YouTube commenters who noticed were a little less kind.

But I was only mortified for a moment. After all, I was just a guy working at a tech company with very little experience who had no right to be interviewing the president of the United States in the White House. Yet, because of YouTube, here I was.

As an upstart, YouTube was free from corporate overthink. The fact that a scrappy group of entrepreneurs had built a video website so good that it had surpassed tech behemoth Google's own video solution—leading to its acquisition by Google for $1.65 billion—was a huge source of pride at YouTube.

"Only in Silicon Valley could such a story take place," people said. And I believed it. All this momentum was possible because of the culture of Silicon Valley. Build things fast, try them out, and don't worry about making money until you have an audience. Let people try things, and don't get in their way. If you think you have a shot at interviewing the president of the United States, just ask him and then go do it.

It felt like I'd stumbled into the center of the universe, and I couldn't imagine I'd ever want to leave. Years later, after I did leave, I looked back at Silicon Valley's culture and couldn't help but compare it with my new home in Minnesota. Why was Silicon Valley so special?

What might I take with me as I ejected from the world's most dynamic economy and launched a new life working in government, two thousand miles away?

I had discovered Silicon Valley by luck, but I came to learn later that there was nothing accidental about the culture of innovation there. It grew from decades of investments and hard work by people, the government, and institutions. If you wanted to, you could trace the genesis of Bay Area culture back to the Gold Rush, which brought a flood of entrepreneurial hustle to the region. The proximity of shipping routes to Asia was an obvious advantage that helped grow the economy through the 1800s, but it was the founding of Stanford in 1885 that set the foundation for the culture that was to come.

Stanford became the anchor for research and talent in the region, and it set the stage for the tech economy's growth. The school focused on growing technology talent and built the world's first university research park in the early 1950s. When the Korean War hit, the Department of Defense started funding advanced technology research on the campus. Defense contractor Lockheed Martin moved there from Burbank, as did several others, to take advantage of the funding opportunities and talent. Like so many things in American life, the government played an outsized role in jump-starting growth.

The expanding ecosystem spawned startups like Hewlett-Packard, and it attracted private companies like General Electric and Sylvania to set up shop to benefit from the burgeoning market. Entrepreneurs like William Shockley, who is widely credited with having started the semiconductor boom that led to the term "Silicon Valley," helped grow the region's reputation. Successful chip companies thrived in this innovative culture, including Fairchild Semiconductor, a company that produced so many engineering leaders that it inspired over ninety spin-off companies. All those startups growing next to each other were able to trade talent and feed off one another's success.

With this combination of academic research, government investment, and ecosystem development, Silicon Valley had momentum. Decades later when I moved there, the advent of the internet put the region firmly on the global radar. Every year, the Valley pulls in by far the highest percentage of venture capital in the nation, often reaching upward of $80 billion in a single year.

From there came a unique brand of Silicon Valley swagger. When billion-dollar companies are being started almost every year out of people's garages, how can you not feel like your community is invincible? That kind of confidence drives a risk-taking culture that you need to build a dynamic startup ecosystem. And it helps entrepreneurs persevere through hard times—because building new things is really hard.

Now in Minnesota as a rookie state government official, I wondered if there was something I could do to help encourage that type of innovation in my new community. After all, the government had played a key role in Silicon Valley's success. Why couldn't we do the same in Minnesota?

I needed to ask only one person how to get started, and fortunately she lived under the same roof as me. Back at Google, Mary had traveled the world with her Google for Startups team to help entrepreneurs succeed, from Madrid and Paris to Seoul and Dubai. Now at Rise of the Rest, she was doing the same thing in venture capital, in a list of cities that looked a little different: St. Cloud, Minnesota; Indianapolis, Indiana; or Columbus, Ohio.

After she got back from one of these trips, this time to Fargo, North Dakota, for the Prairie Capital Summit, I asked Mary what she thought about the startup scene in the Midwest so far. She started unpacking, giving it some thought.

"Entrepreneurs here complain about a lack of venture capital, which is true," she said, pulling conference swag out of her suitcase. "And there's no shortage of good ideas in the Midwest. But sometimes I find the startups here are specific solutions to a problem, rather than a platform or product with potential for global scale."

She thought about it a bit further.

"I actually find that refreshing, but sometimes it can make it harder for those companies to land big venture investments."

A corporate sensibility in the area was another reason that startup culture was held back here, she offered. With the highest number of Fortune 500 companies per capita in the nation, the Twin Cities boasts successful established businesses, but their stability creates opportunity for a different kind of value proposition for engineers or technology leaders: tech jobs that are rewarding, but comfortable.

For those who do start companies, the businesses they choose felt different from those Mary saw in Silicon Valley.

"I met this company that detects mastitis in cows, called EIO Diagnostics," she shared, explaining their name came from the refrain of "Old MacDonald Had a Farm."

"They measure their growth not only in revenue, but in UUM," she said, explaining the acronym: "Udders Under Management."

It was a solid business and Mary was fascinated by their technology. But, of course, it did not intend to become the next Google or Facebook.

"Many entrepreneurs in the Midwest are trying to hit singles or doubles, not home runs," she reflected. "That creates a different environment that doesn't have quite the same risk-seeking culture that makes Silicon Valley such a magnet."

To explore how I might help make Minnesota more of a magnet

for entrepreneurs through my new job, I went to the office of Republican senator Eric Pratt, the chair of the Senate Jobs Committee. Pratt was a tall, dark-haired former banking executive who'd built a career on fighting fraud at Target and U.S. Bank. He had a reputation for being focused on his principles, and lived in the exurbs just southwest of Minneapolis.

As I sat in a chair across from his desk, I noticed a photo on his shelf of him in a Colorado Buffaloes football uniform.

"You played college football?" I asked.

His eyes lit up. "Linebacker," he confirmed.

I'd played wide receiver in college, so we traded some football stories. I found myself wondering what kind of a competitor Pratt might be in politics, and if we'd be able to find a way to work on the same team.

The truth is that we needed each other, because in the last election, Minnesota had voted in the only split legislature in the country. The Democrats controlled the House and Republicans controlled the Senate. It was a very Minnesota result: voters here have no problem splitting their ticket to signal that a divided government makes more rational decisions. That same sober mindset from our startup ecosystem was also prevalent in our politics.

That meant that anything we wanted to pass through the legislature, we had to convince Republicans in the Senate to vote for it as well. That's why I was sitting in Senator Pratt's office.

After we'd swapped a few football stories, I told Pratt about "Launch Minnesota," a program my team and I had been conceiving, based on some of Mary's insights, to incentivize startup growth.

The basic idea was to de-risk the startup journey for entrepreneurs. It included grants to pay for housing and childcare for early-stage tech founders so they could take the leap. It had money for community-building organizations across the state to provide startup training. And it would deliver grants and research dollars to help startup founders get going. Built into the program was a preference for founders of color, women, and veterans.

Pratt nodded; he seemed genuinely interested. I knew he'd need to convince his Republican colleagues to vote for it, some of whom might not get it like he did. Inside my bag was a book I'd been carrying around by an economist named Enrico Moretti, who showed that for every "innovation job" an economy creates, five new service sector jobs are created alongside it. I told Pratt about the research.

"Launch Minnesota isn't just about helping startups, but helping the whole state," I offered. He shook my hand and promised to think it over.

It was the beginning of my education in state legislative politics.

The Minnesota state legislature is part-time, and meets for only the first five months of the year. But in a split legislature, my team told me, no bills get signed until the final week. Each side passes its preferred legislation and doesn't want to make any "gives" until all the ideas have made it through committees and are on the table. While Pratt may have been receptive to Launch Minnesota, we'd still have to negotiate its passage alongside dozens of other priorities in the final budget deal.

With two days left before the session ended, Pratt and I joined a handful of other legislators and staffers in a large room on the third floor of the state capitol to negotiate the final jobs bill. Sitting across from each other at a large wooden table, the two of us debated funding to workforce nonprofits, incentive packages for businesses, and unemployment insurance law. We slid offers to each other across the table, printed out on pages from the capitol printer. In between conversations, Pratt and I would each retire into separate rooms with spreadsheets to reconfigure deal points and come back with counteroffers. But several sticking points remained.

When the negotiation turned to Launch Minnesota, Pratt said he didn't like one big item about the program: the inclusion of health insurance and childcare coverage for early-stage entrepreneurs.

"I don't like wedging social benefits into programs designed to grow our economy," Pratt told me. "Those kinds of programs belong in the health and human services bill."

To our team, those ideas were central to the program. They addressed one of the very issues holding back Minnesota's tech community—risk aversion from would-be startup founders working at established companies with generous benefits programs. But Pratt wouldn't budge.

As the final night of negotiations wore on before the end of the legislative session the following day, we still didn't have a deal. It was after midnight, and time was running out. Finally, around 1:00 a.m., the governor called us into the Cabinet Room, where he was working with the leaders of the Democratic House and Republican Senate on the overarching final budget, spread across several committees. It turned out the jobs bill wasn't the only one held up in this divided government. Still, it felt a little bit like being called into the principal's office. I could tell that Pratt felt the same way.

We returned to our negotiation, and the intensity only mounted. And it wasn't just about DEED's budget—there were heated disagreements about a wage-theft law that our Labor Department was pushing. Pratt gave a passionate speech about how it was too punitive on businesses; the labor commissioner gave a passionate speech to the contrary. You could feel the heat emanating from everyone's heads in the stuffy late-night air.

Yet it turned out that the pressure from the governor and other legislative leaders was what we needed. A deal started to come together. On Launch Minnesota, we agreed to keep the housing benefits and lose the childcare benefits.

By two o'clock in the morning, we reached a deal on the entire jobs bill, which would be voted on the next day.

I drove from the capitol in St. Paul back to our home in Minneapolis and collapsed into bed at around four in the morning, muttering to Mary that we'd gotten Launch Minnesota across the finish line before falling asleep.

A few hours later, I drove back to St. Paul. Sitting in my office with my team to finalize the bill's language, I got a call from Senator Pratt. He was calling to point out a clarification. "We removed both the childcare and housing benefits from the final Launch Minnesota agreement, right?"

I was surprised—I was certain we'd compromised to keep the housing benefits and lose the childcare benefits. Maybe we'd both been too bleary-eyed the night before to get clear on the details, or maybe the language we'd used was too vague, but Pratt was clearly frustrated. I was, too. It was too late to change anything now, the bill was already heading to the floor and would be voted through soon.

A few days later, I got a letter from his office. It was an official data practices request, asking that I turn over every single email and text message that I'd ever sent to anyone about Launch Minnesota and its formation. The excitement I'd felt about our compromise was jolted. I was back to being the fish in the aquarium.

When I called Pratt about the letter, he brushed it off. "We're just taking a look," he said nonchalantly, as if fishing through all of someone's emails was the most normal thing in the world.

In the weeks that followed my team would provide Pratt with all the emails and texts he requested, and we never heard anything back from him about it. But I would never send an email or a text message through the same eyes again. It was my first lesson in the battle of building trust across the aisle, something that would get much harder in the months to come.

Getting Launch Minnesota off the ground was the fun part. We held a kickoff event in front of a packed house of founders and investors at a new coworking space in Minneapolis, where Senator Pratt, the governor, and I all thanked each other and the entrepreneurs who'd advocated for launching the program. The debates over details had faded. We took our victory lap together.

This new program, designed to make Minnesota more like Silicon Valley, gave me a chance to meet more of the state's entrepreneurs. But the more I explored, the more I started to realize that Minnesota's startup superpower was the fact that it wasn't like Silicon Valley at all.

———

One spring afternoon, I walked into a biotech company called Miromatrix, nestled in a nondescript office park just off the freeway in a suburb of Minneapolis.

Inside, something remarkable was happening.

The startup's energetic founder, Jeff Ross, greeted me in the lobby and took me on a tour of their laboratory. When I peered through the large pane-glass windows, my jaw dropped. Floating in plastic buckets of red fluid on dozens of metal tables were bioengineered human organs. Human livers and kidneys that had been grown from pig cells, awaiting a chance to be transplanted into humans some day.

"We're dedicated to ending the organ transplant waiting list," Jeff told me in the same matter-of-fact tone you might use to tell someone what you had for lunch that day. He explained that over 20 percent of people on organ transplant lists die because they can't get an organ in time. If his startup's technology could get approved by the FDA for live transplants, that number could drop to zero.

Jeff was about my age, and had graduated from the University of Minnesota's PhD program. He'd been at Miromatrix working on this technology for over twelve years, first as a product development lead and then as CEO. To succeed in this field, you not only have to be an expert in regenerative medicine, but also have the patience to keep moving toward a goal year after year.

Jeff's company was making progress. Today was a ribbon-cutting ceremony for an expansion to their lab that our agency had helped fund. Jeff's team set up a podium and some red and white balloons in the lobby, where a few dozen Miromatrix employees and investors were mingling.

Jeff introduced me to a kidney transplant patient named Tim, who was enthusiastic about the potential of this technology.

"I've had my human donor kidneys for thirteen years, but they only last for fifteen or twenty," he shared. "I can't even get on the list for a new donor until my kidney is failing, and even then I might not get one from a live donor."

That meant an uncertain future. If a bioengineered kidney were readily available, that would change. When the ceremony began, Tim took the podium and addressed the Miromatrix employees.

"Your technology is a game changer," he told everyone as he shared his personal story. "You are all going to improve millions of people's lives." He had to pause to catch his breath and compose himself.

I could feel a lump growing in my own throat and looked around the room to see tears in the eyes of several in the crowd. Behind those tears was also a look of pride. The human impact of this startup's technology was in front of them. Their persistence and sense of purpose were palpable. Somehow it felt different to me than the feeling I got when I'd gone to events in Silicon Valley. It felt more . . . human.

As I left the event, I wondered how a company like this ended up getting founded in an office park in suburban Minneapolis. To find the answer, I went back to study how Minnesota's technology economy had emerged.

The more I learned, the more surprised I was to discover that Minnesota had its own technology boom around the same time as Silicon Valley. Mid-century, it was in Minnesota where the first distinctive computer industry in the United States formed, anchored by firms like Control Data Corporation and Honeywell. That spawned a collection of computer hardware companies that blossomed under a new super-computer boom.

These Minnesota tech companies gave the world innovations like the pacemaker and the black box flight-data recorder. Later, pioneering talent at the University of Minnesota created the internet "Gopher," which was hosting more of the internet than the entire World Wide Web in the early days. In fact, its visionary founder, Mark McCahill, was the one to coin the phrase "surfing the internet."

However, Minnesota's early tech companies didn't pivot well from hardware to software innovation, and the state's technology economy lost some of its momentum at the turn of the century. But what did come out of that supercomputer boom was a nation-leading medical technology sector that eventually sprung such companies as Miromatrix.

My home state's technology community had other unique ingredients. If Stanford is the anchor institution of Silicon Valley, then Minnesota's is the Mayo Clinic. Mayo is the number one hospital in the world, and it's located in Rochester, just over an hour outside the Twin Cities. The clinic pioneered a model for patient care that has drawn the top medical talent to Minnesota for decades. They serve over 1.3 million people every year, from all fifty states and over 130 countries.

I'd seen this firsthand. My dad had eye surgery at Mayo. My sister had lung surgery at Mayo. In both cases, it felt like going to the Google of hospitals—they focused on their patients and created a seamless experience for people at the most vulnerable moments of their lives.

Meanwhile in Minneapolis, the University of Minnesota (U of M) has become a top research and development university in the country, with more than 50 percent of the startups it spins out being in the life sciences.

The talent market created around Mayo and the U of M, combined with the engineering talent that had built America's supercomputer boom, has helped sprout hundreds of medical startups and led to the formation of Minnesota's Medical Alley, the largest cluster of medical companies in the world. Companies like Medtronic, 3M Medical, and Smiths Medical have all grown from that ecosystem. Today, Minnesota ranks first in the country for medical device patents per capita.

There's something deeply purposeful that comes with having a technology culture so focused on saving and improving lives. Maybe that was what made my new community different.

I began to see this purpose-driven culture everywhere I looked. One night at a startup community event we held for Launch Minnesota, an entrepreneur came up to me holding a blue-and-orange robot stuffed animal. At first glance, he seemed a little out of place.

He introduced himself as DeLonn Crosby, the founder of a company called SayKid. Behind wire-rimmed glasses and a tight crew cut, he was gregarious and passionate.

"A few years ago, my son got kicked out of preschool for behavioral issues," DeLonn said over the rumble of the packed event. "It changed everything for me. I started looking into how schools help children grow. If we took all the science of child development and just did the opposite, that's what American education looks like!"

DeLonn decided to do something about it, so he invented a toy robot stuffed animal to interact with kids, using all the best insights on how children learn. It talked with kids using voice-activated technology, playing games and answering questions in ways that helped kids open up in a comfortable environment.

SayKid would go on to win several awards, including the Amazon Alexa EdTech Skills Challenge. He continued to tote his SayKid stuffed animal with him wherever he went, the perfect prop for his persistence.

The more entrepreneurs I met, the more Minnesota felt unique. If swagger is the defining feature of Silicon Valley's startups, then maybe a sense of purpose was the defining feature of Minnesota's. People like Jeff and DeLonn were building things that solve real problems and make life better for their communities.

"What a lot of people don't know about Minnesota is that startups here are all about persisting," DeLonn shared. "That matters because rarely do people get the right answer on the first shot. . . . Ultimately you want to be in a place that has people who can think big and come together to work together. We found those people in Minnesota, so that's why we're here."

That purpose-driven startup culture has built one of the highest business survivability rates in the nation. Maybe it has something to do with the state's history. A hundred years ago, an agrarian economy in a cold-weather climate meant people had to help out their neighbors to survive. The humility and stoicism that comes from generations of building a life on the frozen prairie has bred hard work and a commitment to helping your neighbor that turns out to come in handy when starting a business.

There's a certain no-nonsense sensibility to entrepreneurs I was meeting in Minnesota. Life's too short and the winters are too cold to chase something that doesn't matter.

Yes, Minnesota can learn a lot from Silicon Valley: the risk-taking, the velocity, the swagger. But Silicon Valley can learn just as much from Minnesota: the determination, the focus on solving real problems, the conscience to do the right thing for your community.

At a time when technology growth continues to change our lives at a pace unseen in human history, tech companies could do a better job of balancing their swagger with a sense of conscience and purpose.

I was reminded of an app that had been all the rage in Silicon Valley around the time Mary and I had left. Called *Yo!*, the app literally had one function—to say the word "Yo" to someone else in your contact list. While some treated the app as a joke (it was launched on April Fools' Day), it quickly got $1.5 million in investment at a $10 million valuation. All that for an app whose utility was essentially to steal your attention with a gimmick.

"*Yo!*" would never have been invented in Minnesota.

———

The desire that Mary and I had to be part of a community that felt more rooted in purpose was part of the reason we'd left Silicon Valley for Minnesota in the first place. When we did, we became early participants in a growing exodus from the Bay Area. In recent years, tens of thousands of people left the region. According to research by the Hoover Institution at Stanford University, high tax rates, high labor costs, and declining quality of life are contributing factors.

As communities across America strive to grow tech markets, so many are looking to copy Silicon Valley. Arizona wants to be the Silicon Desert. A group of Midwestern states has leaned into Silicon Prairie. Heck, we even named our nonprofit Silicon North Stars.

What I learned is that these efforts will do best if they develop their own identities. When you're trying to build a community, you have to lean into your unique strengths. Copycat cultures don't stand out. Being different does.

That's what's begun to happen here. It seemed to me that our startup community was updating the Minnesota Model for a new generation. Mary put it best:

"What I love about startups here is that they solve real problems, invest in outcomes that have impact in their community, and focus on sectors central to a high quality of life. Especially healthcare."

Recently, a group of leaders in Minnesota successfully lobbied the federal government to become one of thirty-one "Tech Hubs" across the country. Their focus is medical technology. Dubbed "Med Tech 3.0," the collaboration between big med tech companies, early-stage startups, and research institutions like Mayo and the U of M is designed to further build a growing market. Artificial intelligence, data science, and device manufacturing are the focus of this effort to deepen the state's status as a global center for Med Tech.

Building a strong community is a lot like building a startup. You borrow ideas from lots of places, try them in new ways, and mix in your own concepts to do something unique. The best communities, like the best startups, succeed when they're rooted in what makes them special.

I never would have appreciated that if we'd stayed in Silicon Valley. Moving out of our bubble was starting to give me a much better sense for the rest of America.

Chapter 6

Boomerang

Halloween is the best holiday of the year when you have little kids. The whole concept is perfect. You get to dress up in whatever costume you want, go right up to people's houses to get free candy, and then stay up late eating that candy. It hits just about every button a little kid has.

In our house, Halloween bred a yearlong obsession with costumes. Violet and Luke wanted to dress up all the time, and we soon collected a giant bin of costumes in our basement, from Batman to Lion King to Thomas the Train. My favorite was a pair of hot dog pullover costumes we got for them, which Mary and I complemented with adult ketchup and mustard costumes.

What's the point of having twins if you can't dress them up in embarrassing matching outfits from time to time?

Of course, in Minnesota it's pretty cold by October 31, so the universal costume that every kid also wears is "winter jacket." People here still talk about a Halloween blizzard that happened in 1991, when we got three feet of snow.

But the weather doesn't stop anyone from going out. On our first Halloween in our new home, Mary and I met up with my youngest sister, Mary Beth, and her husband, Forrest, who'd also recently moved back to Minnesota, from Chicago. Mary Beth is a labor and delivery nurse, and Forrest is a data scientist working at a Minnesota-based logistics startup. With their two toddlers, we walked the neighborhood. My parents drove up from Northfield to join us.

My dad pushed our double stroller down the street as we walked past trees that had been blanketed with a fresh coat of snow earlier that day. Luke and Violet, now almost three, scampered between houses to load up on candy, retreating back to the stroller every once in a while to nestle under blankets and warm up. My mom walked alongside my sister and Mary, chatting in the evening air. When the cold did us in, we packed up and went home.

It all seemed very normal—another night with the family we'd moved across the country to be closer to. But if you'd told me when I was a kid that I'd be trick-or-treating with my parents and my own kids one day, I never would have believed it.

When I was a kid, we weren't allowed to trick-or-treat. My parents thought Halloween was a satanic holiday. And in our community, they weren't alone.

I grew up in the heart of what would later be called the "satanic panic," a strange period in our nation's history in which the idea that satanists were trying to infiltrate society through culture and institutions spread widely. Wild rumors grew that there was an underground effort to kidnap children for ritual sacrifice. Halloween was especially fraught. A girl in my fifth-grade class had to go home from school on Halloween because she was scared of getting kidnapped and couldn't stop crying.

As members of a conservative evangelical church, my mom and dad heard these tales and more from fellow congregants and our preacher. One Sunday night, they took me to a special sermon by a pair of traveling evangelists called the Peters Brothers. They were from St. Paul, and had gained national attention for their work to expose the dark side of rock and roll music's influence on young people.

Their presentation, "The Truth About Rock," had gained so much popularity that it landed them an interview on *Nightline* with Ted Koppel. Tonight, they'd come to Northfield for a presentation in front of a packed audience. My sister Kelly and I were six and eight, too young to be listening to much rock music yet. But the Peters Brothers scared us anyway.

"We're here tonight to talk about what the devil is wrong with rock music," the two clean-cut brothers began. They flashed heavy metal album covers and crude song lyrics on the projector screen, images we weren't used to seeing in the chapel. The congregation went silent.

The Peters Brothers criticized Elton John for promoting homosexuality. They took Cat Stevens to task for converting to Islam. They railed against David Lee Roth for promoting a promiscuous lifestyle during Van Halen concerts—so promiscuous, they claimed, that he'd taken out "paternity insurance." I didn't even know what that meant.

But what really got the crowd worked up was their explanation of "backward masking," a technique they claimed rock bands were using to put subliminal satanic messages into their music that could be heard when you played them backward. When the Peters Brothers played some examples and put the lyrics they'd deciphered up on the screen, a collective "Oooh" echoed across the crowd. Kelly and I fidgeted in our seats.

Years later, it would be shown that most of these messages were due to something called phonetic reversal—words that just sound different when played backward. In other cases, bands inserted messages as marketing stunts. Geraldo Rivera, the bombastic talk show host who produced a two-hour prime-time documentary for NBC on satanism that touched on these topics and more, apologized in the late 1990s for contributing to the national scare.

But at the time, the Peters Brothers had us believing satanists were using rock music to turn the whole nation against God.

"The Truth About Rock" struck a chord with my dad. A week after the Peters Brothers presentation, I walked by my parents' bedroom to find him going through his old record collection, taking a razor blade to almost every album he owned. He showed me some of the album covers of his favorite bands that he now felt were bad influences. And it wasn't just heavy metal bands.

"Look at this," he said, showing me the album cover for *Whipped Cream & Other Delights*, by Herb Alpert and the Tijuana Brass, which had a picture of a woman covered in whipped cream on it. Looking back, it's hard to imagine a 1960s brass band had a satanic influence, but Dad wanted to do the right thing.

Dad's tendency to go all in was just how he was built. He never did anything halfway. When he started a landscaping business, he pushed past his more introverted personality to knock on every door in the neighborhood to find customers. He built wooden ramps out of plywood so that he could run wheelbarrows of rock up into the truck. He bought and grew his own seedlings so he could save money; soon a nursery of potted plants lined the perimeter of our small backyard.

Things were lean at home for several years. We were on the reduced-priced lunch program in elementary school. Lacking health insurance, my parents paid for my sister Mary Beth's hospital bill by bartering landscaping services with their doctor.

Yet Dad seemed invincible to me. At over six feet two, he had a wiry, muscular frame. He loved playing games with us and was wildly creative, building forts and creating imaginary worlds that stretched our own creativity. The summers were different; he worked ten- or twelve-hour days, then came home and drew landscape plans for customers until he went to bed, only to wake up and do it all over again the next day. I rarely saw him in the summers until I started working for him in middle school.

Working for Dad was a daily lesson in hard work and efficiency. Point your wheelbarrow in the direction you're going to push it before you start loading it with rock. Park the truck in the location that minimizes the number of steps you have to take to get to it.

"If you lose ten percent of your efficiency every day, you've lost half a day of work by the end of the week," he told me once as we were driving to a job site. His hard work, alongside my mom, who was an equal partner in the business, provided a middle-class upbringing for us that helped send four kids to college.

Dad brought that same intensity to his faith. Though he'd been raised Methodist in a small Iowa town, he wasn't very religious until he became born again in his mid-twenties. From there, the church became a central influence in his life. My mom had grown up Catholic and had stayed faithful in her practice. After Dad's conversion, they explored both the Catholic Church and a protestant evangelical denomination, eventually deciding to raise us in the latter tradition.

I was a sensitive kid with a big imagination. The more I learned about the influence of Satan on the world, the more it felt so full of evil. When I was twelve, a boy my age named Jacob Wetterling was kidnapped in St. Joseph, Minnesota, just two hours away from our house. The tragic case wouldn't be solved for thirty years, and is one that affected every Minnesotan of my generation. His mother, Patty Wetterling, became a national advocate for child protection and one of the most inspirational Minnesotans of our generation.

To hear about a kid my age snatched off the side of the road in a small town just like ours terrified me. For years, I asked my sister to sleep on my bedroom floor with me at night.

Fear became a central emotion I grappled with for much of my youth. It gripped me so strongly that my parents and I started to call them "My fears." They asked me to see school counselors. On routine trips to Target, they encouraged me to walk a lap around the store by myself, something that made my stomach turn. The world was full of evil, and I wasn't ready for it.

When another traveling evangelist came to town for a Sunday-night service just like the Peters Brothers had, my parents brought me forward at the end and asked him to exorcize my fears. I sat trembling in the pew as this gray-haired man I'd never met before put his hand on my shoulder and demanded that the demons of fear leave my body.

Things got really weird when the evangelist started speaking in tongues. I'd heard about this before, but had never witnessed it. I peeked through closed eyelids to see him looking upward, fervently reciting what sounded like a garbled foreign language.

Switching back to English, he claimed to see demons rising out of me.

"There goes the fear of school," he said, as if giving a play-by-play of the exorcism. "There goes the fear of the night. And there goes the fear of your father."

It was unsettling. I left the church that night even more spooked about the world, not less. And those last words he said were haunting— was I really afraid of my dad?

In the years that followed, I started wondering about the world outside the church. By the time I was in middle school, the satanic panic was fading. By the time I was in high school, I was tired of being afraid. I was also angry at my parents for sheltering me from other ideas, and angry at the church for what I began to see as sanctimony. Mostly, I was just an angry teenager.

As my horizons expanded, the world felt less scary, but more unfair. The idea that there was only one path to salvation no longer made sense to me.

Was Gandhi really in hell because he wasn't a Christian? (Yes, my dad said.)

How could a god who said he loved people allow so much suffering? (God works in mysterious ways, said Dad.)

If other religions had the same moral lessons as ours, why were they so bad? (Jesus is the only way to heaven, Dad urged.)

My questions had my parents worried I was straying. Ten years after slashing his record albums, my dad went through my collection of CDs. He noticed that it included bands he thought were bad influences and took them away from me, then put me on a two-week Bible study. I was too mad to read a single word.

Later that year, when my grandma came for a visit, she and Dad took me to the Happy Chef restaurant in Northfield for breakfast. I suddenly got the sense that this was a planned intervention. But I wasn't having any of it and tried to head them off.

"There are so many different ways to live," I urged. "People around the world have all kinds of ways to find God."

There was a look of genuine concern and frustration on my dad's face.

"I just don't understand why you'd look for answers anywhere else, when all the answers are all right in front of you," he said, exasperated.

After I graduated, I left Minnesota for college in California. I did not plan to come back.

———

Leaving home, for me, was a revelation. Everything about California seemed perfect—the weather, the food, the people, the culture. Maybe it was just because it was different, and different felt good. From the moment I landed, I wanted to become Californian.

In my first week at football practice in college, I was sitting in a dark classroom with my teammates, watching film of a scrimmage from earlier that day with our coach, a dry, sarcastic man named Rick Candaele. After each play, he'd stop the video and share his critique. On one clip, I saw something I had a question about and raised my hand.

"Hey, say, Coach . . ." I began in a thick Minnesotan accent that drew out the long *o* in "Coach." The room erupted in laughter, and Coach Candaele got up from his chair and walked over to the light switch and flipped it on, turning toward me with a grin on his face.

"What the hell was that, Grove?"

My face turned red, but I laughed with the rest of them. One of our linemen nicknamed me, "Hey Say Coach," and he called me that for the rest of the season. I played along, but quickly trained myself to drop the Minnesotan accent. By the end of my first semester, there were no more long *o*'s.

My new teammates introduced me to punk rock music and board shorts. Many of them skateboarded to class, even in December. We all wore flip-flops every day. It felt like living on another planet.

But my connection to home and family was not easily erased. Near the end of the football preseason, a few teammates told me they'd scored some weed. Eager to try anything new, I got high with them. A few hours later, when the high swung toward a low, I suddenly became agitated and nervous. I became convinced I'd made a terrible mistake and wanted to make sure I never did again.

It was after midnight in California, the middle of the night in Minnesota. Without thinking, I picked up my dorm room phone and dialed home. My dad answered.

"Dad, I'm really high," I told him. "I never want to do this again." He talked me through the bad high before I fell asleep.

I woke up embarrassed. Neither of us ever mentioned the phone call again.

After I graduated, I moved even farther away from home. I got a job teaching English in Tokyo, and moved to Japan on my own. Though I thought I'd built up some tolerance for being away from home, living in Japan was hard. My tiny three-hundred-square-foot apartment felt isolating. Even though I'd taken Japanese in college, the language barrier was strong.

Every day I rode the subway to work and pored over my college Japanese textbook, practicing what I learned on the passengers sitting next to me. Yearning to meet some people, I thought joining an aikido class might help me branch out, so I went to the local government office to find out what classes were available. A kind, middle-aged government official named Tatsuo Takano took me under his wing to help me find a class. He even bought me the aikido uniform and invited me out to dinner with his family. We became fast friends.

In Japan, as in many parts of Asia, multigenerational families (families with more than one generation living under the same roof) are common. Takano's mother lived with him and his wife and daughter. Within a few months, we started talking about me moving in with their family, too. I could teach them English and they could teach me Japanese.

I left my tiny apartment behind with no regrets. The second half of my year in Japan was far better than the first.

Later in the year, my parents came to visit me. Now conversant in Japanese, I was able to show them around the country. We rode the bullet train to Kyoto, saw the sites, and ate new foods together. When we visited temples, we avoided the topic of religion. At the end of the visit, I took them to the airport. Before boarding the plane, my dad gave me a hug.

"I'm proud of you, Stever," he said. Instantly, I burst into tears and couldn't stop.

Sitting alone on the train ride back to Takano's house, I marveled at the weight of Dad's words. If I was so bent on being independent, why did his words carry such power?

I traveled Asia for several months afterward, spending months in India and Thailand. When I came back to the U.S., I had nowhere to go but Minnesota. I moved back in with my parents and worked for the family business while I figured out what was next.

Every day after I got home from work, I scoured the internet for jobs outside Minnesota. Mostly I looked for reporting jobs at newspapers. I applied everywhere from the *Queens Courier* in New York to the *Charles City Press* in Iowa. The editors who read my applications must have wondered why in the world this guy from Minnesota was applying to work at their local papers. I lost count of the rejection letters when they passed eighty.

A feeling of darkness began to come over me that I couldn't describe. Everything felt heavy. I'd built my vision of success on independence. Living with my parents and working for my dad was the opposite of that. I felt trapped.

One day while building a flagstone wall with my dad, I felt my arms grow weak. I couldn't lift the flagstone slabs up onto the wall anymore. The weight in my chest, which was always there when I spent time at home, was growing unbearable. I thought I might have mono, so I left the job and drove to the doctor, whose diagnosis was different: I was depressed.

He prescribed me Prozac. I went to the pharmacy to pick it up, but couldn't bring myself to take a pill. I probably should have. But it didn't fit my stubborn narrative of independence.

Maybe I could work my way out of the feeling. I started writing for the *Northfield News*, our small local newspaper that came out twice a week. It was an unpaid internship, but it was something. I covered high school sports and local news. Eventually I wrote a series about the effect of Hispanic immigration on our small town, a topic of much discussion given the influx Northfield had experienced in the previous decade.

Writing about a global topic through the eyes of my hometown felt a little less parochial. I poured my heart into the stories like my life depended on it. To me, it felt like it did. When the series won a small Minnesota Newspaper Association Award for "Best Social Issues Series," I felt like I'd won the Pulitzer Prize.

The small win gave me enough credibility to apply for another unpaid internship, this one at *The Atlantic* in Boston. When I got it, I couldn't pack my bags fast enough. I'd figure out how to make money once I got there.

———

The drive for independence is a foundational American ideal. Leaving home and striking out on your own is a rite of passage for lots of young people. For the last century, for example, the U.S. has had a lower rate of multigenerational families compared with other countries.

But was my journey of leaving my extended family for a different state, and then coming back to Minnesota years later, a common one? I decided to talk with some experts to see what I could learn.

The foremost researcher on the structure of the American family happens to be at the University of Minnesota. Steven Ruggles is a historical demographer who won a MacArthur Genius fellowship for his work creating the world's most extensive database of population statistics. When I reached him, I learned that he himself had recently escaped Minnesota, for a winter sabbatical in Barcelona. We hopped on a video call together.

I was a little nervous to be in the presence of a bona fide genius, but Ruggles's gray beard and jovial smile put me at ease. He looked a lot like the friendly theme park creator in the movie *Jurassic Park*.

I asked him what was important to know about family structure and mobility in America.

"First, I'm a believer that culture follows economics," Ruggles told me. "In the nineteenth century, you had largely agricultural households where family businesses kept extended families living together under the same roof out of necessity. But that's no longer the case."

The trend of people leaving their extended families and forming nuclear ones took off in the twentieth century, he explained, brought on by the shift in our economy from agriculture to industry. When you no longer needed all members of the extended family to manage the family farm, leaving home to get higher-paying jobs in industrial centers became popular.

The Groves were farming people in South English, Iowa, for many generations, and stayed near home until my grandfather Lyle, who served in World War II, left the family business and got a job selling insurance in a town nearby. My dad left Iowa for Minnesota and started his own family business, the landscaping company, but never pressured me to follow in his footsteps. If anything, he encouraged me to find something to do with my life that wasn't such hard physical work.

Despite the trend toward nuclear family and independence in America, most people who leave home to chart their own path don't go very far. The number of Americans living within an hour of their extended family is over 50 percent. That rate is even higher in the Midwest, at 62 percent.

To find out more about people leaving the Midwest altogether, I reached out to Minnesota's state demographer, Susan Brower. Now that I was officially a government nerd, Brower's job struck me as one of the coolest gigs in government. Being the state demographer means she spends her days examining reams of data and survey work to determine demographic and migration trends for Minnesota, which helps policymakers make decisions on everything from social service programs to economic development.

Brower was gracious to host me at her sparse, sun-splashed office behind the state capitol. Drinking coffee from a paper cup with a picture of the globe on it, Brower wore black glasses and was full of insights, which she shared with an exceedingly cheery demeanor that softened her scientific disposition. She was fresh off publishing a new paper about migration trends in Minnesota.

"People have been leaving the Midwest for decades," Brower explained to me. "It's a seemingly immovable trend." Her research showed that for the past twenty years, Minnesota has consistently lost residents to other states. It's part of a broader regional phenomenon—states in the "Frost Belt" have been losing people ever since the economy moved from agriculture to industry. Opportunities in bigger cities, and the coasts, drive some of the movement.

Out-migration in Minnesota, like in other Midwestern states, is most pronounced among young people. College-age kids leave the state at a greater rate than others. Many come back, but not all.

For those who do stay in the Midwest for college, the next challenge that states face is the so-called brain drain. This phenomenon has been well documented by the Center for Public Affairs Research at the University of Nebraska, tracking out-migration of people twenty-five years of age and older with a bachelor's degree since 2010. Their most recent findings show that college graduates leaving their extended families to chase jobs and opportunities in other places is an especially strong trend in Nebraska, Iowa, North Dakota, and Wisconsin. The U.S. Census Bureau reports that 43 percent of all interstate moves are motivated by new jobs.

What's different about migration in Minnesota, Brower told me, is that even if on the whole more people are leaving than coming, it's a "stickier" state than most. She reminded me of a statistic I'd read before.

"Something like seventy percent of the people who live here were born here, which is higher than most places," she said. The national average of people staying in the state they were born in is 64 percent; most Midwestern states fall well below that—North Dakota, for example, is at 48 percent.

For the Minnesotans who leave and come back, so-called boomerangs, they mostly do so in their twenties. Making a move later at age forty like I did is far less common, Brower shared.

"Once you have a stable job and your kids are in school, for most people, that's the moment they're settled in," she said.

I asked her about people who've never lived in the Midwest before choosing to live here. "I don't think moving to the Midwest is even on people's radars," she offered, sharing a recent experience she had trying to recruit a data scientist for her team from out of state to move here with his two young children. She had to convince both the data scientist and his ten-year-old son that Minnesota was right for them.

"That's why it's called flyover country," Brower laughed. "People in Connecticut aren't sitting there thinking, 'Gee, I should move to the Midwest!'"

When I lived in California, I had to point out my home state on the map to people quite often. To them, Minnesota was just one of those places in the middle of the country, indistinguishable from its neighbors.

However, when it comes to people making choices of where to live, Minnesota truly stands above all the rest with professional workers.

When Mary and I decided to move here, I was surprised to discover the nation-leading density of Fortune 500s in the Twin Cities. It's a place rich with managerial talent.

Myles Shaver, a business school professor at the University of Minnesota who left a tenured post at NYU to move here a few decades ago, was also floored by the unique density of corporate headquarters. Shaver and his wife, Susan, a native Minnesotan, moved to the Twin Cities because they wanted to start a family near family, and thought this was a place where they might both be happy in their careers.

As he began his work at the university, Shaver started meeting with local business executives and heard a common refrain: "It's hard to get people to move here, but once they're here, they never want to leave."

Shaver wanted to see if the data backed this claim. His research led to a book, *Headquarters Economy*, which showed that in fact it did. Surveying almost three thousand college-educated workers in management jobs at twenty-three Twin Cities corporations, he discovered a regional phenomenon that helped Minnesota punch above its weight: an economy of opportunity for professional workers.

Shaver and I met in his office at the university, just along the Mississippi River, which separates Minneapolis and St. Paul. Over a cup of Caribou Coffee (founded in Minnesota in 1992, now the fifth-largest coffee chain in the U.S.), he described to me the "virtuous cycle" that led to Minnesota's status as a corporate mecca.

"The Twin Cities is the number one metro in the country for dual-career households," he told me. "The economic opportunity not only leads to opportunities for both spouses, but creates opportunity for managers to leave one company and join another without having to leave the state."

Shaver's research showed him that only 15 percent of the managers who work in the Twin Cities were born here, suggesting that professionals come here for work, and then stay. An economy with opportunity creates a tax base that provides amenities like great public schools and outdoor recreation. When Shaver shared that almost 90 percent of those in his survey send their kids to public schools, his out-of-state colleagues at other business schools nearly fell out of their chairs.

This cluster of managerial talent feeds a "headquarters economy" that can retain talent due to density of career opportunities and amenities that, despite bad weather, make it worth it to stay in the state. The Twin Cities out-migration rates for professionals turns out to be the lowest of any major metro area in the country.

Reflecting on my conversations with these experts, I compared my journey with their insights: I, too, had left for college like many Minnesotans, but had stayed away far longer. We moved back before our kids were in school, which made the transition easier. The professional market in the Twin Cities made it more enticing for Mary, but I ended up leaving the private sector for government. My experience tracked the trends, but also didn't.

That escape from Northfield to Boston for the internship at *The Atlantic* had set me on a new course. I worked for a year doing odd jobs and freelancing, then went back to school to get a master's degree. After that, switching coasts to take a job at YouTube just felt like one other step in an adventure.

To get to Silicon Valley, I first took a train from Boston to Minnesota, where I stopped only long enough to buy a used car in Northfield that I drove the rest of the way to California. Living near home wasn't even a consideration. I needed to find my own way. Plus, the weight in my chest returned every time I was back in Minnesota.

Moving back two decades later was an entirely different proposition. I had made progress elsewhere. I was married with kids. Things felt more settled. I'd done something with my life and felt more certain about myself.

But I began to sense I was also part of a newer trend. In recent years, Americans have chosen to live near or with families more often than before, especially in the Midwest. Multigenerational families in America have steadily grown in the last few decades. Slowing economic growth and older marriage ages are both factors.

But I think something else is going on, too. At a time when the world is changing faster than ever before, living close to family provides comfort. The stability that existed in the social compact, and in our visions of the American Dream in the post–World War II era, has shifted. Rapid changes in society and technology have left the country feeling unsettled.

Susan Brower pointed out to me that mobility is decreasing across America in the past several decades.

If the nineteenth-century farm economy drove families to live together, and the twentieth-century industrial economy drove people to live separately in nuclear families, how is the twenty-first-century technology economy going to change how families live, with or near each other? Lack of housing and decreased economic opportunity are leading more people to marry later and live alone, while also driving more people to move back in with their parents. Ruggles, the demographer, thinks it's too early to tell how these trends will evolve.

"I'm a historian, not a futurist," he joked to me.

Neither am I. But what my heart was telling me, twenty years after desperately escaping home, was that building a community near family was a powerful force. A more powerful force than economic opportunity. Maybe culture does follow economics, but there's something deeply human about wanting to feel connected to your family in a place you can truly call home.

Trick-or-treating with my parents, my sister, and our twins in Minnesota, so many years after I'd left the state, I marveled at how much was changing for me. Dad and Mom had moved beyond the idea that Halloween and rock music were satanic. Conversations with them no longer felt like walking on thin ice all the time, waiting for religious topics to break things apart. The old familiar weight in my chest had gotten lighter.

Maybe I'd just grown up. Maybe it was having kids of my own. Maybe it was that my parents and I had found ways to accept each other over time. Or maybe our silent pact to ignore the topic of religion was our safe new normal.

At Christmas, Mary and I drove the kids to Northfield to my parents' small farm to spend the holiday with my brother and sisters and their families. We all squeezed into my parents' small house in the country for Christmas dinner. We played euchre and watched football. My dad dressed up in a full Santa costume and brought presents to the grandkids. Later, all the men went outside behind the barn and hung an old Green Bay Packers jersey on a stick, then put a jar of gasoline behind it and took turns shooting a .22 rifle until the jersey exploded into flames. Some good, stupid fun.

As I watched Luke and Violet wrestle with their cousins, who doted on them incessantly, the benefits of being back in Minnesota fully sank in. They could see themselves as part of a broader network of support. The connections with their grandparents, aunts and uncles, and cousins were special, something we couldn't have given them in the same way in California.

On Christmas Eve, the whole family packed into our cars to drive five minutes to my parents' church, a different congregation than we'd grown up in. It was just assumed that we would go to the service, but not just because of my parents. My brother-in-law, Kelly's husband, Abe, was the head pastor.

Though we had the same parents, Kelly had gone the opposite direction from me. She always believed in God, she attended a Christian college, and she married a man of faith right after graduation. Despite our different paths, I admired her journey. She always seemed at peace on matters of faith.

And Abe was a catch. We became fast friends, and I never felt awkward talking with him about religion. Maybe it's because we kept our conversations intellectual. They were never judgmental. Our relationship became rare: a family member I could talk with about religion, without things blowing up.

Going to church with my entire family, however, still made me uneasy. As I strapped the twins into their car seats in my parents' driveway, I could feel the old familiar weight on my chest. My parents didn't directly ask me to come to the service; I could have stayed back.

As the Grove family shuffled into the pews to hear Abe preach, I took a seat and looked down at my shoes, striving for minimally viable participation. A gifted speaker, Abe gave a kind and thoughtful Christmas message, far from the fire and brimstone I'd grown up with. He had no guilt in his words, didn't speak in tongues, and no exorcisms occurred.

Yet I still felt uneasy. Just being in a church made me feel judged. The idea that you had to believe a certain thing in order to avoid eternal damnation felt so binary, so dogmatic. How could a loving God demand such obedience, punishable by hell? And why was personal salvation the central purpose of church communities? It seemed like churches should exist to serve people, not convert them.

Relieved when the service was over, I watched people embrace their neighbors and share holiday greetings. I had to admit that this was a powerful community for its members, where people cared about each other. Their shared beliefs sustained them, made them feel connected and comforted.

Although uncomfortable to admit, I longed for that same feeling of community. With a family of my own now, I was hoping that we could feel rooted. But that weight in my chest held me back. The trade-offs felt too great. Joining a spiritual community meant I'd have to be spiritual myself, and I wasn't sure just what that path looked like.

When I told Mary on the drive back to my parents' that I still had feelings of being the black sheep in the family, she tried hard to understand. But to her, it didn't compute.

"Your parents don't seem like they pressure you on religion at all," she observed. "Why is this still a thing for you?"

I had trouble explaining it, even to myself.

Chapter 7

Stuck

Nothing screams "government" more than a messy, convoluted flowchart.

As if government processes weren't already complicated enough, trying to map them in a picture is often an exercise in futility. Yet I'd decided to try anyway. Standing at a whiteboard in my office along with my team at DEED, I asked them to help me understand how our workforce development system worked. I got out a marker and tried to draw what I heard.

Hamse Warfa, a talented and thoughtful Somali immigrant who led our workforce development team, walked me through the dozens of steps required to issue a grant to a workforce organization. Kevin McKinnon, the ex-hockey player, tried to explain how the fifty different workforce centers operated, with a series of regional partners who all had different ideas on how that system should run. Darielle Dannen, our legislative director, educated me on how the legislature directed funding from the state's workforce development system to fund job-training programs.

When we were done, the whiteboard was a tangled mess of arrows, boxes, and diagrams that seemed to melt together. If the system was this complicated to me, how would it seem to someone trying to navigate that system to find a job? I let out a groan.

"Are you regretting your life choices, Commissioner?" joked Darielle.

I laughed, but also gritted my teeth. The complexity of the agency could be maddening, and so many things needed fixing. Ever since I started, I'd been compiling a long to-do list: *Modernize our website for job seekers. Simplify and speed up our process for delivering grants. Expand the number of disabled Minnesotans we can serve in our programs. Shift our business-incentive funding to industries of the future. Fix our department of disability services leadership structure.*

Plus, staffing our agency was a challenge. Government salaries make it hard to recruit great talent. Our office burned through three schedulers in my first year.

"You're going too fast," Hamse told me when I asked for his advice. "There are many things to fix, but you can't do all of them at once." He was right, of course. But it was hard to prioritize when I saw so many areas that deserved attention. Some days felt like there were dozens of fires to put out, but I only had one squirt gun and I had to get a hundred approvals just to get to use it.

The pressure I put on myself to succeed was substantial. I felt like I'd traded a lot to be in this position, and I wanted to make it count. That made finding patience elusive. A year into the job, I was gaining a more sober perspective of what was possible, and what might not be. There was no way I was going to leave this job accomplishing everything that needed to be done.

With every big change, you're bound to have a honeymoon period. The romantic notion of moving to my home state and doing public service had sustained me through my first several months on the job. I got plenty of "attaboys" on my decision. The early momentum that comes with learning a lot of new things at once, and having the early social capital of being the new person, gave me a sometimes unrealistic sense of potential.

But almost a year into working in government, the honeymoon

was starting to fade. I still didn't understand so many parts of the job. I oversaw a vast agency, with hundreds of programs created over decades by thousands of legislators and stakeholders—all on top of a system that was messy and often opaque.

I started telling Mary about the challenges. The more I told her about the struggle with inertia at the agency, the more I started missing the speed of Silicon Valley. Impulsively, I started an email newsletter to send to friends and former colleagues in California. I called it "The View from Minnesota."

It felt cathartic to talk about life in the aquarium, what I was learning about making change, and the challenges of government culture. I wrote about our kids and how we were navigating this new place. What I wrote last, however, was the most important:

> Having a great partner is everything. For us, changing so much about our life has required belief in the step we're taking and a sense of purpose about what we're doing. Mary is doing incredible work to grow the startup ecosystem here in the middle of the country. And we're figuring it all out together. No matter where this chapter leads us, it feels like a unique part of our adventure together.

Neither Mary nor I could have made this transition without each other. Every day we shared stories about our discoveries in our new community, and consistently traded advice about how to make it here. We'd both gone all in on trying to meet people and were making progress, but it felt slow.

When our second Christmas hit, we decided to return to California for a visit. One of my best friends, Nick, worked at Meta and lived just a few blocks from our old house in Menlo Park. He and his family were traveling for the holiday, and he kindly offered up his place for us to crash. We jumped at the offer.

As soon as we settled in, we set out to visit our favorite places in the neighborhood. We took our kids to the Magical Bridge Playground, a massive sunny jungle gym, where they frolicked with the other kids, who were also wearing only T-shirts in December. We took a hike through the redwoods near Kings Mountain, and retraced our steps at our favorite weekend walk at Bedwell Bayfront Park. We jumped on the trampoline in Nick's backyard, and got burritos at Tacos el Grullense, our favorite Mexican restaurant (it's hard to find good Mexican food in Minnesota).

The feelings of déjà vu were strong. Things felt eerily familiar, yet different. It was like transplanting ourselves into a life that we would have had, if we never left. I found it impossible not to compare this vacation with our old life with the new one we'd created.

Walking barefoot in the park was a far cry from pulling on snow boots just to go out and get the mail. Eating ramen on the patio at our favorite ramen stand felt glorious compared with ordering pizza to the house on a dark, snowy winter night. Swinging by Google to show the kids giant Android statues and buildings with slides inside of them felt very different from pulling a suit on every day to testify at a hearing in the basement of the state capitol.

I kept telling myself that this was a vacation, not real life. But I couldn't help but feel wistful about our old life.

For Mary, it was worse.

"I almost wish we hadn't come here," she said one night after we put the kids to bed. Tears welled up in her eyes. "Being here just reminds me of all the great things we gave up. I miss our old life."

I did, too. But I didn't want to admit it. I felt like one of us had to defend the decision we'd made to reinvent ourselves in the Midwest.

"It's probably just the winter blues," I reasoned. "It'll feel better once we get home and settle into our routine again."

This did not go over well.

"You're not listening to me," Mary shot back. "I'm a California girl. Everything here feels so familiar. The people, the culture, the energy, the diversity. Things back in Minnesota still feel foreign to me."

It was hard to hear. We'd just moved our whole life to Minnesota, but these were serious doubts. Though it was painful, it wasn't shocking. Both of us had been trying hard to find our groove in Minnesota, but it hadn't all clicked yet. Making friends was taking time, even for extroverted people who are assertive by nature. We hadn't found our community yet.

And then, of course, the weather. The woman I'd once nicknamed "Sunshine" pulled out her phone and asked me to guess the number of sunny days per year in Minneapolis. I winced. Maybe 150?

"It's ninety-five," she said, looking up from her phone dryly. "In Menlo Park, it's two hundred fifty-five."

Mary's disgust with the cold weather carried all the more weight because she'd been trying so hard to acclimate. She'd bought all the right winter gear to stay warm, even picked up some figure skates to try ice-skating. I'd gotten an indoor lamp that mimics the sun to put in her office, but it didn't work very well and was collecting dust after a few months.

Mary had also been trying more meaningful ways to make it work. Turning her focus outward, she had started making meals for other people. Food had always been a way of expressing love in her family. On the first snowy day of our first winter in Minnesota, Mary made a lasagna for a new friend she'd met through the kids' preschool, a woman who'd just had a baby. She covered the pan in tinfoil to keep it warm, then bundled up in a puffy purple parka and hopped in our minivan to drive it across town to her new friend's house.

It was her first time driving in the snow, and I stupidly forgot to mention anything to her about how to navigate the slick roads. Just a block from our house, she came to a small hill, where the minivan skidded and fishtailed down the incline and ran smack into the bumper of a black Audi sedan parked at the bottom.

It ended up being a few thousand dollars' worth of damage and an unhappy end to her good deed. I kicked myself for weeks for not telling her more about the hazards of winter driving.

To make our new lives work, we had to figure out how to get through the winters. The truth is, even though I grew up in Minnesota, I was struggling with them, too. After we moved to Minnesota, I learned that I had something called Raynaud's syndrome, a condition that decreases blood flow to your fingertips and toes when it's cold out. The slightest drop in temperature and I'd find my fingers quickly turning white, and then numb. Holding them under hot water to regain feeling felt like a million pinpricks through my skin.

The cold weather had made everything about our new home seem a little less romantic, even my new job. A typical day meant hopping in my car before sunrise to drive to St. Paul in the morning darkness on a snowbanked freeway. I'd hold my hands up to the dashboard heater to keep them warm, sometimes steering with my elbows if both hands were freezing. I'd park my car on a rooftop parking lot in sub-zero weather, then trudge over snowbanks to get across the street to the capitol building. From there I'd shuffle into some committee hearing to take questions from state legislators about whatever the issue of the day happened to be. My hands would usually thaw out about halfway through the hearing, then I'd head back outside and drive to the agency for a day of meetings. The next day, the same thing all over again.

It felt adventurous at first. But on some winter days, it felt like a complete and utter slog.

We returned to Minnesota from our "old-life vacation" unsettled. For a month, we ignored the conversation. There wasn't an easy solution and we both had a lot to digest. But on a cold February night, we settled into the big couch in our living room after putting the kids to bed and the topic came up again.

"I don't know if I can do this," Mary admitted, picking up right where we'd left off a month earlier in California.

I could see the stress on her face. I could feel the pressure building inside my head. It wasn't just one thing, it was many things. It was the winters, the pressure of trying to meet new people and build a community, and the intensity of new jobs that were radically different from our old life.

For Mary, the biggest challenge of her new job was travel. Rise of the Rest had been a great experience for her to learn the venture capital business. But the firm was based in Washington, D.C., where the other partners were living, and she felt distant from her colleagues.

One of them was J. D. Vance, who managed their small team of four venture partners under their founder, Steve Case. Vance clearly had political ambitions that seemed to go beyond venture. He often appeared on television and was happy to keep an aggressive travel schedule. The other two partners spent a lot of time on the road, too. But with two small twins at home, Mary found that her natural proclivity for travel had waned. Plus, it wasn't helping make Minneapolis feel like home.

With Mary's travel schedule, and the late nights and unexpected hours of my new job in government, we found ourselves relying on my parents and babysitters for help more often than we'd planned. It was great to be near our extended family here, but we were actually seeing less of our kids in Minnesota than we did in California.

We both had to believe this was the right decision. I was starting to think Mary might not anymore.

This time, though, I didn't try to defend the decision, or reason away the feelings of doubt. We needed to honestly discuss our options.

"What if we made plans to eventually move back?" I found myself saying. "Or at least explore what that might look like?"

The mention of retreat felt like breaking the ice on one of Minnesota's ten thousand frozen lakes. We began to fantasize about what we'd do if we went back to California. We could probably get jobs at Google again, or maybe Mary could work for a venture capital firm. Or what if we tried San Diego, Mary's hometown?

Neither of us was sure if we were serious. But it felt surprisingly cathartic to imagine other futures. My nervousness to admit we might have made a mistake, and my desire to defend the adventure we'd chosen, gave way to the liberating feeling that can come only with honest and constructive conversation with a partner you love and trust.

Mary felt it, too. We brainstormed ideas, timelines, and spoke further about how we felt. After an hour, she suggested something that surprised me even more.

"What if I left my job and started my own venture capital fund?" she offered. "I could set my own hours, travel a lot less, and make more time for the kids."

I loved the idea. It felt very Mary. The daughter of immigrant entrepreneurs, she'd always had the itch to start something of her own—it was in her blood. She'd been a natural at starting ambitious new programs at Google and inspiring people to follow a vision, and now she had even more experience in the venture capital space and exposure to incredible talent and ideas across the Midwest, and the country. She talked a little bit more about what it could look like, reasoning that the shift would also help us see if Minnesota was right for us long-term.

"If we're going to give Minnesota a real shot, then I should be working from here, too," she argued. We discussed it more and decided it was worth a go. If after a few years it didn't work, we could revisit our path again.

The conversation was a humbling breakthrough. To see someone I loved so much struggle, but then double down on our new life, was moving. Her selflessness and tenacity made me want to make this new adventure work even more. It was a fresh dose of inspiration, and made us feel even closer.

Reinventing our lives in Minnesota may have seemed like a romantic fantasy at first. But our new life wasn't a fantasy, it was real life. Having a partner to figure it out with, and being completely honest, vulnerable, and open to all options, was the only way this was going to work.

Mary left her job and got to work starting her own venture capital firm. She partnered with another local investor and they started raising their own fund. They called it Bread & Butter Ventures—an homage to one of Minnesota's nicknames, "the Bread and Butter State." With a focus on the industries the state is best known for—healthcare, agriculture, and food tech—they started investing in companies across the country, with a special eye on startups based in the middle of America.

We changed a few small things in our family, too. We bought some snow tires for the minivan. I picked up a pair of battery-powered mittens to keep my hands warm. And we splurged on a hot tub for the backyard, which allowed us to be outside in the winter without our limbs going numb.

It felt like betting on Minnesota again. Since we'd arrived, we both found new jobs based here, both focused on trying to build up the new community we'd chosen for our family. We promised each other we'd keep talking openly about how we felt. If things didn't work out, we could always move back to California.

But if we were going to take a real shot at living in Minnesota, this was it.

Part II

Crisis

Chapter 8

No Playbook

Have you been following this virus in China?" Governor Walz said to me, looking down as he scrolled through his phone. We were sitting inside a small jet in St. Paul, about to take off for a short visit to a broadband internet provider in central Minnesota. It was January 2020.

I told him I'd read about it.

"We had a few of these to manage when I was in Congress," he reflected. "Ebola and Zika. The important thing is to stop them early. It's hard." The governor looked back down at his phone. "Apparently, they think this one can be contained." He didn't sound very convinced.

The coronavirus had been spreading fast in China, and had started appearing in a few countries in Europe. Scientists didn't know much yet, but what they did know was that the fatality rate was high. If it did hit our shores, it sounded like the kind of problem the federal government would be counted on to handle.

The plane took off, and soon we landed in Melrose, Minnesota, and drove to the small headquarters of the broadband provider, a company called Arvig. There, we began the typical "formula" for a government visit: A clutch of local officials greeted us at Arvig's headquarters, where a sampling of local business leaders were gathered to share their testimonials. A tour had been arranged for us to see the business, nod our heads, and point at things while asking questions. A roundtable with name placards had been arranged for a discussion after the tour, surrounded by local news cameras on large tripods, ready to capture sound bites.

The Formula maximized time with local leaders and churned out local media hits that demonstrated your government in action, working for you!

The governor followed the company's leaders into a cool, windowless room, where dozens of computer servers stood on metal racks. Over the whir of large cooling fans, we learned about the company's work to expand broadband internet access in rural Minnesota.

A recent DEED grant would help them expand their coverage beyond where they would have normally provided service. Our office's broadband program had already built one of the leading models for rural internet expansion in the country, issuing hundreds of millions in grants over the last decade to connect hundreds of thousands of homes, businesses, and schools to high-speed internet. It was designed to give matching dollars to fill a market gap of rural pockets of the state that companies would otherwise overlook.

"The market does wonderful things, but there's also that final mile," the governor reflected as we sat down for the roundtable.

A company called Farm Systems, which installs robots and other equipment on dairy farms, shared that they couldn't troubleshoot their technology remotely without broadband. Next, a boat manufacturer named Chuck told us that he'd held off on growing his sales efforts because the company didn't have the broadband needed to mount an internet advertising campaign.

"A strong broadband connection helps us manage our website, our Facebook page, our ads," he said to the cameras, praising the grant.

As a town of fewer than four thousand people, Melrose was no metropolis. But these business owners and their neighbors loved living there for the quality of life, access to the outdoors, and the benefits of small-town living. None of that is possible without access to high-speed internet, a utility as important as water or electricity today.

Using state dollars to help Melrose connect with the rest of the world also connected it with the rest of Minnesota. It gave people in communities like this one a belief that they were part of a larger community that looked out for each other, a sense that rural and urban parts of the state shared the same Minnesota identity.

The governor gave a few interviews, then we got back on the plane. We were bound for St. Paul, but we were also flying into uncertainty. In the coming days, the coronavirus crisis would change everything. It would challenge the foundation of American communities everywhere. It would strike doubt in those who believed harmony between urban and rural places was possible. And it would throw my new world into chaos, teaching me more about the new community I was trying to build than anything I'd learned so far.

The Formula we just executed in Melrose went out the window. There wasn't a playbook for what lay ahead.

———

The first health briefing I attended on the coronavirus was terrifying. Our health commissioner, a seasoned state government veteran named Jan Malcolm, brought together scientists from the University of Minnesota to share what they knew. The governor invited me because of the effect the growing pandemic might have on the economy.

"Unchecked, we estimate this virus will kill 74,000 Minnesotans by August," said the lead researcher. "With mitigation measures, we could get that number down to 50,000."

The call went silent. Even the governor was quiet. I did the math—that was the equivalent of about twenty-five 9/11s, just in Minnesota alone.

As the federal government shut down the borders, the NBA

canceled its season, and news reports flowed in of overrun hospitals in New York City, it became clear that the coherent national plan we'd expected from the federal government wasn't coming soon. In its place, the governor started calling daily press conferences to share what we knew, and what state government was doing about it. Jan and I joined him every day.

Each day the governor made a new, mind-boggling announcement. First he shut down schools. Then bars and restaurants. Then he issued a "stay at home" order for the whole state, which shut down all businesses not deemed "essential" by a federal government database we consulted. In a matter of days, we lost over 400,000 jobs across Minnesota. Not the statistic I had suspected we'd ever hit when I became head of the jobs department.

All of the governor's executive orders had optimistic timelines of a few weeks at most. We hoped scientists would figure out a solution by then.

Without a clear national plan, every state had to figure out the best approach on its own. It was like fifty different science experiments playing out alongside each other. And overnight, like state government officials everywhere in America, I had a new job: to help navigate my new community through a crisis.

Every day at 2:00 p.m., I stared out at dozens of reporters, who sat socially distant from each other in a large conference room at the Department of Revenue, where the press conferences took place. A row of local news cameras pointed at the podium, capturing every word. Millions of Minnesotans watched from home. It all happened so fast that at first I felt like an actor playing a government official on TV.

I took my cues from Governor Walz, who seemed calm, decisive, and honest in the briefings. His training as a schoolteacher came in handy as he explained in clear terms what was happening and why we were taking the actions we were. People started calling him "Minnesota's Dad."

I tried my best to project the same confidence and calm. The primary topic I was tasked with addressing first was unemployment insurance. Hundreds of thousands of people were applying to a complicated government program for the first time. They not only needed to know how it worked, but if it would work at all given the flood of applications pouring in.

Truthfully, I hadn't known much about the program before I entered government. And I certainly hadn't taken the job to focus on an eighty-five-year-old social benefits program that seemed to be humming along quite nicely. But now it was job number one. I had a lot of studying to do, and fast. It turns out unemployment insurance is a complex program, run differently in every state, with layers upon layers of rules designed to prevent fraud.

But my lack of detailed background with the program proved to be an advantage. It forced me to understand how it worked with fresh eyes and explain it in a way that people could understand. Once again, being an outsider in government helped.

"The scope and scale of this is stunning," I acknowledged from the podium when the governor asked me to step forward. Carefully, I walked through how the program worked.

"Unemployment insurance helps workers who are separated from their jobs by no fault of their own, which is what so many Minnesotans face today," I explained, reading from notes I'd scribbled down hours earlier. "Employers pay a tax into a trust fund that is used to issue payments to workers who are unemployed."

The governor had just signed another executive order to ensure employers didn't get increased tax rates to expand the trust fund, because a pandemic was clearly not the fault of any employer, either.

"Our trust fund is healthy," I added, hoping that it would remain the case. "It's one of the largest funds per capita that any state has."

A barrage of questions followed and I did my best to answer them. Again, I tried to follow the tone the governor had set earlier—be empathetic, be confident, and don't be afraid to say what you know and don't know.

It felt surreal. After a few days of press conferences, I started getting recognized in grocery stores.

Back at the agency, we had to figure out how we were going to expand unemployment insurance so broadly. Six months earlier, when the previous program director had retired, I'd promoted a seasoned government bureaucrat named Jim Hegman to lead the unemployment insurance division. With a black-and-gray-speckled beard, he spoke with a precision and speed that reminded me of engineers I had worked with at Google. I soon trusted him deeply.

We gathered Jim's leadership team in a conference room at DEED and sketched out a plan on a whiteboard. One person would be in charge of staffing support. A group of three would form a technology SWAT team to make sure our website wouldn't crash. A point person for communications and reporting took the lead on building a nightly report for the governor on our progress. And a daily meeting would ensure we monitored progress and raised issues as needed. Jim would handle the most complicated cases and oversee the department's effort.

Watching Jim direct the response was like watching a great conductor command an orchestra. The frustrations I'd had with government red tape melted away as I saw him snap the bureaucracy into action. Program adjustments that would have taken months to happen before were now processed in minutes as Jim made one decisive move after the next.

We shifted staff to work from home as quickly as possible to keep them safe. We asked customers to apply on particular days based on their Social Security numbers, in order to manage website loads. We started processing applications on Sundays for the first time ever. We added two extra servers to manage the massive influx of web traffic and began the process of moving the entire system over to the cloud to keep it stable.

Jim kept the team focused. When I suggested we create a chatbot to help respond to the influx of customer questions and complaints, he wasted no time telling me what a bad idea it was. "We have a good system for customer service and a stable website," he said. "But a chatbot is going to be distracting, and it will frustrate customers."

He spoke with the confidence of someone who'd spent decades running our customer service department and consistently winning national awards for excellence. Minnesota's seasonal economy had forced our program to be both stronger and more nimble than lots of other states. In a typical year, the department would have to quadruple the number of accounts it handled when the weather got bad and construction and other trades couldn't work outside. That meant we were used to big changes in our customer base, a muscle memory that came in handy now.

At Google, we had a mantra: focus on the user. But I didn't need to teach that to Jim and the team. Their mantra, which Jim repeated often, was almost the same: "Everything we do inside this building is for the people outside this building."

For the first time, I was seeing what a powerful and stabilizing force a well-run government could be. For all its frustrating policies and procedures, when a crisis strikes, the machine of government can have the capacity to respond with speed and scale. It can come to the rescue of its citizens, the most basic function it serves. The decades of experience that were common for people working in the agency, and had often frustrated me in my first year on the job, were suddenly a huge asset. Career professionals knew how to move a complicated system when disaster struck, and they knew where to push for innovation—and where not to.

I found myself wondering why government couldn't always operate with this kind of speed and precision. Essentially it all came down to risk. In normal times, the risk of going fast and breaking things will put your department in hot water with the public. People don't want government breaking anything. But in a crisis, the risk of going slow and not delivering will put your team in even hotter water. You wanted an agency that could flex its appetite for risk when the moment demanded it. I was amazed to see that happening now.

When federal government support for unemployment insurance did come, I watched Jim direct his team to swiftly adapt the new programs. Each was complex to administer: an extra $600 in weekly benefits, an expansion of benefits to independent workers and contractors, and an extension in the number of eligible weeks. But Jim and our team navigated the federal government and other state agencies for support, and within days Minnesota had become the first state in the country to enact all three new programs.

The weebees were getting the job done. Remarkably, the early days of this crisis were growing my faith in the bureaucracy.

———

As two weeks of shutdowns turned into two months, which morphed into "indefinitely," our crisis management efforts grew. The days and nights blurred together. Every day began with a singular focus: How can we help get people through this and keep the state intact? And every day ended with a singular question: Are we doing this right?

Of course, it also changed life at home. I started getting threats online from social media accounts that were trolling me for the pandemic information I was sharing online. I was used to trolls by now, but when they began mentioning Mary and the kids, it started to get uncomfortable.

I knew I wasn't alone—the governor and Jan had it far worse. I'd seen reports of state government officials in other states confronting angry protesters at their homes. Our commissioner of public safety contacted the Minneapolis Police Department, and they started driving by our house on a regular basis. Sometimes they'd park on the block for a few hours. I told the neighbors it was just a precaution. Mary and I were glad that the kids were too young to notice or understand. But I felt terrible for the stress this was bringing to our family.

Mary had found herself in a position we never agreed to: the primary caregiver for the kids. We'd prided ourselves on being equal parents. But now I had no way of giving as much as she could. After dozens of meetings a day, I tried to at least be there to tuck the kids in at night. But after that I was right back in meetings with the rest of my colleagues.

One such night, after putting the kids to bed, I trudged down to our basement, where I'd set up a work-from-home office. I flipped open my laptop to log in to a regular meeting that I had come to dread: the Safe Reopening Group.

The Safe Reopening Group was a collection of state government leaders whom the governor had asked me to bring together to make recommendations on reopening the economy after his initial stay-at-home order. Shutting down "nonessential" businesses wasn't going over so well. How do you tell a small business they aren't "essential," when their very existence is essential to their own livelihoods? Thankfully, the governor wanted to follow the science, but also keep a close eye on our economic health. It was our job to help advise him on how to best do that.

The Safe Reopening Group almost never agreed. Health officials were incentivized to keep the economy locked down. I was concerned about losing jobs and businesses forever. We had endless debates based on shifting understandings of the virus and the data surrounding it, and usually ended up suggesting a range of options for the governor to consider. It was all a deeply uncomfortable exercise in social engineering.

That night was especially tense. I'd been hearing from shuttered businesses for months that we needed to open up the economy or risk losing entire industry sectors. But I knew health officials would be strongly opposed. I set a cup of coffee next to my computer as it booted up the video call.

As the faces of my colleagues began to pop onto the screen, everyone looked exhausted. Epidemiologists had strained looks on their faces. An assistant commissioner who led the children's cabinet held her young child on her lap. Our IT commissioner—who was leading our outreach to Minnesota's sports teams simply because he'd been a high school basketball coach and wanted to help—pulled big head-phones over his ears so as not to wake up his four-year-old sleeping in the next room.

"What's in that coffee cup, and can I have some?" a deputy health commissioner joked to me. I chuckled. There was an occasional air of gallows humor in these meetings that helped us get through them intact.

We then began what had by now become a familiar ritual. An ep-idemiologist from the health department walked through the latest COVID data—how fast it was spreading, where it was spreading, and what the problem spots were. Next, a staffer from the governor's office pulled up a slide with detailed grids we'd created outlining different business types: bars and restaurants, barbershops, gyms and fitness centers, and so on. Next to each business type were listed options for restrictions we were evaluating:

Percent capacity allowed. Total number of people allowed. Masking requirement. Social-distancing requirement. All variables in our social engineering experiment.

As my eyes scrolled through the list, I grimaced. Eager to get more businesses open, I recommended we allow restaurants to open at 50 percent capacity.

That wasn't a random suggestion. I'd gotten it after speaking with hundreds of restaurant owners in regular calls I was hosting with busi-nesses. Every day I held different roundtables, staring through my screen into the businesses of people across the state who were desperate for a lifeline.

A pizza shop owner in Fergus Falls sat in front of his redbrick pizza oven. A steakhouse owner in Wayzata sat at her bar with a bottle of tequila sitting next to her. A bowling alley operator in Mankato dialed in from her empty arcade.

None of them were fans of our orders to put restrictions on busi-nesses. Once, a call with hotel operators got so intense that I had to ask one of the participants to leave.

"You're killing our businesses—there's no way we can come back from this!" he kept shouting into the call, talking over everyone else.

But the restaurants were the most persistent. The regulations we'd put into place in their industry were among the most complex. Social-distancing requirements, masking imperatives, table size restrictions, percent capacity limits. It was too much to navigate. They were constantly pushing back and wrote letters imploring us to change our course.

"Hospitality is a force for good in our communities, and the Governor and his administration would be wise to leverage that force, rather than watch it flicker out," wrote the head of Hospitality Minnesota in a public letter. Most felt they could easily operate at 50 percent capacity while still accounting for social-distancing requirements.

I shared these concerns with the Safe Reopening Group. I told them about the pizza owner and the steakhouse owner and the arcade operator.

A health official who had her video camera turned off jumped on my suggestion of 50 percent capacity, suggesting we start at 30 percent instead.

I sighed. I shared again what the restaurant owners told me earlier that day—that opening up at less than 50 percent capacity wasn't worth it.

The health official cut me off. "I don't believe that," she shot back sharply. "We should set the limit at thirty percent capacity first, and make them prove they won't reopen under that guideline. Businesses tend to buckle under pressure."

It sounded arbitrary to me, and condescending to people whose livelihoods were at stake. I leaned back in my chair and asked how we knew that 30 percent capacity was significantly safer than 50 percent. It was a genuine question, though in my fatigue it probably came off as combative. The health official exploded.

"People are dying, Steve!" she screamed back.

The meeting went silent. Tired faces turned to shock. We'd had plenty of disagreements, but not like this. The pressure was getting to us all.

Finally, someone deflected to another topic (a very Minnesotan Nice way of managing conflict).

Looking back, it seems darkly comical—two government officials yelling at each other over a few percentage points in a guideline. But when your whole community feels like it is sinking, every person on that ship counts. The same passion that had brought us together in that very first government orientation session over a year ago was now colliding with the biggest test of our careers.

When I trudged back upstairs an hour later, Mary was still awake. I told her about the exasperated health official's outburst. And about the equally exasperated business owners who seemed on the verge of tears each time we met. She listened for as long as I needed to talk.

When I finished, she said, "What do you think, is all this worth it?"

I was surprised by how quickly I answered yes. Everyone in the world was struggling with the pandemic. Beyond the sheer terror of the health crisis, the feeling of helplessness was just as pervasive. But I got to wake up every morning and do something about it. It was messy and difficult. But working in government during this crisis was giving me a chance to be useful at a time of hopelessness.

Chapter 9

Coming Apart

C risis can pull people together, and it can tear them apart. Often, I discovered, it does both at the same time.

The dueling tensions of meetings with angry business owners and meetings with exhausted colleagues were persistent. But the even bigger rift growing across the state was the fault line between rural and urban Minnesota.

Though we lived in Minneapolis, I was raised in rural Minnesota, and felt like I understood the differences intuitively. Growing up in Northfield, I knew that my parents and our neighbors cherished our independence. One of the reasons my dad had started his own landscaping business is that he believed in self-reliance, being his own boss. He didn't want to work for anyone else.

My parents had moved us from town to a small three-acre property in the country when I was in sixth grade. They wanted to raise us in a more rural setting, and they wanted enough room to run their business without having to depend on others to rent land to store landscaping materials. I grew up playing on giant piles of shredded bark, and watering the plants that we potted and grew on our own land. Having a small business meant my parents got to live by their own schedule, set their own prices, and make their own way.

They worked harder than they ever would have if they worked for someone else. But they liked it that way.

Government programs were not my dad's favorite. Unemployment insurance was something he understood, but hated paying for in the offseason, when his employees didn't find winter jobs. Excessive regulations were an impediment that chipped away at already narrow margins. And new taxes that didn't consider how hard it was to start a small business made most liberal politicians seem out of step.

Though my dad had retired before the pandemic hit, I often imagined how he'd have reacted to all the emergency business restrictions coming out of St. Paul. He was a man of reason, but more government mandates would have been frustrating.

I saw that frustration every day in the business owners and people I met with in Greater Minnesota. The restrictions that rained down from the capitol exasperated rural Minnesotans. Having someone dictate your every step runs in direct opposition to feeling independent. Being told by your government how many people could sit in your restaurant or how closely you could stand next to your neighbor went against the whole reason people enjoyed living in rural towns in the first place.

Similar to the rest of rural America, Greater Minnesota has a much higher percentage of small businesses and self-employed workers. Years of American economic policy has rewarded massive growth and big business, which by definition had more resources and cushion to navigate a catastrophe like this one. Now, smaller business owners were suffering the most, and more of them lived in the rural parts of our state.

Compounding this frustration was the simple physical fact that life is less dense in small towns.

"Living in Greater Minnesota is a natural form of social distancing," was a refrain I heard often. "We don't need restrictions to stay safe."

When I drove outside the Twin Cities, I saw billboards that expressed people's frustrations. One had a picture of a man's head twisted around his body and shoved up his rear end. It read, "Governor Walz: Northern MN is trying to see things from your point of view."

I shook my head as I drove by. I knew how hard the governor was trying to do the right thing, and how impossible the decisions were. No vaccine existed yet, there was no end in sight, and the death toll was climbing every day. At the end of one very difficult Safe Reopening Group meeting, in which he'd made a tough call to increase restrictions due to a spike in COVID cases, the governor told a few of us, "That's probably going to cost me reelection, but it's the right thing to do."

The vitriol in Greater Minnesota felt far away from the governor's winning campaign slogan of just a year earlier. "One Minnesota" was an ideal that had resonated with the state. It had tapped into a long history of shared identity in being Minnesotan, no matter where you lived. And it was fueled by an approach to state government that was more robust and active than almost any place in the country.

The broadband program we'd highlighted in Melrose was just one example of what I discovered was a history of significant state government investments across Minnesota. In the 1920s, the legislature began investing to build one of the most expansive highway systems in the country. That meant state dollars went into making roads that connected towns and cities directly with each other, without requiring you to go through Minneapolis–St. Paul first to get somewhere else.

Investments in infrastructure didn't stop with roads. Minnesota was one of the first places to put state dollars into water and sewer infrastructure. Through a series of grants and low-interest loan programs, the state helped communities across Minnesota accelerate their infrastructure, which attracted more companies to set up shop here. That helped places like Rochester entice IBM to build its second headquarters here in the 1950s. And it gave places like Thief River Falls, a hamlet in the northwestern pocket of the state with just over 8,500 people, the chance to grow major employers like DigiKey and Arctic Cat.

How this Minnesota Model for urban-rural connections came together owes much of its origin to the formation and dominance of the Farmer-Labor Party in the first half of the twentieth century. The unlikely coalition between rural farmers and urban laborers would become the most successful third party in American political history.

It started as a movement. Drought and economic depression had created catastrophe for farmers, plummeting the price of wheat and leading many to lose their farms. In the city, jobs were hard to find and those that did exist had low wages from owners who worked hard to prevent unionization. Though their professions were very different, the two groups shared a dislike for monopolies, inequality, and middlemen.

That's when a St. Paul labor leader named William Mahoney met a farmer and Sunday school teacher named Susie Stageberg. Mahoney was the publisher of the *St. Paul Union Advocate*, and Stageberg was the editor of the Red Wing *Organized Farmer*. Both were seeing that neither the Democratic nor Republican Party seemed to be paying attention to their concerns. Both groups felt like big business was ripping them off, and the simple insight that they'd be stronger together drove a unique urban-rural coalition. The broader surge in populist sentiment in America brought more and more people to their cause.

The movement galvanized when a streetcar strike in 1917 brought laborers to the streets, fighting for higher wages and better working conditions. Farmers joined them, seeing a shared purpose in their cause. Large-scale protests across Minneapolis and St. Paul ensued as thousands of people marched over the course of several months. The demonstrations often turned violent, and the federal government took notice. While the strike ultimately wasn't successful, this watershed moment in the labor movement showed urban and rural interests could work together.

A year later, the Farmer-Labor political party was officially born. Over the next twenty-eight years, the party would produce three Minnesota governors, four senators, and nine congresspeople. At its peak, the Farmer-Labor Party was far more dominant than the Democratic

Party in the state, until the two finally merged in 1944. No third party in American politics has ever landed that many candidates in state and federal government. The legacy of the coalition lives on today in the name of the Democratic Party in Minnesota, which goes by DFL: Democratic-Farmer-Labor Party.

The more I learned, the more I realized that Minnesota's investments in connecting the urban and rural parts of our state helped create a sense of community here that's different. That bleeds into culture as well—many Minnesotans living in the Twin Cities own cabins "up north" in lake country. Often people in Minneapolis care about environmental protection in northern Minnesota, because that's their home, too.

And in late August, the entire state converges on the Twin Cities for the "Great Minnesota Get-Together," or the Minnesota State Fair. It's one of the biggest and most popular state fairs in the entire country, a literal example of Minnesotans coming together to connect from across the state.

But, of course, the state fair was canceled in 2020, robbing us of our annual chance for a statewide block party.

This idea of "One Minnesota" was the result of decades of focused efforts by people, government, political movements, and businesses to make the most of a resource-rich patch of land in the cold, northern plains of America. It helped fuel a sense of Minnesota pride that I'd sensed, but could never quite explain.

I now understood Minnesota exceptionalism a whole lot better.

The arrival of a crisis did not make the unraveling of that sense of community inevitable. Past moments of hardship had actually brought the state closer together. In 1910, a fire that took nearly 300,000 acres of land near Minnesota's northern border and killed dozens of people led to the founding of the Forest Service, to engage in active forest management and conservation. In 1997, a flood of the Red River on our border with North Dakota drew scores of volunteers to the area and billions of dollars of investment in forecasting and satellite technology that made future floods far less disastrous. And in 2007, when the I-35 bridge collapsed in Minneapolis, killing 13 people and injuring 145, volunteers again flocked to the scene, and the wake-up call led to more investments to repair bridges statewide.

But the pandemic was different. It was neither acute nor simple to fix. It was dragging on indefinitely. It required decisions from state government that got to the core of what kind of society we want to live in. And it was coming after a decade of increased polarization in the country that was chipping away at Minnesota's sense of unity even before the pandemic arrived.

That polarization, between a blue metro and a red Greater Minnesota, often devolved into debates over who was paying their fair share. Metropolitan Minnesotans would complain that tax dollars from urban areas subsidized life in rural ones. Purely from a math perspective, that's true: for every tax dollar it receives from the state, Minneapolis generates more than three and a half dollars in tax revenue. But the Twin Cities are dependent on rural economies, too. Minnesota's manufacturing industry—the second-largest contributor to state GDP—has almost half its jobs in Greater Minnesota. If Minnesota's rural economy crumbled, the state would be in deep trouble.

We were connected to each other, whether people liked it or not.

The more towns I visited in Greater Minnesota, the more concerned I became by the lack of credible information sources across the state. The rapid decline of local newspapers was at the heart of the problem. When I convened groups of businesses to get feedback and share the latest on our government's efforts, I consistently heard people say, "Where can we find this information? We're not getting enough information from the capitol!"

At first that was frustrating, given the number of blogs and emails and media outreach we were doing to keep people informed—not to mention the fact that the internet puts the entire world's information just a click away.

But expecting someone to read a government website, or a metro-based newspaper, wasn't enough. In the last twenty years, the number of journalists working in rural Minnesota has dropped by almost 65 percent, and 35 percent of rural newspapers have completely disappeared. When you don't have a trusted source of local news in your community, it changes how you get information that you trust and believe in.

In place of trusted local journalism, misinformation was growing. The politicization of the pandemic, often wrapped in misinformation about bizarre cures for the disease, for example, or about the end of the pandemic always being just a few weeks away, filled a vacuum left by decaying local news organizations.

The politics were changing, too. A few years earlier, the rise of Trump's candidacy had capitalized on many of the growing national divisions between urban and rural America to change the political map in Minnesota. In 2016, Trump turned counties that had long been Democratic strongholds into pockets of conservative populism. According to Ballotpedia, of the 206 counties across the U.S. that flipped for Trump after supporting Obama, almost 10 percent of them were in Minnesota.

The Iron Range, with its heavily unionized mining industry that had long been a DFL stronghold, began to turn red. Republicans successfully lifted up concerns over the economy as the cyclical mining industry teetered. The Farmer-Labor coalition in rural Minnesota seemed to be unraveling before our very eyes.

A polarized political landscape, an indefinite crisis, increased government regulation, and deep grievances over fairness mixed into a toxic stew that was driving a state that once felt broadly unified into one that, now, felt more divided by the day.

———

And then came the masks. There was no more visible division between people's views on the pandemic than masks. When the governor decided to issue a mask mandate for the state after many blue and red states had already done so, we knew it wouldn't be easy.

I called a team meeting at DEED to discuss how we could smooth the transition to the mask mandate set to go into effect in a week. We brainstormed a few ideas, but kept coming back to one: What if we shipped masks to all the businesses across the state, so they could offer them to customers? It might be a great olive branch, especially to small businesses who'd been so hurt by our restrictions.

We'd been hosting a regular call with all of the chambers of commerce across Minnesota, and realized we could work with them on distributing the masks. I called the commissioner at the Department of Administration, who was in charge of the state's PPE supply.

"You're in luck," she told me. "We have four million masks in storage that we can spare, and I think we can move quickly. Just give me names and addresses."

A few days later, we'd gotten most of the chamber leaders on board and our team built a plan to distribute the 4 million masks to each of them, based on county population. Spreadsheets were built, calculations made, outreach strategies kicked into gear. Once again, it was beautiful to see the bureaucracy snap into action. The scale of government was far more intoxicating than the scale I'd worked at in tech; reaching an entire state with our work could save lives and strengthen communities. It really meant something.

The governor's office loved our mask program. They were busy creating a broader advocacy effort to encourage allies to write letters to local media to encourage mask use. The communications team drafted email templates that groups could use if they wanted, sending me one in case we wanted to use them for our mask program.

In the frenzy of building the distribution program on a tight deadline, I neglected to read the template letter closely, and simply attached it to a mass email I sent to the chamber leaders.

"To make this work—we need your help," I wrote, encouraging them to use the attached letter template to spread the word:

"On behalf of ORGANIZATION NAME, I/we stand in support of Governor Tim Walz's statewide masking requirement," the letter began. It went on to say, "We applaud Governor Walz for issuing a mask requirement . . ."

Whoops. Asking business owners who were bucking at restrictions to applaud the governor for another mandate was like asking your enemy to present you with a gold star.

Soon after, someone shared the template letter with the press. And so, on the same day we'd secured a front-page headline to champion the herculean effort the team had built to distribute millions of masks, there was a competing headline next to it, criticizing me for sending the letter template. I buried my face in my hands.

The leader of the Senate Republicans, Paul Gazelka, called my move a "poor decision."

"The public needs to see a reprimand and explanation of this abuse of power," he said. Some Republican lawmakers started calling for my removal.

The Senate, which is required to confirm commissioners at some point during their terms, had confirmed hardly any of us so far. It was a calculated move. It made it feel like one misstep and the Republican-controlled Senate could call a vote to oust us from our jobs.

Nancy Leppink, the labor commissioner and veteran regulator with a steely spine who had clashed repeatedly with Senator Pratt on our jobs committee, was the first to go. Pratt claimed she wasn't working collaboratively with businesses on COVID policy and the new wage-theft law, and led a movement with his colleagues to deny her confirmation on a party-line vote. We all saw something different: this was clearly a move to get back at the governor for his approach to the pandemic.

Just a month later, the Senate ousted the commerce commissioner, another veteran of state politics, Steve Kelley. More seemingly manufactured reasons came with the decision, but it was the same tactic—to strike a blow to our efforts to mitigate the pandemic.

One by one, they were dismantling the governor's cabinet. It was an unprecedented move that threatened to derail state government. This was Minnesota, a place that prided itself on getting along, on bipartisanship. What was happening to us?

In a speech on the Senate floor, Gazelka said the Republicans were considering other commissioners, too. Fresh off my fumble with the masking letter, he mentioned my name.

I knew I needed to call him to save my job. So I closed my office door, gritted my teeth, and dialed his number.

I was shocked by how calm and kind he was on the phone. "I appreciate all you're doing to work with businesses, Commissioner," he said. This did not sound like the same person I'd heard railing against me and my colleagues on the Senate floor. I explained my mistake and he thanked me for making the call, saying it meant a lot to him. It was hard to reconcile this thoughtful voice on the phone with the passionate speeches in the Senate. It was an insight into the different personas politicians use when they feel they need to.

Luckily, my job was safe, for now.

But these were becoming such strange jobs. Commissioners were hired by the governor and traditionally confirmed quickly so that they could do the work of leading the government. Now the pandemic had thrust us into the political spotlight. It wasn't just in Minnesota—government officials across the country felt pressure, in particular commissioners of health. The confirmation battle in Minnesota was more pronounced than in most places, however. It felt out of step with the kind of place the state had aspired to be.

A few months later, I went to a backyard goodbye party for Myron Frans, the MMB commissioner who'd given me the whiteboard lesson on government when I started. Myron had decided after ten years as a commissioner at two different agencies that it was time to move on. Though his job was never under threat, ten years was a long time to be in the hot seat and he was ready for something new.

The party was held at the home of Laura Bishop, the Pollution

Control Agency commissioner, who'd also been under fire from the Senate. A dozen or so of my fellow commissioners were there. I found Laura standing by her backyard grill and we chatted for a while, pulling down our masks to take sips of sparkling water as we commiserated about this strange new world we were living in.

"These jobs are impossible," Laura said. I nodded. The Senate had been unhappy with her because of rules she and the governor had made requiring dealerships to sell electric cars—something that was within the agency's purview, but that some legislators and auto dealers didn't like. In normal times, the disagreement might have played out in other ways, but in the current climate the Senate felt compelled to go straight to the nuclear option and suggest her removal. It was particularly strange because Laura had come from the private sector and was as business-friendly a commissioner as you were going to find in an environmental agency. And this topic wasn't even related to the pandemic.

"You know, if they think someone else can do the job better, they can have it!" Laura joked to me.

A few months later, she, too, would be forced out by the Senate—the third commissioner to go. Every time a commissioner was removed by the Republican Senate, it set off a storm of debate.

We were in new territory. The job I'd signed up for was no longer the job I had. I was frustrated. We'd moved to Minnesota to help build and invest in a community. I'd taken a job focused on building the state up. I knew this was a place that was uniquely connected. And now I was watching it come undone.

One afternoon, the governor called my cell phone unexpectedly. I wondered for a moment if another catastrophe had taken place. But the governor wasn't calling with another emergency. He was calling to apologize.

"I'm sorry you have to go through all of this," he told me. "I know this isn't what you expected when you signed on. I'm sorry it's been so hard. I'm grateful for your service."

It was a small but touching act. I felt like my fuel tank had just been refilled. I thanked him and told him I was all in.

And I was. Our unemployment insurance payments were keeping families afloat. Emergency small business loan programs were helping some small businesses survive. Our pandemic mitigation was saving lives, and it was less harsh than it could have been given the economic concerns I was allowed to bring to the table every day. It may have been maddeningly difficult, but it was deeply meaningful.

The crisis was also giving us an opportunity to move faster and more decisively, unsticking bureaucratic inertia in favor of life-saving actions. The arrows we took from the public every day were hard to absorb, but being honest and showing up was making a difference. People knew we were in an impossible position and didn't expect perfection.

Day by day, I was discovering something about myself that I would have otherwise never had the chance to learn: I liked working in a crisis.

The realization came at just the right time, because more crisis was to come.

Chapter 10

Inflamed

One afternoon in late May, I picked up my phone to see a news alert that a Black man had died at the hands of the police, just a few miles from our home. When I clicked on the link, there was a video filmed by a bystander named Darnella Frazier that captured it all. Watching George Floyd lie helpless on the ground for nine minutes and twenty-nine seconds, under the knee of a white police officer, was horrifying. COVID was already stealing the last breaths from thousands of people every day. How could an officer of the law so callously do the same, to a man lying helpless on the ground, crying for his mother?

As the video of Floyd's murder quickly spread across the internet, it caused nationwide shock. Locally, protests formed across the city, concentrated on Lake Street in Minneapolis. As I watched people gather in massive crowds to speak out against the murder and racism, suddenly our internal debates over the proper size and social-distancing protocols of outdoor social gatherings—which had seemed so important just days earlier—felt oddly quaint.

A few nights later, Minneapolis went up in flames. Mary and I put the twins to bed and turned on CNN. From our open window we could hear sirens. On the TV, we saw protesters destroying Lake Street.

Store owners rushed to get plywood up on their windows to protect their businesses. Though our home was far from the center of the action, the moment felt dangerously unpredictable. I thought about the kids sleeping upstairs, and wondered out loud to Mary how far the violence would expand. I started texting with people I knew who lived closer to the chaos to see if they were okay.

We stayed up most of the night watching it all unfold on TV, devastated. Devastated at yet another killing of a Black man by law enforcement. Devastated that our city was being destroyed. Devastated that the racism behind the Minnesota Paradox was so viciously persistent. And devastated that in a moment of crisis, we seemed powerless to prevent our community from going up in flames.

The next morning, I went over to Lake Street. DEED had a workforce center right along the corridor where the riots were happening, and I wanted to see the office and try to understand what had happened in our community.

What I saw was chaos. Charred window frames sat empty on buildings that had been gutted by fire. Many structures had collapsed entirely, their twisted beams lying tangled on the ground amid smoldering embers. The signs of small businesses and restaurants, once brightly welcoming their customers, were melted and barely legible. *El Nuevo Rodeo Restaurante. Minnehaha Liquors.*

A black plume of smoke drifted out of the 3rd precinct police station that protesters had breached the night before. Where the makeshift plywood shields hadn't been broken by rioters, spray-painted messages remained: *FUCK 12, I Can't Breathe* and *JUSTICE FOR GEORGE* were painted hundreds of times along the street, calling out the police. Another set of messages simply pleaded for rioters to stay away. *PLEASE DON'T BURN, BLACK HOME NEXT DOOR, THANKS* read a hastily painted message sprayed on the plywood of the O'Reilly Auto Parts store.

I made my way toward the DEED workforce center at the corner of Chicago Avenue and Lake Street. The center, like dozens of others across the state, was our outpost to help people in the community find jobs. It was meant to be a beacon of light in the community. But it had not been spared. Several windows on the tan-brick building had been smashed in, their white accordion blinds bending awkwardly into the open air. An alarm blared inside, and I peered into the lobby to see our sprinkler system spraying water on workstations, where damaged computers sat silent amid broken cube walls.

Standing next to a Humvee across the street, two National Guard soldiers held machine guns and scanned the street for danger.

Later that day I met with legislators in the House and Senate jobs committees and we walked the streets together, talking with business owners. Jim Davnie, the House member who represented the neighborhood, walked me and Mohamud Noor, a Somali immigrant legislator who represented the district right next door, down the street. Soon we ran into the jobs committee chairs of the Senate and House, Senator Pratt and Representative Tim Mahoney. It was strange to see them together here on the streets, instead of in suits at the capitol.

We stopped at a small restaurant that had been decimated the night before. The owner, a Black woman who was rummaging through the debris on the floor of her burned-out dining room, let us step through the broken window and talk with her. Senator Pratt asked if she had insurance.

"I think so, but I'm not sure what it covers," she told us. The tables and chairs and stools were all burned to a crisp. As we walked farther down the street, we saw business after business destroyed beyond repair.

Representative Mahoney, a union plumber who represented a district in East St. Paul, reached down to the curb and picked up a bullet shell from a .22-caliber gun. He handed it to me.

"I've been seeing these everywhere," he said from behind a mask.

We began to see people emerge from their homes with small brooms and dustpans. Soon a line began to form, a makeshift broom brigade. People from all corners of the city descended on Lake Street to help sweep up the mess. It was a small step on a long road to rebuild.

When we finished our walk, I broke off from the legislators and zigzagged through the side streets to where I'd parked my scooter. On the short ride home, I kept thinking about these business owners—most of them people of color and so many of them immigrants. They were the same people who experienced the kind of discrimination that lay at the root of George Floyd's murder, and the violence against Black people across the country. And now they were suffering even further.

I wanted to help. And I wanted to understand how a community could seem to turn on itself in such catastrophic fashion in its hour of greatest need.

———

As the governor, the mayor, the Minneapolis police, the National Guard, and the Department of Public Safety scrambled to help Minneapolis quell the violence, a group of us were asked to help with outreach to the community. I called Tawanna Black, the CEO of the Center for Economic Inclusion and a prominent Black voice in the community. I wondered if she would help us convene a meeting of leaders to speak with the governor. By Saturday afternoon, we had a group of about a dozen community leaders, preachers, and business leaders on a video call. The governor and lieutenant governor both joined.

Tawanna helped start the discussion.

"The Black community has been hurting for a long time, as you know, Governor," she began. "It's important when you're speaking with our community that you recognize this crisis didn't come out of nowhere. It's the result of decades of systemic racism against Blacks in Minnesota."

The governor nodded, pursing his lips resolutely. I'd seen that look many times over the past few months. He wasn't here to talk, but to listen.

Other leaders chimed in and gave him advice. They reminded us this wasn't just one death at the hands of police. Since 2010, eleven people had been killed by Minneapolis police officers. The killing of a man named Philando Castile at a traffic stop in 2016, captured on Facebook by his girlfriend in what became one of the first viral live-streamed breaking-news events on the platform, had brought global attention to the state. Yet nothing had changed. At a certain point, the leaders told the governor, people without options feel they have no other choice than to strike out—even if that means setting their own city on fire.

"This isn't just about George Floyd," Tawanna said. The others nodded. Later that afternoon, Tawanna texted me an invitation she'd discovered online inviting a group called "the Original Black Panthers" to meet up on Chicago Avenue later that day. Many different groups with many different motives were coming from out of town to Minneapolis to join in the destruction.

That night, the protests roared for a second time. Governor Walz deployed the National Guard in force. The governor and mayor called a curfew. The effort was more coordinated. Mary and I watched again, still shocked that this was happening in our backyard.

With each passing day, we became less shocked. The gap between life for white and Black Minnesotans that we'd seen through the lives of our Silicon North Stars wasn't just a travesty, it was a crisis. All the injustices of Minnesota's past that I'd read about in books suddenly seemed much closer. The hanging of the thirty-eight Dakota men in Mankato. The running of the freeway through a historically Black neighborhood that had cut it off from other communities. The discrimination by banks that prevented homeownership in Black and brown communities. Each event added more tension and strife. Eventually, that pent-up tension was bound to explode.

The state I'd returned to as an adult had diversified more since when I last lived here in high school. The 1990s saw rapid growth in international immigration to Minnesota. Only this time, the immigrants weren't coming from Scandinavia or Germany like they had at the state's founding. They came from Somalia, Southeast Asia, Mexico, and Latin America. Today, the state boasts the largest populations of Somalis in the country. The Twin Cities has the largest concentration of Hmong population in the U.S.

One of the strangest graphs you can look at in Minnesota is a line chart that tracks a decline in international immigration from 1920 to 1980, which then increases from 1990 to today. It looks like a giant *V*. In fact, in the 2000s, immigration from abroad was the only reason Minnesota had positive migration rates at all. That's why even the Minnesota Chamber of Commerce—an organization that usually aligns itself with Republican political priorities—is an outspoken advocate for more immigration to the state. We need the talent.

This rapid influx of people of color into Minnesota in such a short time has put a historically very white state more closely on par with the ethnic makeup of the country as a whole. But the state's culture and systems haven't flexed fast enough to keep up with that rapid change. Not that those systems had ever been in a strong place—communities of color had faced discrimination since the state's founding.

Only Washington, D.C., and North Dakota have higher rates of "income persistence"—a lack of mobility on the income ladder—according to a study run by the Minneapolis Fed. Black Minnesotans make just 60 percent of the median income in Minnesota.

Stubborn Minnesota exceptionalists might gloss over these facts by pointing out that Black people in Minnesota have fared about the same as those in other states on measures of quality of life, and that it was simply the relative gaps between Black people in Minnesota and their white counterparts that were out of whack. Or they might point to the slew of nonprofits that have worked to create a welcoming immigrant and refugee resettlement environment. I've heard others mention how great it is that Minnesota is regularly in the top three states in the country for international adoption.

All of these things are true. Yet the underlying systems were still rife with discrimination. The inequality in wealth is still stunning.

How had my home state gotten to this point? Desperate for answers, I decided to reach out to Samuel L. Myers Jr., the Black public policy professor at the University of Minnesota who coined the phrase "Minnesota Paradox." He had authored the study I'd read earlier about the loan applications at banks that had disproportionately rejected Black applicants.

Sitting in his office at the university, Myers was dressed in a stylish blue tweed suit and a black tie. Because he is deaf, he brought along a captioner, who typed my questions out for him as we spoke. He spoke with an engaging and powerful passion. While I expected Myers to dive into his research, he instead started with a story.

"The Minnesota Paradox begins with swimming," he began. "I was a competitive swimmer in high school and college. When my wife and I moved to Minnesota from Baltimore in the 1990s with our daughter, we wanted to find a good swim team for her. So I wrote to all the teams and asked about their commitment to diversity. Most didn't respond. One wrote back that they were offended by the question. Only one team wrote that they valued diversity on their team, so we joined that one."

Myers began following his daughter to swim meets, sitting in the stands with white parents. As he watched his daughter compete in the 100-meter butterfly, he began to wonder why swimming was the whitest sport in America, even more than fencing and lacrosse. When he asked other parents, they either denied the fact or half joked that "you Black people have taken over every other sport, this is the one sport where our kids can actually succeed."

As if to prove discrimination didn't exist in swimming, they'd point to the fact that half of the state records were held by Black swimmers. But that was a singular Black swimmer who'd been phenomenally successful. Myers knew there was something else going on.

When the Centers for Disease Control (CDC) released a report sharing drowning rates by state and by race, Myers discovered Minnesota had the highest drowning rate for Black people of any state in the country. And it wasn't because of the state's ten thousand lakes. A vast majority of deaths by drowning occur in swimming pools. Drowning deaths among kids between the ages of five and nineteen is over five times higher for Black people than for white people.

Along with a few of his graduate students, Myers traced the drownings to a lack of Black lifeguards, which stemmed from a severe lack of Black competitive swimmers, like him and his daughter. Systemic racism is insidious, going back to segregated swimming pools in the twentieth century and the underlying racial disparities in swimming. Some of this discrimination was overt, other aspects of it were more subtle. But it mattered.

"Having Black lifeguards at a pool is important in the same way it's important to have a Black teacher, a Black police officer, or a Black social worker," Myers told me. It expands what people can see in professions designed to help and protect people.

"The more I studied, it became more prevalent, and obvious, that the nature of racism in Minnesota is very different from the nature of racism in Baltimore, Alabama, Texas, Florida, or Mississippi," Myers shared. "People here like to believe they are progressive, that they believe in equality, fairness, and social justice. But they have some hidden, unconscious biases, too. Sometimes they believe if you simply take some poor, impoverished child of an addicted mother and put them in a nicer neighborhood, then miraculously racial inequality will disappear. It doesn't work like that. The underlying systems need to change."

Myers leaned forward in his chair. "I like to call it racism without racists," he said.

The murder of George Floyd revealed these broken systems in Minnesota to the world. Nowhere was this more on display than in the Minneapolis Police Department.

News organizations, working to shed light on officer violence against Black people in Minneapolis, reported on a multitude of problems within the MPD: Officers serving in a community they don't live in. A culture of discrimination in the department. A union with entrenched leadership invested in preventing reforms. Overworked officers often asked to do jobs in the community that far extended beyond the policing they were trained to do. All these issues and more would surface in a series of state and federal investigations in the coming months.

The more you looked, the deeper the problems seemed. I felt for the community and I felt for the officers. When systems are broken, it's harder for people to call on the better angels of their nature. It's why reform is so hard, but so important.

Two years into my new life in Minnesota, I was getting a clearer picture of the downsides to Minnesota exceptionalism. The state had drunk the Kool-Aid on our own story, and it was blinding us to the real challenges we faced. Yes, Minnesota's relative success was an outlier in flyover country. But all the top rankings and quality-of-life awards gave the state, at times, a delusional sense of self.

Beneath the Midwestern humility and hardworking, purpose-driven sensibility was a pride that we'd figured something special out here and it was working just fine, thank you very much. No need for major change. Minnesota Nice is such a pleasant phrase, but residents here know its deeper meaning: a kind veneer with a passive-aggressive underside. A smile and cordial greeting that never leads to an invitation for dinner. It's much clearer to call the underside of Minnesota Nice, *Minnesota Ice* instead.

Minnesota Ice protects the status quo and ignores things that challenge it. It celebrates that we'd made a "state that works," like *Time* magazine said, but is uncomfortable changing how it works, and for whom. It chooses passive-aggressive approaches to problems over direct ones. The Minnesota Ice that makes it harder for transplants to chisel into social circles has much deeper and more serious implications when it comes to chiseling through broken systems that drive racism in our community.

When George Floyd was murdered, the chaos that followed should have surprised no one. The community wasn't doing this to itself. It was doing this to cry for help and melt the Minnesota Ice that had for so long ignored the causes of our deepest problems.

As a white Minnesotan myself, who grew up in a rural pocket of the state in the 1980s and '90s, I had a lot to learn. The fact that I'd married the daughter of immigrants and started an organization that helped Black and brown high school students didn't mean I could truly empathize with what my new community was going through. Being white, I knew I would never be able to feel what my Black neighbors were feeling. What I did know was that I needed to listen.

———

At the agency, the fissures were starting to show. The same teams that had rallied together to respond to COVID were now hurting like the rest of the state and country. The unrest had stirred something in everyone, which perhaps was the intended effect. After the protests had subsided, I called an internal town hall. The only plan was to listen to each other. Several hundred people dialed in, many with their cameras turned off.

It took a while to get the conversation started. The only way to break the ice was to lower the pressure. I told everyone the truth—that as a white man leading an agency whose job was to drive opportunity in our economy, I knew I had a lot to learn, and that the only way to do that was to keep talking with each other, even when we don't know what to say.

A few brave voices started to speak up. People shared frustrations with getting passed over for promotions, pay gaps between white people and people of color, lack of Black or brown faces in key leadership roles. But some went a layer deeper.

"My opinion is often dismissed in meetings, and I wonder if that would be the same if I was white?" shared a woman in our workforce division. I saw nodding heads.

"DEED is not a place where people of color can raise issues," another person shared. "We fear retaliation. The truth is, we just don't feel welcome or valued here."

Another woman, whose camera was turned off, told the story of getting into a conflict with her boss that got heated. Finally her boss said to her, "This is not Somalia—why are you here?"

I winced. She explained that the issue had been reported to HR, who had taken disciplinary actions. But the damage had been done. "I don't feel safe being who I am here," she said.

The conversation went on. People loosened up and shared even more. Some shared their thoughts in the group chat, feeling more comfortable typing than speaking. A frustrated woman typed, "The color of our skin only goes an inch deep. Why can't we all just ignore it and move forward?"

A thick tension returned to the air. I saw lots of furrowed brows on the screen. The group chat started popping as people piled on to denounce the statement.

"How can you ignore decades of racism?" someone implored.

"Ignoring the problem doesn't make it go away," another person wrote in exasperation. The call went quiet for a while.

"We have a long way to go before we get to 'One Minnesota,'" someone finally said.

After we all hung up, I felt uneasy. The racial tension that had boiled over in the state was also boiling within the agency. I felt a responsibility to do something, but didn't know exactly what.

I asked my team for ideas on how we could make progress. Someone suggested having everyone at the agency take an assessment called the Intercultural Development Inventory. The IDI was a fifty-question assessment designed to help people understand their strengths and weaknesses working with people from different backgrounds. The assessment told you where you were on a spectrum from "denial" to "adaptation," with navigating cultural differences and similarities.

What's more, the IDI was also designed to tell you where you *thought* you were on that spectrum, so that you could see the gap between your own perception and reality.

I was asked to answer whether I agreed or disagreed with every statement that appeared on the screen, on a scale of one to five. I realized that the questions were all open to interpretation, without a way to game the results to seem more culturally aware.

One statement read: *People are the same—they have the same needs, interests, and goals in life.*

Another stated: *When I am with people of a different culture, I act differently than when I am with people of my own culture.*

Others were more conceptual: *I do not feel I have a culture.*

I did my best to answer honestly. A few weeks later, a consultant came in to help me interpret my results. It turned out that on that spectrum, I was on the border between something called "minimization" and "acceptance." Minimization meant that I tended to minimize differences between cultures rather than engage with them, a very Minnesotan result.

Meanwhile, my results showed that I *thought* I was in the adaptation category, which defines someone who's able to bridge across differences. If the IDI was right, it was humbling that I thought I was more competent with cultural differences than I actually was. The blind spot for "minimizers" was focusing too much on emphasizing commonalities, without recognizing differences.

It gave me a lot to think about. As I reflected, the results started to resonate. I did often find myself trying harder to find connections between people of different backgrounds than I did understanding the ways that we were different and bridging them. The fact is, I needed to do both. Especially because I come from a dominant culture and race in my community.

The self-reflection was powerful, giving me pause for introspection. I thought deeply about the racial reckoning, the tension between Greater Minnesota and the metro, and my own journey of trying to find a new community in a state and a country that seemed to be unraveling. There would be no easy answers.

But there were opportunities for breakthroughs. This felt like one. It changed how I saw the journey I was on. What makes us different also makes our communities richer.

We ended up offering the assessment to everyone at DEED who

wanted to take it. The point was not to shame any person or group, or to level judgments of any kind, or to get caught up in DEI jargon. No one had to share the results with anyone else. It was a very personal exercise that gave people a chance to see the world through a new lens. It created more space for conversation, and kept the ice melting.

Hamse Warfa, our workforce development leader, called me one afternoon. A deeply connected community leader, he not only had a pulse on where the agency was, but also how the community was perceiving our role in the state during the second big crisis we were facing in just a few months.

"We've got to use this moment for transformation," he reported. "People want to know how government is going to do things differently after George Floyd, and we have to show this is not business as usual."

We talked for a long time. We could advocate for programs and policies in the next legislative session, but at an even deeper level we needed to address how the agency operated day-to-day. All the culture change we'd engaged in so far was powerful, but this was a moment to go further.

Hamse and I got a group of people at the agency together to discuss what needed to change in our approach in order to meet the moment. We mapped out what we were doing and where the weaknesses in our approach were. In the end we settled on five commitments that we could make to Minnesota as an agency to address the inequality we were grappling with. Hamse and I wrote them up in a blog post, and we started sharing them with the community.

Drive dollars to targeted communities. Increase outreach and engagement. Reform programs to address systemic barriers. Make equity everyone's job. Change from the inside out.

Each commitment was followed by a series of steps we'd take to make it happen. It covered a lot of ground, and it wasn't perfect, but at least it was the start of something new. It gave the public something to evaluate us on. At a minimum, I hoped, it showed where our hearts were. The real work lay ahead.

The town halls, the IDI, the five commitments, it all felt . . . clumsy.

But there was a power in clumsiness. It meant we were trying even if we didn't quite know the way forward. That we could be vulnerable enough to be clumsy together.

I was learning that movement was most important, progress over perfection. Clumsy was okay, as long as you were trying something real with other people. What would hold our community back would be to get stuck and let inertia take over. To let Minnesota exceptionalism explain away our challenges and ignore them. Or worse, to say that nothing could ever really change.

Rather than throwing up our hands or staying silent, some earnest clumsiness might be the only way to break the Minnesota Ice.

———

After the riots in the streets of Minneapolis were behind us, conversations turned to how to rebuild our city. To do that, we first had to understand what the damage was.

A Minnesota-based construction giant, the Mortenson Company, sent a team to walk up and down Lake Street to assess the damage. Other neighborhoods had been hit, but Lake Street was by far the worst. They swept up glass and helped business owners install new signage and impact-resistant windows and doors. David Mortenson, the third-generation chairman of the family business, contracted with firms owned by people of color to help, and the company's risk managers helped small businesses understand their insurance policies and negotiate claims.

Mortenson called me to share what they'd learned.

"Five hundred million in damage, when you add it all up," he said. Over 1,500 businesses had been hit. The Lake Street Council, a community development nonprofit, estimated 60 percent were uninsured.

The governor applied for FEMA disaster assistance, but President Trump denied the request. The state had a disaster relief fund, but it was much smaller and wasn't intended to help repair damage to private property.

The state government clearly needed to do something to help, and those dollars would likely need to come through DEED. Fortunately, almost a year after Floyd's murder, the economy had bounced back to the tune of a $1.6 billion budget surplus for state government. In other words, we actually had resources to help rebuild.

The governor and our team put together a proposal for $150 million in state bonding dollars—money the state government regularly raised from selling bonds to investors to be paid back over time—for the neighborhoods that had been hit.

But it was going to be a battle. A powerful Republican state senator from rural Minnesota, Julie Rosen, proposed a bill that would prohibit local governments from getting state aid for public infrastructure after a riot.

"I've heard over and over again from Greater Minnesota, from my constituents, that 'Please, do not pay for this out of our taxpayer dollars,'" she said during a Senate hearing for her bill.

The Republicans had, for months, been blaming the riots on Governor Walz and Minneapolis mayor Jacob Frey. They said both were at fault for not responding forcefully enough to stop the destruction. Both the governor and the mayor conceded that the response, especially early in the crisis, had been inadequate. But there was some disagreement between the city and state government about who was responsible. I hadn't been involved in the crisis response to the riots in the governor's office, so I didn't know how exactly things had played out. But it was clear to everyone that the response could have been swifter, stronger, and better coordinated. The frustration from legislators wasn't surprising.

Senate Majority Leader Gazelka, who lived in a rural northern Minnesota district, agreed with Rosen. "Many of us don't think that the entire state should be responsible for some of the costs Minneapolis is asking for," he said.

Democrats, meanwhile, compared giving state aid to help rebuild Lake Street to providing state disaster relief.

"I couldn't fathom the thought of not supplying disaster relief to Greater Minnesota when a tornado comes down, or a major snowstorm has an impact on those communities," said Cedrick Frazier, an up-and-coming member of the House from the metro area.

This went on for days. It became clear that our bonding proposal was going nowhere. As the legislative session drew to a close, the governor and Senate and House leadership agreed the jobs committee should address the destruction, but left it for us to negotiate exactly how much money to dedicate, and by what mechanism to deploy it.

I would represent the governor in the negotiation, once again working with Republican senator Pratt. From the House, we'd be joined by Democrat representative Mohamud Noor, the new House chair of the jobs committee whom we'd walked Lake Street with during the unrest.

A Somali immigrant who represented a district in central Minneapolis, Noor was about my age, but grew up in very different circumstances. He had taken asylum in Kenya when the Somali civil war started. In 1999, his family immigrated to America, settling in Minnesota. He studied computer science and worked in the private sector before getting into politics, winning a seat in the House a few years earlier. He was new to state government just like me, and was full of passion, especially about rebuilding immigrant businesses destroyed in the riots.

Even though most legislative committees were still meeting via video conference due to COVID, the three of us decided to meet in person.

Being back at the capitol was eerie. Usually buzzing with legislators, lobbyists, and press, the building was now nearly empty. I could hear my footsteps echo on the marble tile as I walked down the hallway to meet with Pratt, Noor, and our teams. We had our pick of any room in the building, and chose a large Senate hearing room, where we could sit socially distant from each other behind an expansive horseshoe-shaped dais.

For months, I had tussled with Pratt on dozens of different issues and programs to navigate the crisis. We'd negotiated unemployment insurance extensions, small business assistance packages, and of course spoke often about the governor's COVID mitigation policies. Pratt was no fan of the governor and took every opportunity to let me know. Even when I'd travel to his suburban district to meet with him, he'd always wedge a line into the conversation about the governor's failure to get the COVID crisis right.

He wasn't alone in his frustration. Legislators from both parties knew they were elected to lead, so when the governor needed to use emergency powers to move fast and lead the state through crisis by issuing executive orders, rather than negotiating legislative outcomes, it was bound to frustrate other elected leaders like Pratt.

Negotiating to build assistance for Lake Street was going to be even more complicated. Pratt set the tone early.

"I don't see how we can deliver funds for these areas that got hit by the riots that the governor couldn't contain, without also looking at the neighborhoods across the state that are still suffering due to his COVID policies," he said from behind the dais. I took a deep breath and looked over at Noor, who sat between Pratt and I, about ten feet away. I imagined him gritting his teeth underneath the blue surgical mask he was wearing.

"We have to rebuild Minneapolis," he implored. "As Minneapolis goes, so goes the rest of the state. The destruction on Lake Street hurts not only the businesses of immigrants and people of color in this city, but businesses everywhere."

He was right. The economic engine of Minnesota, Minneapolis is the front door to the state for many people and businesses considering growth here.

Pratt knew that. He was very smart about economic development and had been right on the streets alongside Noor, me, and others as the city was still smoldering. But he also had to represent his entire Republican caucus, many of whom felt differently.

Many hours in, Noor and I realized that if we were going to get the

Republican Senate to agree to money to repair the corridors hit by riots, we were going to need to also designate more money for neighborhoods outside the metro that had suffered from COVID lockdowns.

Pratt brought in a large white easel pad and a black Sharpie. His training in banking came in handy as he sketched out a plan for a loan guarantee program, which would backstop banks that made riskier loans to business owners trying to rebuild. But that rubbed Noor the wrong way.

"These businesses need cash, not loans," he said. I agreed with him. Having met with business owners and developers in these neighborhoods, I'd heard that refrain again and again—don't give us a loan, we need grants to get back on our feet.

The legislature blew past its deadline and the governor had to call an extension to the legislative session to prolong our time at the capitol. Every day, Pratt, Noor, and I, with our teams, came into the empty building to hash out the details. We traded dress shoes and slacks for sneakers and jeans.

I was keenly aware that Pratt and I were two white guys negotiating with a Black man who lived in an immigrant neighborhood. As passionate as we were, to Noor this was personal. And every time we hammered at the deal points, I was reminded of all the people who weren't in the room with us but whose lives and businesses were on the line. In between offers, all three of us reached out to stakeholders, who reacted to the deal points and helped us refine them.

I got David Mortenson on the phone again, along with Minneapolis Foundation president and former Minneapolis mayor R. T. Rybak, to walk us through their damage assessment in more detail. Noor called business owners and other legislators to walk them through options on how grant or loan programs might work. Pratt engaged community leaders, bankers, and businesses, too, and continued to stand at his easel, running the numbers on a loan guarantee program.

Rybak suggested to me that we use "Main Street" to title the program, to signal it could benefit main streets across Minnesota—and be easier for Republicans to vote for. I jumped on the idea, and Pratt and Noor liked it.

It took weeks, but by the end of June we'd hammered out a program. Actually, two programs.

The Main Street Economic Revitalization Program would give $80 million to developers who could help rebuild main streets across the state, using their choice of matching grants or loan guarantees. Another $70 million would go into a lottery system designed to go directly to business owners across the state. Both programs would be split, roughly by population, between the metro and Greater Minnesota.

Gone from any of the language was a reference to George Floyd or the riots that followed his death. In a less-than-elegant turn of phrase, we said that eligible projects included those "that are designed to address the greatest economic development and redevelopment needs that have arisen in communities across Minnesota since March 15, 2020."

Like anything in government, they were not perfect programs. Just $150 million for the whole state was far less than what was needed for Minneapolis alone, and no amount of money was going to upend decades of discrimination that had led to this in the first place. But it was a start.

Divided government was hard, but it forced us to collaborate in ways that benefited far more people with a lot more buy-in from them. I left those negotiations exhausted, yet with a deep sense that they were worth it. I also had a new respect for the work of Noor, Pratt, and other legislators. If our community was going to rebuild, we needed to work with people from different backgrounds, including different parts of the state. Building something statewide gave us a shot at helping the entire state feel a little more connected.

I was learning the power of working with people who aren't just like you. In fact, I was becoming convinced that it was the only way we were going to strengthen our community after so much pain and chaos. Focusing only on our common purpose wasn't enough—we needed to recognize our differences and unique needs, too. I was becoming a believer that you could in fact do both, even when it was clumsy.

A year after I'd first taken the IDI, I took it again. I was curious to see if I'd made any progress. As the questions flashed up on the screen, I answered honestly. This time, my results came back different. I was in the adaptation stage, though just barely. All these experiences were changing how I saw the world. Working in government in a crisis was stretching me to see differences and find ways to bridge them. It was difficult and messy, but it was growing my faith that communities could find ways to strengthen in hard times.

One Saturday morning in the middle of all these debates with legislators, I laced up my running shoes and went for a run to clear my head. I headed for Lake Bde Maka Ska, in the heart of Minneapolis. When I arrived, I ran across a grass field to the footpath that surrounded it. Up ahead I saw another runner a hundred yards in front of me. My natural competitive instincts kicked in, and without thinking about it I made it a goal to pass him—something I did often on runs to motivate myself.

I made up ground quickly, and as I got closer, I could see it was a Black man, about my age. But he wasn't running alone, like I thought. Strapped to his body was a heavy athletic weight-training vest, with large cylindrical sandbags that bounced on his chest with every stride he took.

I felt embarrassed for trying to pass him. We may have been running around the same lake, but we were running very different races.

Chapter 11

Catching Each Other

S tretching out on the couch on a Saturday morning, a cup of coffee sitting on my chest, I watched my parents play on the floor with Luke and Violet.

For the first time since the pandemic, we'd gotten away for a short weekend, to a small cabin on a lake in western Minnesota. The kids had packed every stuffed animal they could fit into the back of our car, and we'd all quarantined for a week so that my parents could join us. It wasn't exactly an exotic vacation, but just driving a few hours away to get outside our own house for a couple of nights felt like a luxury. We'd been looking forward to this for a while.

It was November, eight months into the pandemic and six months since Minneapolis had burned. Everything felt heavy. The summer was supposed to bring some relief, with COVID standards relaxed. But the fall brought on a surge of cases, with no vaccine yet available.

As I watched heavy gusts of wind blow a light snowfall across the backyard of the cabin, I tried to put it all out of my mind. Then I heard my phone buzz. I looked down and saw it was Chris Schmitter, the governor's chief of staff. The call could only mean one thing.

"We need to get the Safe Reopening Group together," he said. "The health department thinks we need to take drastic measures, and the governor wants us to put together a plan."

I shouldn't have been surprised. It had taken Minnesota over six months to record the first 100,000 coronavirus cases, but only the last 42 days to add an additional 100,000 new cases. With the holidays coming, more people would be gathering together, which would only worsen the situation. I put down my phone and looked over at Mary, who knew exactly what I was going to say before I even said it.

"Go," she said without skipping a beat.

Setting up shop in a spare room in the back corner of the cabin, I spent the rest of the weekend in video conferences with colleagues, debating what we should do. We looked at numbers, debated our options, and put together a recommendation. This time, there was less to argue about—the data that Health Commissioner Jan Malcolm and her colleagues shared made it clear we were heading for disaster unless we did something quick.

On Sunday night, we met with the governor to share our recommendation. I could see the pained look on his face as Jan walked through our recommendations over the video conference.

"Governor, we need to shut down most businesses other than those critical for survival," she said with conviction. "And we need to limit social gatherings to only people within your immediate family, for at least four weeks."

Effectively, we were recommending that the governor cancel Christmas.

The next day, I met with businesses to share the news in the run-up to another 2:00 p.m. press conference.

"How can you be shutting down movie theaters when there's not a single documented case across the country coming from theaters?" a theater owner desperately complained.

A St. Paul restaurant owner wiped away tears. "You're asking us to furlough our employees within forty-eight hours. These people are like our family," she said.

An irate bar owner tried dark humor. "You'd better absolutely promise us that you're going to reopen after four weeks, or I'm going to need a *lot* more alcohol than this," she said, holding up a bottle of booze.

The leader of Minnesota's hospitality trade association, a veteran lobbyist named Liz Rammer, concluded with the most important point.

"You've got to offer us some help, and now."

How a community comes together to take care of itself when things get bad says a lot about the kind of place it is, and that it aspires to be. There's no better measurement of that aspiration than the social safety nets we create for managing life's hardest moments. Whether you're for big government or small government, everyone wants the government to be able to respond when there's a crisis.

The governor asked me to see if we might use some of the federal pandemic relief dollars we'd gotten to pull together an assistance package for small businesses, and an extension for unemployment insurance for workers. It would have to pass through the legislature to take effect. That meant working with both Democrats and Republicans to get something done.

For the next three weeks, I hosted an almost nightly video conference with legislators and leaders from both parties. Everyone desperately wanted to land a package. As our canceled Christmas approached, we finally agreed on a deal of over $200 million for a small business relief program and an unemployment insurance extension.

We all breathed a sigh of relief. No one felt the package was big enough to match the moment. State governments rarely have the resources to respond to disasters like this because, unlike the federal government, they can't borrow money indefinitely or literally print money like the feds can. But we were desperate to do something and help with the resources we had.

Three weeks later, as COVID cases had declined thanks to the lockdown, the governor asked me to come to the State Emergency

Operations Center in St. Paul for a press conference. We were going to announce the loosening of business restrictions once again. After weeks of isolation, this was a rare moment to share good news.

On the drive, I turned on the radio and heard about protests that were getting out of control in Washington, D.C., outside the Capitol Building.

The date was January 6.

By the time I got to the press conference, protesters had stormed the Capitol. The governor and I stood side by side, scrolling our phones, shocked.

We scrapped the press conference plans. Governor Walz called Republican Majority Leader Senator Gazelka, the same leader who'd led the ouster of three of his commissioners, for a short conversation. Then he stepped up to the wooden podium to speak, flanked by American and Minnesota flags. He didn't use a prompter, or the prepared remarks we'd written to announce the loosened restrictions.

"Good afternoon, Minnesota," he began, looking straight into the camera. "As you're well aware, there's been developments in D.C. over the past few minutes as we prepared for this announcement around COVID-19. I wanted to take just a moment to assure Minnesotans that the situation here is calm and stable. I just was speaking with Senate Majority Leader Gazelka, a man of honor, a friend, and the two of us are in absolute alignment that the sacredness of our democracy, the ability to disagree agreeably, is fundamental."

I sat just off camera, one of the only people in the room besides the press pool cameraman.

"As you're watching things unfold, know that here in Minnesota we understand that when our politics gets to the point where everything becomes so fractured, it's very difficult to run society that way. And so I wanted to acknowledge that eyes are on what's happening in D.C., but also to acknowledge here that the Minnesota way of doing things is still stable. We disagree on certain things, but our values are the same."

When the cameras turned off, I got up from my chair and shook the governor's hand. I was moved by his phone call to a rival, and his calming presence at the podium. I wanted desperately to believe he was right that our community could be different than what we were seeing unfold in Washington.

The aid package we'd just passed was one hopeful sign. But it was only temporary, a reaction to a crisis. Working together on something that more permanently strengthened our state would be much stronger proof that we could make our community better. After months of division, we desperately needed that proof.

––––––

Driving into the Youthprise parking lot, I was nervous to meet with the teenagers waiting inside for me. A small nonprofit of twenty youth activists had just taken our agency to court with the support of the state attorney general—and won. They had every reason not to welcome a government official who'd denied them unemployment insurance payments for months.

At issue was a technicality in a law from 1939, stating that high school students weren't eligible to receive unemployment insurance payments, even though their employers were paying into the program on their behalf. At the time, the cost-saving measure was based on the idea that high school kids didn't need the money if they were laid off, since their parents were the ones who supported them.

But the world has changed a lot since 1939. Today, many high school students, especially immigrants whose parents were part of the surge of migration in the 1990s, held jobs that supported their entire families. And while our department hadn't been paying high school students unemployment benefits for the last eighty years, the recent federal funding that had expanded the program during the pandemic had far fewer restrictions. It was there to help workers who might slip through the cracks of the traditional system—self-employed workers, contractors, and others who didn't pay into the program in the same way. But the federal funding didn't mention high school students, so this was a gray area.

Cole Stevens, a high school senior with an Afro and a budding goatee, had been let go from his job at a coffee shop after we shut down the economy. At first, our team at DEED sent Cole several thousand dollars of unemployment insurance payments by mistake. But when the department ran a correction to comb the system for mispayments, they found Cole and sent him a letter demanding he pay the state back. The letter had driven him into action, and he quickly became a leader in the movement to challenge our decision in court.

When I heard about Cole's case, and many others just like it, I was mortified. No one gets into public service to steal money from kids. Especially in a crisis. When we lost the case in court and were required to pay almost $35 million in back payments to high school students across the state, I was thrilled. Losing never felt so good.

Now Cole and his friends wanted to wipe the 1939 law off the books so that even in normal times it wouldn't apply. This would require growing a benefits program that was already under fire. Many felt the government's expanded unemployment insurance program was keeping people away from work longer than needed, and that people were gaming the system.

As I got out of the car to walk inside the building, I hoisted Violet out of her car seat. A COVID case at the twins' school meant that Mary and I didn't have childcare for a week, so she took Luke for the day, and I brought Violet with me. Maybe she'd bring me good luck.

Inside, Cole and his friends greeted me. Most, like him, were Black or brown. Several were immigrants who supported their families, and all were impressive. Hayat Muse, a Somali immigrant who was one of nine children, was headed to Harvard that fall. Walter Cortina, a Mexican immigrant who'd been working since he was fourteen and sent money back home to his family, was the valedictorian of his high school class. Like the other students assembled, both had been denied unemployment insurance after losing their jobs.

Cole was clearly the ringleader. Dressed in blue jeans and a baggy black T-shirt, he leaned forward and gave me a big hug when he saw me. I breathed a sigh of relief.

"It's great to see you, Commissioner," Cole beamed in a baritone voice that made him seem older than his years. "We're so glad you're here!"

We spoke for a while about the campaign, and the unfair law. He told me how shocked he was when he got our letter, and how desperate the situation felt. If he'd had to pay back the money, he wouldn't have been able to pay his family's heating bill. The prospect of getting your utilities turned off during a Minnesota winter is no joke.

I instantly liked Cole. He seemed wise beyond his years, a savvy operator even at seventeen. He was passionate, bright, and clearly comfortable in his own skin. It put me at ease, too.

We chatted about our lives, and I told him about our work with Silicon North Stars. He was interested and instantly agreed to be a guest speaker at a future meetup. We were warming up now.

"I'm glad we lost that lawsuit," I admitted. "Clearly, we didn't get this one right."

Cole didn't blink, he just smiled. "But we got the chance to change the law for good!"

He led me to a set of tall stools the team had assembled on a patio just outside their offices. The local TV stations we invited had their cameras set up in front of the makeshift stage. Someone found a small folding chair for Violet and set it next to my seat. I hit play on an episode of *Blaze and the Monster Machines* on her iPad and pulled a pair of bright blue headphones over her ears.

I opened the panel and thanked our guests, then asked Cole to share his story.

"The realities of today's economy are completely different than they were in 1939," he said. "The cost of living has gone up, the cost of college has gone up, and so there's this huge disconnect."

I looked out across the crowd. Hayat, Walter, and the other students all snapped their fingers in unison to show support.

"What we're saying is, we're already working just like everyone else, and businesses are already paying the tax, so it's time we get paid like everyone else." More snapping.

Cole and his friends weren't just young and full of idealism, they were smart. Their campaign found allies in the AARP, the powerful lobbying group who also wanted some changes to unemployment insurance law that affected seniors. Together, young and old activists made a compelling coalition. Their team also got businesses and chambers of commerce to write letters to legislators and held events on the capitol steps that drew the attention of the media.

Cole may not have known it, but he was joining a long history of organizers in Minnesota who had fought for worker's rights for decades. The deft organizing capability of the Farmer-Labor Party in the first half of the twentieth century hadn't just changed state politics, but had changed the nature of national labor politics, too.

One of the foundational labor upheavals in American history took place in Minnesota in 1934. Called the "Truckers' Strike," it was spearheaded by a Swedish activist named Carl Skoglund, a union leader in the Teamsters who organized coal truck drivers and delivery workers to fight for higher wages and better benefits with local employers.

Though the Farmer-Labor movement was on the rise, Minneapolis was still considered a scab town. Wages were well below the national average, artificially depressed by big businesses, which had a stranglehold on the economy. So Carl and the Teamsters took to the streets to demand higher wages, using innovative strategies for their time.

First, they worked to unite both craft unions and industrial unions into one coalition. That meant that the truck drivers were picketing right alongside the warehouse workers. This wasn't common, according to Peter Rachleff, a labor history professor at Macalester College in St. Paul.

"The Truckers' Strike was the first time you saw two different union types coming together in common cause," he told me over video conference from his front porch in St. Paul. "That Minnesota model would be copied by national groups twenty years later, when the AFL-CIO was born."

The Teamsters were also groundbreaking in that they organized unemployed workers, too. They stood up for job creation and unemployment insurance benefits, which appealed to those without jobs—and prevented the unemployed from swooping in to take open jobs held by Teamsters when they went on strike.

On July 20, 1934, their strike devolved into a battle with police. In what would come to be known as "Bloody Friday," police opened fire on unarmed strikers and injured sixty-seven people, mostly by shooting them in the back, according to historical records. Two were killed, which set off even more mass demonstrations in response to police violence.

The country took notice. President Franklin Delano Roosevelt, fresh off his New Deal that gave workers the right to collectively bargain, even rode a train through Minnesota to show support. Four months after it started, the strike ended as negotiations resulted in a minimum wage and stronger union rights. Minnesota had become union-friendly almost overnight. A year later, the National Labor Relations Board was formed to create a structure for collective bargaining that was peaceful, a direct response to the violence in Minneapolis.

"Once the Teamsters had won the Truckers' Strike and brought national recognition to Minnesota," Rachleff told me, "they used that momentum to grow their movement."

The leaders next shifted their focus to the creation of an unemployment insurance program. Our neighbors in Wisconsin had enacted the first-ever state-run unemployment insurance program. Even some enlightened private employers were experimenting with their own programs in the U.S.

But social safety nets don't work so well when they're piecemeal. It's the collective action and shared risk that ensures they're stable and fair. In the thirties, there was a growing sense that a national program was needed to make sure states weren't competing with each other. Several

Minnesota political leaders became outspoken advocates to the federal government to start such a program. By providing benefits to workers when they were let go, Uncle Sam could keep the economy moving in times of hardship by stabilizing the buying power of workers while helping them to find their next job.

In 1935, FDR signed the Social Security Act into law, which included the creation of a national unemployment insurance program. States needed to follow basic federal guidelines to receive federal assistance, but could modify their programs in certain ways. Thus, quirky laws like Minnesota's 1939 prohibition against high school students receiving payments were born.

It can be rare in life to get a chance to directly make up for a mistake. When Cole and his team decided to take on the cause of changing the 1939 law, I saw a chance to do just that. As he and his team organized, forming a new nonprofit called Bridgemakers to grow their efforts, I jumped forward to help. Together, we crafted an inside-outside game strategy. While the students lobbied individual legislators with their cause, putting a face and a story to the challenge, my team and I put together plans for changing the law. I met with legislators on both sides of the aisle to show our support, and my team did the research that showed how changing the law would have a minuscule impact on the state budget. I testified at every committee hearing, backing up the passionate stories that Cole and his friends were telling legislators.

Most important, we reached out to Republican senators for support. For the past year, Republicans in Minnesota—and across the country—had been claiming that unemployment insurance was keeping people on their couches and hurting business. So it was hard to be optimistic that we'd win anyone over to actually expand the program.

But with young people leading the charge, the conversation started to change. Cole and his friends reached out to Jason Rarick, a Republican senator from Pine County, which is a unique pocket of Greater

Minnesota that's a little less red than most. Rarick is a union electrician and a solid Republican, but accustomed to working with Democrats in his district, and often felt he had more in common with rural Democrats than Republicans in the metro. He was quickly sympathetic to the cause of the students, in part because their argument just made sense.

"If employers are paying into the system for these kids, why shouldn't they get the money?" he told me.

After hearing Cole's story, he wanted to help them out. First he had to persuade Senator Pratt. To his credit, Pratt's principled nature made him a convert on the logic alone. Next, they had to explain to their Republican colleagues why they should actually expand unemployment benefits to this one group, after months of advocating that benefits should be curtailed.

"It was the way those young people activated that made the difference," Rarick shared with me. "They made it easy to advocate for them because they were so willing to tell their story."

The students kept up the pressure, speaking on the front steps of the capitol, showing up to hearings, and getting coverage in every major media outlet in the state.

Inside the capitol, as the jobs committee negotiated a final package for the session, I found myself once again trading deal points with Senator Pratt and the Republican coalition. By this point, they were even more frustrated by the governor's pandemic rule by executive order. But Rarick had done his research, and worked behind the scenes to keep the bill alive on the Republican side of the room.

The media picked up the students' case and made them heroes. Something must have resonated with legislators, who saw the chance to right a wrong. Somehow, we all managed to hold the package together, and the 1939 law was permanently changed as part of the final jobs bill.

The students were elated. The rest of us were inspired. They showed what a powerful force young people can be in politics.

Driving home from the event at Youthprise with Violet in the back seat, I marveled at these young people. I was learning that it takes a lot of different people to make lasting political change in a community—and not just people in power.

We needed Cole and his friends to drive the campaign for change. And they needed us to navigate the state government and change the law. A Black teenager working at a coffee shop, a rookie state government official fresh from Silicon Valley, and a rural Minnesota electrician turned state senator may not look like they have much in common. But working with people who are different from you is exactly what makes lasting changes in community possible.

———

"Today's the day, are you ready?" asked the nurse, who was wearing bright pink scrubs. Mary and I nodded. Hanging on the wall here in the fertility clinic hung a sign that read *It's an Eggcelent Day in Minneapolis.*

Mary and I were giddy about the idea of growing our family. Not only did it feel like there was a space waiting for another person in our home, we also felt there would be something special about having a baby in our new community. What else could deepen our sense of connection to this place more than having a child in it?

When our long fertility journey had given us twins three years earlier, Mary and I had finally felt like we'd gotten over the hump on our fertility journey. Now the eight frozen embryos that we'd flown from Colorado to the clinic just a few miles away from our new home in Minneapolis were ready. It seemed inevitable that at least one of them would become our newest family member.

The door opened and the embryologist came in, pushing a large cart that held a petri dish under a microscope. She leaned over and peered into the lens, turning a dial to focus the machine until suddenly a circular bundle of cells was projected on the viewing monitor. Mary squeezed my hand, and we both beamed. Even the nurses oohed and aahed.

I remembered this same moment from our experience with Luke and Violet. It was magical. To see your potential children at this early stage of development was surreal. From those eighty little cells might come a brain, a heart, arms, and legs. A personality, a sense of humor, likes and dislikes, hopes, fears, and ideas. A spirit. Gazing at those little cells now and imagining their future was an act in believing in miracles.

After the transfer, we drove home and waited. Nine days later, Mary took a blood test to see if she was pregnant. Negative.

We tried to hide our disappointment. Even though we had dozens of negative pregnancy tests behind us, it was impossible not to get our hopes up each time. Still, we took comfort in knowing that we still had seven more frozen embryos to transfer. Surely one of them would work.

But in the coming months, more and more attempts ended when negative test results came back. Doubt began to creep in. This was turning out to be more complicated than we had thought. Looking for answers, we went to a doctor at the Mayo Clinic and discovered a new barrier in our fertility journey—Mary had a uterine condition that would require surgery if we wanted to try again. She didn't even have to think about it; we booked the surgery for the next month. Our journey to grow our family would need to take a detour, but we hoped staying the course would pay off eventually.

A lot of life happens at once when you're a young parent, or trying to become one. What seems like decades' worth of emotions and life lessons get compressed into just weeks or months of time. Between trying for another child, navigating a surgery, raising our toddler twins, and facing crises at work, life felt more occupied for Mary and me than ever before.

But we knew we weren't alone. Every parent of young kids faces a balancing act they've never had to manage before. We knew that compared with most families in our community, we were the lucky ones. That luck had started a few years earlier when Violet and Luke were born and we were able to step away from work to take care of them.

Google, like many big companies in America, had a generous paid family medical leave program. Mary got almost five months off, I got three, and we were able to add vacation weeks to those numbers to take a half year off to take care of our infant twins—with no hit to our paychecks. It was impossible to imagine having gotten through those first six months with two infants at home if we weren't both able to take that time together.

The social safety net of paid family leave is another example of how communities take care of each other when people need it the most.

In most countries, getting paid time off when life happens, like a new baby, is normal. But in America, such benefits are available only to the privileged few. For over 75 percent of Americans, paid family medical leave is an out-of-reach luxury. That means most parents have to reduce their work hours, take unpaid leaves, or quit their jobs altogether in order to take care of their baby. The same is true for those who face an unexpected medical issue, or the need to care for a sick loved one.

In the case of pregnancy, not getting time off to spend with your newborn flies in the face of everything we know about child development and economic growth. The absence of paid leave is a triple whammy—it deprives babies of the chance to bond with their parents in an important window of brain development, it creates hardship for parents right when they need the most help, and for those who quit their jobs to take care of another, it derails their career growth.

Women, of course, bear the heaviest burden of losing pay to take time off, falling behind professionally. Nationally, if women participated in our labor force at the same rate as men, we'd have $650 billion in additional economic activity every year. It's just dumb policy that we don't have a national paid family leave policy to do the same thing that unemployment insurance does: to help our neighbors when life happens to them.

In the absence of a national paid leave program, the governor and lieutenant governor had made creating a statewide program one of their priorities. If it passed, DEED would be the agency to administer it. The program would be run just like unemployment insurance, as a payroll tax on employers to create a trust fund to draw benefits for workers who qualified.

The Republican Senate was not interested. They lined up with Minnesota's powerful corporate community, who had concerns about funding a state-run program. Their case was that creating a new state tax on business, in a place that already had too many taxes, was going to drive growth away, to states that didn't have those programs.

The debate wasn't too different from the one over unemployment insurance in the 1930s. If states have to stand up social safety net programs on their own, you get counterproductive competition between citizens of the same country. And you undermine the sense of basic fairness in a country that's founded on the idea that all people are created equal.

But absent a national program, we were determined to fight for one in Minnesota. The governor believed the opposite of corporate concerns, that it would attract workers to the state to work in a place that took care of its workers in ways neighboring states did not.

Just a few blocks from our house in Minneapolis, at an oil and vinegar shop owned by a middle-aged entrepreneur named Sarah Piepenburg, the governor gathered a group of small business owners to make the case for paid leave. We wanted to deploy the Formula that we'd used back at the broadband event in Melrose before the pandemic, this time to raise awareness for paid leave.

But with COVID, it was a little more awkward. Surrounded by silver tanks of flavored oils, the governor and lieutenant governor and I sat with our masks on, alongside a collection of small business owners and medical doctors, trying to stay six feet apart from each other and the TV cameras that had arrived. Thankfully, Sarah was a compelling storyteller who told us about one of her employees named Linda, who had suffered a hip injury that took her out of work. Without a paid leave program, Sarah dipped into her savings to pay Linda out of her own pocket while she was in the hospital.

"When you have a small business, your employees are like your family," she told us, tears welling in her eyes. "There was no way we were going to stop paying Linda. But to afford it, we had to stop paying our mortgage. If we'd had a paid leave program like big companies do, we'd have been able to keep our business moving." Sarah had looked into what a private market insurance solution might look like for a small business, but found nothing she could afford.

For months, I joined the governor and lieutenant governor on visits to small businesses like Sarah's. I testified at the legislature to argue for a state-run program, telling my own story of our infant twins and my paid leave experience to make the case. But we couldn't get the votes. Passing an entirely new social program in the middle of the pandemic was hard. There just wasn't the same urgency to apply to paid leave as there was to unemployment insurance or emergency assistance for small businesses. A pressing crisis seemed the best tool to spur action on social reform in a divided government. Without it, it's a lot harder to move government to make big changes.

I was also learning something deeper about how communities view their responsibility for each other. Having grown up in a small business family, I wanted to live in a place where competition was healthy and the government mainly stayed out of your way. But playing a part in our state government's response to these crises was broadening my perspective.

When faced with something big or challenging, you want your government there to help you out. Minnesota had a history of rising to those moments in unique ways. But updating that social safety net to meet modern demands was a slog every time. It got to the heart of deep questions about how we want our communities to take care of one another, and who is responsible for what.

Perhaps those questions shouldn't have felt as complicated as they sometimes did. Taking care of each other at life's most vulnerable and important moments is simply what community is all about.

As the vaccines arrived and spring approached, we finally began to trend toward the better. We ended all COVID restrictions, and the uncomfortable period of social engineering came to an end.

Mercifully, we disbanded our Safe Reopening Group. Despite the hardships, I knew I'd miss working with my new government co-workers so closely. The struggle had brought us closer in ways only a crisis can.

Building a playbook for a global health pandemic, or navigating a racial reckoning, was never on my radar when I took the leap to join government. But I was learning and growing more from the experience than anything I'd ever gone through before. I was learning how to be calm in the hot seat. I was learning how to spot real crises from fake ones. I was learning how to listen better, how to translate between groups with different perspectives, and how to work closely with people from different backgrounds. I was getting better at learning to disagree without being disagreeable.

So much of this came from watching talented leaders in government show up every day because they cared about the future of the place where we live. They didn't forget that sense of community that had been so fundamental to our state's identity. It also came from seeing concerned citizens step up and do what seemed impossible. I never would have had the opportunity to learn from them if I hadn't given this new job a shot.

In a way, I'd glamorized public service before I went into government, partially to get myself excited about taking the leap—only to spend the pandemic doing very unglamorous work. Yet that work gave me a much stronger sense of purpose in my new home, a connection to the community I was becoming part of, and a much deeper appreciation for anyone who does public service than I ever had before trying it myself.

The crises that had ravaged Minnesota were impossible to ignore. The state we'd moved to just a few years earlier now felt different, with more division than before and more uncertainty about the future. I'd seen my new community go through chaos and try to hold itself together. After all the time we'd spent reacting to that chaos, our community desperately needed something to run toward, not just run from.

I did, too. An all-consuming job, at a time when meeting up in person had been on hold for two years, had stunted my own efforts at building a community and new friendships here. Neither Mary nor I felt like we'd settled in yet.

What would our community look like? How could I make real friends in this new place? Could I reconcile my religious differences with my parents?

I wasn't sure about the answers to those questions, but I was ready to find out.

With spring in bloom, we decided to plant a garden in our backyard. I drove to the hardware store with the kids and picked up some long planks and a few cinder blocks. In our backyard next to the trampoline, we built a small rectangular garden bed. I asked the kids what they wanted to plant in it.

"Strawberries, tomatoes, and cucumbers," they agreed after some debate. They slipped on little green gardening gloves, and we all spent an afternoon planting our new garden. Later that night, Luke had another idea for the garden.

"Could we plant poison ivy?" he asked. He'd recently become fascinated with poisonous plants, and we'd been watching YouTube videos about them. I'd never heard of anyone actually trying to grow them before, but why not?

I went online to discover that, yes, you can order poison ivy seeds. A garden center in North Carolina sold them in small packets. I placed an order and a few weeks later we planted them in a clay pot next to our garden. The kids painted pictures of poison ivy on the sides of the pot, and giggled at the prospect of growing a poisonous plant.

"I bet I'm not allergic," Luke said proudly.

Mary and I laughed as we watered the garden bed, and the poison ivy seeds, wondering how it would turn out. The months ahead would show us what we'd be able to grow.

Part III

Hope

Chapter 12

Breaking the Bubble

Do you think it's too early to text him back?" I asked Mary sheepishly.

We'd just returned from a holiday party hosted by one of the families in the kids' elementary school, and I had what I thought was a good conversation in the kitchen with the dad, Kevin. He was a transplant from Oregon by way of New York, and was working as a successful musician. Concert posters from his past shows hung on the walls of their home, and a piano was parked in the middle of the living room.

He seemed very cool. I wondered if he might be a potential friend.

Gracefully, Mary treated my question with sincerity. "Let's see, it's been two days . . . I think you're okay to text him."

I carefully typed out a thank-you text, wishing him a happy holiday and vaguely suggesting we get together in the new year. Then I waited. Two hours later, he replied back warmly, remembering our conversation and agreeing to my faint invitation to meet up sometime. He even included three emojis. My heart jumped.

"He wrote back!" I sang to Mary.

She laughed and gave me a hug. "Congratulations, honey!"

I blushed and put my phone down, plotting my next move. It would probably have to wait until after the holidays, but I was hopeful.

Finding new friends in your forties, especially in a new community, can feel a lot like dating. You don't have a lot of time, there are awkward barriers to cross, and truly getting to know someone takes vulnerability and commitment precisely at a time when those things are being demanded of you by your family and job, too. Experts estimate it takes more than two hundred hours for a stranger to become a close friend. That's a lot of time and effort that is hard to come by given the modern demands of adulthood.

Add to that the Minnesota tradition of long-standing social circles that can be hard to crack, and the challenge felt daunting.

Moving near family had been powerful, but for Minnesota to feel like my chosen home, I knew I needed a chosen family, too. I needed friends.

When we'd first moved to the state, Mary and I had gotten off to a good start, hosting barbecues and inviting people over often. A year in, we felt like we were making some progress. But then the pandemic hit, grounding everything to a halt. Instead, I retreated to groups of friends from previous stages of my life, keeping in touch over group texts.

One of them was a group of friends from grad school. Eight of us had become very close over our two years in school together. Most of them now lived on the East or West Coast, having found careers in D.C., New York, or the Bay Area. Our group chat, which we jokingly named "Safe Space," was a lively, active conversation that covered the gamut from reactions to daily news to advice on books, fitness, parenting, even fashion. Most days I could barely keep up.

The men in the group had racked up an impressive, inspiring collection of career experiences with a national or global focus. Sean worked as an American diplomat, traveling the world and trying to negotiate solutions to such intractable problems as the war in Afghanistan. Jeremy lived in Salt Lake City and ran a national real estate impact investment fund. Luke had worked for President Obama on counterterrorism before starting a national research consultancy that had grown to sixty people. James lived in Singapore, where he ran an Asian geopolitical think tank and wrote books. Dallas worked on nuclear policy. Others had big jobs in tech, development, and business. Nick, my close friend whose home we'd stayed at on our trip back to Menlo Park, built and ran Meta's entire media partnerships division.

I'd been through something big with each one of these friends over the years. Our experiences in school came at a time when we were each trying to figure out what we wanted to do with our lives. We'd spent a lot of time with each other, in the classroom and outside it. We'd blown through the two-hundred-hour rule pretty quickly, building a jocular affinity for one another that can come only from becoming friends at a fresh yet uncertain time in your life.

Mostly, we had a lot of fun together. When the school handed out a group project to craft a response to the avian flu epidemic, we got a nine-foot-tall inflatable chicken mascot suit and a closet full of medical scrubs, then staged an elaborate prank in which another friend, Dave, got into the chicken suit and stormed into a large lecture hall during a packed class, only to be tackled and beaten down by the rest of us, dressed up like doctors. Scott, a friend who would go on to start his own outdoor retreat business, wore a chef's costume.

None of us knew where life would take us. That commonality alone strengthened the bond. Scattering after school meant we had a group of friends we shared something with, but didn't live close to. Safe Space gave us a way to stay connected, and a place to get advice from trusted friends on how to do life.

No question was off-limits. How do you deal with anxious kids? What do the geopolitics of Eastern Europe mean for the rest of the world? Is it okay to wear dress shoes with white rubber soles? Having a group chat with friends I trusted was a lifeline not only during the pandemic, but throughout adulthood, an extra life guide in my pocket anytime I needed it.

When the pandemic started, a few of us bought rowing machines. I'd often escape to our basement for a quick row when I needed to work out some stress. We traded workout ideas over text, and compared our times at various distances.

Yet I was still rowing alone. Staying close with friends from other chapters of life was enriching, but it wasn't the same as having friends in my neighborhood. Why did that seem so much harder?

As I pulled through a workout on the rowing machine one morning, I listened to a podcast that referenced the nationally acclaimed book *Bowling Alone*, which I'd read twenty years earlier. In it, the political scientist Robert Putnam coined the phrase "social capital" and charted its decline in the twentieth century. He used the metaphor that participation in bowling leagues had declined by 40 percent since 1980, while overall bowling had risen by 10 percent, to show an American community that was spending less time joining activities and making new friends, and more time doing stuff on their own. That was a problem, Putnam said, for our mental health as well as our democracy.

Putnam cited many factors that led to a decline in social capital, from urban sprawl to television to two-career families, to time and money pressures. A few decades later, on the heels of an isolating global pandemic, we seemed to have only gotten worse.

Turns out, Putnam thinks so, too. He's written a lot more since *Bowling Alone*, including another book called *The Upswing*, in which he charts the peak of American feelings of community in the mid-1960s and asks why it felt different then. According to his research, the 1960s had very low levels of polarization and much higher levels of equality than previous generations, or generations since. But today polarization and inequality are leading to more fractured communities and, most important, less trust. When the system doesn't seem fair, or you disagree deeply with others on politics, overall social capital deteriorates.

"To what extent do we think that we're all in this together?" Putnam posed on the podcast I listened to. "What stands upstream of all these other trends is morality, a sense that we're all in this together and that we have obligations to other people . . . We're not going to fix polarization, inequality, and social isolation until, first of all, we start feeling we have an obligation to care for other people."

A society in which isolation is more common than togetherness makes it a lot more awkward to meet new people. Putnam debunks the idea that we're more isolated because we're just too busy. Modern American adults spend on average ten hours a day with media, five of it with television. We've just replaced time we had spent with others with being alone. When I read that, I felt a tinge of regret for giving myself the "I'm too busy" excuse so often.

But while I may have been rowing alone, I wasn't the only one. Many Americans report that making new friends has grown more difficult, especially since the pandemic. A recent survey reported only half of Americans are satisfied with the number of friends they have. Men seem to be in worse shape than women, with 15 percent saying they had no close friends at all, five times higher than in 1990.

At least I had my friends from Safe Space, who, once a year, got together for a guys' weekend, usually at Jeremy's house in Salt Lake City. We made valiant attempts at skiing, but mostly caught up with each other. The first time we resumed the tradition after the pandemic, it was great to see everyone in person again. When a heavy snowstorm chased us off the hills and into a lodge, we grabbed overpriced food from the cafeteria and sat around a table to catch up. I asked the group how they'd navigated making new friends in adulthood.

"I feel like you have to go through something with someone to become true friends with them," observed Sean. "It's not enough just to hang out."

Mike, a natural organizer, had recently moved to West Hartford, Connecticut, and had to make new friends from scratch, too. He told me that coaching his kid's sports teams had helped him.

Luke shared that he and his wife, Rachel, invited the neighbors over to sing karaoke, striking up a friendship over time. Noah, who lived in Boston, had started becoming more active in his synagogue.

"Every year, we hold three Jewish holiday parties at our house," he shared. "One of them is for an obscure Jewish holiday called Lag Ba'Omer. The holiday has this weird connection to archery, so we invite everyone over to eat food cooked over a fire in our front yard and we set up an archery range for the kids. Celebrating it started out as kind of a joke, but it became a tradition."

Everyone was trying something.

Later, on a ski lift, I found myself reflecting with Sean about our life decisions. He and the rest of Safe Space had been surprised when Mary and I had announced we were leaving the Bay Area for Minnesota, and even more intrigued when I left Google for state government. I admitted to him that being with Safe Space and hearing about their global careers often reminded me just how local my own world had become. Sean spent his time navigating complex issues in Congress and the UN, topics that were the stuff of *New York Times* headlines.

Sean listened, then gripped his ski poles and pulled them up to his chest, taking the bait to offer some friendly encouragement. "Yeah, but what you're doing has a tangible impact that's right in front of you. It's helping your community and neighbors. That's something I rarely feel—the impact of my work is often uncertain and distant."

Whether he was being honest or just nice, it was the kind of support I needed.

Having Safe Space was wonderful, and it was helpful that lifelong friends were just a text away. But I knew I also needed friends nearby.

———

One Saturday morning I got in my car and typed in the address of a coffee shop across town. I tried to calm my nerves, and was partly tempted to stay home. A few weeks earlier, I'd signed up online for a Meetup group called Break the Bubble. I'd heard about the group online and when I looked it up, the description seemed targeted exactly at transplants like me:

Break the Bubble was created to solve a big problem: How do you make new friends in the Twin Cities? Making friends here is hard. We're changing that.

When I arrived at the meetup, just ten minutes after the posted starting time, fifty people were milling about in a large open space just off to the side of a coffee bar. From afar, it seemed everyone knew each other, given the number of smiles, head-nodding, and laughter.

I walked over to the check-in table to make a name tag. Next to a pile of markers was a sign that read *Icebreaker: Duck, Duck, _____?* referencing the childhood game Duck, Duck, Goose, which for some reason is called "Duck, Duck, Gray Duck" only in Minnesota. I chuckled and looked up to see a tall man on a stool behind the check-in table. He had a buzz cut, rosy cheeks, and a warm smile. He introduced himself as Jon, the person who organized the event.

"This meetup was started twelve years ago by two newcomers to Minnesota who put up a flyer on a whim, and were shocked when thirty-five people showed up," he told me. "It clearly filled a gap for people."

Momentum built quickly, and today the events, which happen around twice a month, regularly draw over a hundred people. Jon, a transplant to Minnesota himself, took over the organizing duties six years ago. Having grown up in South Bend, Indiana, as a self-described introvert, he found the simple premise of the meetings a useful way to melt away the pressure of doing it entirely on your own.

"It's really 'choose your own adventure,'" he told me. "Some people treat it as a place to meet lifelong friends, others treat it like a college party for adults. Some people tell me, 'My goal today is to see if I can talk with three people, and then I'm going home.'"

He smiled and lowered his voice a little. "I don't advertise it like this, but it's kind of like a low-key secular church."

I stuck a name tag on my shirt and walked over to see who I could meet. A group of three men about my age were gathered next to a pillar with cups of coffee in their hands. That seemed like an easy place to start. I introduced myself and asked what brought them to the meetup. They each had their own reasons.

Rajeev, who worked in marketing and wore stylish black horn-rimmed glasses, said he started coming after COVID. He worked remotely and felt isolated during the pandemic. "It got so bad I started hallucinating. I'm serious!" he said with a laugh. "I needed to get out."

Another man, Chris, looked to be in his fifties. He said he came to the meetup because he wanted to develop a new social circle after a recent divorce. "I can't be 'depressed divorce guy' forever," he joked.

Michael, a bald software engineer in the group, told me he was in lots of meetup groups and even organized one himself. He pulled out his phone to show me the group he'd started, which was titled "40 Plus Social and At Least Slightly Active," which sounded pretty niche to me until I noticed it had 365 members.

As I wandered around the room, I got a little more comfortable approaching people, knowing everyone was here for the same reason. Beyond the shared purpose, however, there didn't seem to be any predominant demographic represented.

I met an older woman named Rochelle, who was here for a second time in the last month. Her daughter had recently left for college and she'd just switched jobs. It felt like a time of change, she told me. "People in my life kind of scattered, so it felt like time to make new friends."

After encouraging her daughter to explore meetups to make new friends, she thought to herself, *Why shouldn't I do that, too?*

Next I meandered over to a table in the middle of the café and sat down with a group of younger people. They seemed much more nonchalant about the whole ordeal. A mountain biker named Eli told me he was headed to a few different meetups today.

"I'm in a mountain-biking group, a climbing group, and a skiing group," Eli shared with me. "I stopped by here on my way over to meet some friends from the mountain-biking group to go for a ride."

I asked him how he made friends.

"I'm in my twenties—it's easy." He smiled. "I have friends in their forties who had kids and then suddenly stopped going out altogether."

For others at Break the Bubble, this was hard work. I met Bennett, a mustached software engineer from White Bear Lake who'd recently moved out of his parents' house and into an apartment. He was soft-spoken and careful with his words.

"I'm just trying to come here and talk to some people," he shared quietly. He told me about an app he was building for an industrial auto parts dealer in town. He'd met people through his job, but was looking to branch out. Later, I saw him sit down in a leather chair and strike up a conversation with a few people.

Watching Bennett push himself to meet new people was inspiring. I hadn't known quite what to expect, but being around others who were looking for community just like me made the world feel less lonely. As I drove home from Break the Bubble, I left encouraged by the people I met. They showed me there was no "normal" way to make friends—you just use the tools you have to reach out and start conversations, and see who you connect with.

While I didn't leave with any new best friends, maybe more important wasn't what I'd gained but what I'd lost: the embarrassment I had for struggling to meet new people. Everyone at that meetup was searching, just like me.

———

A few weeks into the new year, Mary gave me a nudge.

"How's your boyfriend?" she joked, referring to Kevin. We'd been listening to some of his music in the house, but I hadn't contacted him yet about meeting up. It was time to make my next move.

Since he was a musician, I thought maybe a concert could be a good outing. A few local bands were playing at a theater near my house on Sunday evening. I took the leap and texted Kevin an invite, suggesting we bring our kids. I was thrilled when he texted back. He was in.

That Sunday night, I packed up the kids to drive to the show. We'd agreed to meet for pizza beforehand. Kevin and his five-year-old, Flo, were already at the restaurant. We ordered a few pizzas while the kids filled out coloring sheets on the table. When they got squirrelly, they headed outside to the sidewalk to play, and Kevin and I found ourselves alone.

We did the usual trading of brief summaries of our life stories. Kevin had grown up in Oregon, been a talented baseball player in college, but discovered music and took a different turn in life. He ended up in New York, seeing a lot of early success with his band and landing a big record deal. His career took twists and turns like everyone's, and when he met his wife, Marlena, they decided to move to her home state: Minnesota.

Kevin was happy to be here. The Midwest was a great place to raise kids, he commented.

"I love it here. And there's a much stronger music scene than people give us credit for. It's very communal—people come out and support each other," he said. His new band had seen success, with one music reviewer calling Kevin's voice a mix between Bon Iver and Peter Gabriel.

We had fun at the concert. The kids danced in the aisles and Kevin and I traded more stories between songs. He asked great questions and seemed like a genuinely good guy. It felt like it could be the start of something.

A few weeks later, I pushed through my reservations about asking him to hang out twice in a row, and invited him to a Minnesota Timberwolves game. To save on parking, we agreed I'd swing by his place and pick him up, making it a true man date.

Kevin was an easy conversationalist and sports talk gave us plenty to get warmed up on. At halftime we grabbed food and talked more about our kids and our jobs. He told me about a new album he was planning to release soon, and the inspiration for his music. It was fascinating to hear about his process and about how fatherhood and family influenced his creativity.

I also appreciated talking with someone who wasn't so wired into state government and state politics like I was every day. It was a reminder to me of one of the benefits of leaving the tech-dominant culture of Silicon Valley for Minnesota: the chance to make friends from many different walks of life.

Kevin made the next move. He had gotten tickets to a Dave Matthews concert . . . in Denver. Would I want to make a twenty-four-hour journey there to watch the show?

He texted an "out" just in case it was too much. "Couple guys here/ out west I could ask too so no pressure—although Dave will be sad," he couched.

Why not? I thought. A few months later, I found myself getting on a plane for a marathon man date to Colorado. As we took off, I wondered how long we'd keep the conversation going. Should I read a book? Get out my laptop? At what point would we run out of things to say?

But it never happened. We talked the entire flight and continued after landing, learning more about each other's lives and families. With no other plans other than the concert later that night, we figured it out as we went along.

We stopped at a restaurant in suburban Denver. We drove to a state park nearby and decided to jump in the lake. On the way to the show, we picked up Taco Bell like a couple of teenagers.

I liked how Kevin let the moment be the prize. He wasn't constantly checking his phone, or distracted by the world. With twenty-four hours together, we had a lot of time to get to know each other, and it never felt forced.

I left with the simple, pleasant feeling of having made a friend.

Meanwhile, the couple that Mary and I had met at that very first "transplants barbecue" we'd gone to before the pandemic seemed like another good bet for friendship. Justin and Becky had moved to Minnesota from Massachusetts just a bit before we'd arrived from the Valley. I liked them both a lot. Justin and I had some commonalities besides just being transplants—we'd both played college football, we both had young kids, and we both were starting new jobs. He was a doctor, who had been working in urgent care, but had recently started his own family practice. So he was navigating life transitions, too.

When the pandemic hit, Justin and I started going on outdoor runs together around Lake Harriet. We managed to huff out a conversation around the lake, and sometimes grabbed a coffee afterward.

When I got an email from Becky addressed to me and six other men I'd never met before, inviting us all on a long weekend with Justin to visit the Bourbon Trail in Kentucky for his birthday, I found myself nervously excited. A weekend alone with the kids would be a sacrifice for Mary, but it might give me some extended time to get to know Justin better, and maybe his other friends, too. And all seven of the men lived in the same neighborhood in Edina, just five blocks away from our house in Minneapolis.

As the weekend approached, I thought about ways I might quicken the pace of becoming friends with these guys. I took Justin off the group email we were on and wrote a carefully worded message suggesting we surprise him by ordering silly matching T-shirts to wear for the weekend, hoping the rest of the guys didn't think I was some weirdo. Then I waited.

Mercifully, within a half hour, four of them had replied yes. The rest followed. I went online and ordered eight mint-green T-shirts with Justin's name on them, along with a clip art picture of a horse. They looked hideous, but that was kind of the point.

Once we landed in Kentucky, we piled into a massive SUV we'd rented for the weekend to check out distilleries. The group clearly had a rapport going, built on neighborhood inside jokes and a shared love of comedic sitcoms of the nineties, quoting *Seinfeld* lines with impressive fluency. In the back row of the SUV, I tried to engage without trying too hard, falling into the shared language of mid-forty-year-old-guy-ese: dad jokes about pop culture, stories about the travails of raising a family, and the usual banter about current events or sports. But I was still in that nervous state of finding my way in a new group. I found it hard not to evaluate everything I said before and after I said it, hoping I was coming across okay.

Usually when confronted with unfamiliar social terrain, I ask a lot of questions. Talking about other people has always been a lot more comfortable for me than talking about myself. Spending time learning about someone else prevents me from having to share too much, which in turn calms my unhealthy obsession of wondering if people like me or not. If I'm the one asking questions, the other person can't get to know me well enough to decide on my worthiness as a friend. Which is, of course, exactly how not to make a friend.

Justin was the one who clearly held the group together. They described him as the neighborhood organizer; he'd pulled together outdoor movie nights during the pandemic and held barbecues in his front yard. His easygoing manner drew people in and you could see he genuinely cared about each of his friends by the way he spoke with them.

The next morning, I brought out the matching T-shirts and we all surprised Justin with them. He smiled and immediately put his on. For the rest of the day, we looked like a group of forty-year-old guys going to a bachelorette party.

As we hopped between distilleries, sipping tiny flutes of bourbon and gamely pretending to be connoisseurs, I found myself comparing this group with the guys from Safe Space. It had taken a long time to develop the rapport we had, by living through an important moment in our lives together—and sometimes literally living together. We connected before we had families, careers, or other obligations. If nothing else, we simply had the time to hang out with each other.

Could I find that same thing with a group of guys like this? Objectively, it seemed possible. They had interesting lives, warm personalities, were raising families, and lived nearby. If I'd met this exact group of guys when we were all twenty-one—the average age researchers say people meet their best friends—it seemed entirely possible we'd have found our way toward lifetime friendship. But making friends later, when even a couple of days away from family to spend time together feels like a luxury, is a different journey.

As I traveled the Bourbon Trail with these men I'd never met before, little moments piled up that connected us. Some of it was just silly stuff. One of the guys, Dan, got sick going over the rolling hills in the back seat of the SUV, and we had to pull over for him to puke in a cornfield. At one of the distilleries they pumped loud, heavy metal music all day long, explaining that the low bass notes helped joggle the barrels and improve the taste of the brandy, a claim we mocked afterward. We played a game of pickleball at a local court, and Justin pulled his calf muscle five minutes into the game, which we teased him about. At dinner, we discovered we were sitting at a table next to the former drummer of Alice in Chains. A few of the guys were fans and mustered up the nerve to say hello.

Would these little moments become the shared stories that would bond us together as friends? I felt a little sheepish even wondering.

As the weekend wore on, I loosened up a little. I stopped asking so many questions and started answering some. Over a glass of bourbon in the hotel lobby bar, I sat down with Justin and Brian, his next-door neighbor whose son was the same age as our twins.

They knew I'd been through a lot in local government for a few years. "How are you holding up?" Brian asked.

I let myself relax and admitted the toll that the relentless pace was taking on me. I shared the feelings of doubt that were often lurking in my new job, where every decision was so heavily scrutinized and we often didn't know if we were getting things right.

They were kind and encouraging. It felt good to share these things with someone besides Mary. All three of us talked about our families and shared our worries about our kids and how they were doing. I wasn't the only one wondering if I was being the kind of dad I wanted to be amid the craziness swirling around us. We were all just trying to figure things out.

I was coming to realize that there was no secret sauce to making new friends in a new community. It takes time, and it takes the willingness to be open and vulnerable with others. The biggest challenge is that it's much easier today to do exactly the opposite. An American culture that has drastically tacked toward individualism and away from community has made making friends much harder. It's much easier to just get lost in our own lives of work, family, and other obligations. Or whatever show we're streaming.

I'd fallen prey to this, too, finding the excuse that my new work was so stressful and important that I didn't have time for new friendships. And that whatever free time I did have should be devoted to the kids and Mary.

But I was starting to think those were just excuses.

That weekend, I remembered how good it felt to make new friends. How enriching it was to share my challenges with others who live nearby and are willing to listen. Real connection with new people in my community wasn't just a way to steal a few laughs in an otherwise hectic life. It was the chance to learn something more about life, to strengthen the feeling of home I was trying so hard to create.

As Justin and I spent more time together, I found myself confiding in him about things I wasn't even telling my friends of twenty years. I shared my anxieties about our kids, and my questions about how best to help them grow into happy adults. I admitted my worries about whether work was taking too much time away from my family. I talked about Mary, and our ongoing conversations about making Minnesota work for us. I told him about the constant voice I hear in my head—am I doing life right? Justin was a good listener, and he shared his struggles, too.

When I was a kid, having one core crew of friends to spend time with felt so important. Yet different chapters had brought different people into my life. Technology kept me connected with these various friends even when geography could not.

In modern America, adulthood sometimes feels more like a menu of friendships to choose from. When I yearned for different connections in different moments, virtually or in person, I chose different groups to reach out to. It was liberating to know I was never done making friends. It put less pressure on any one friendship or group and allowed me to be open to anyone I met.

The places we call home are varied. Our physical neighborhoods, our virtual social networks, our schools, our community networks, and more are all places we find connection. Yet though we have more ways to build community in America today than we ever have, it often feels like we're more isolated than ever. I was finding that it takes deliberate action and a dash of courage to break through the bubble and meet other people. But once I did, I found others just as eager as me to make friends.

As I stopped telling myself I was too busy and started reaching out to those around me, our community was starting to feel more like home.

After we returned from Kentucky, I stayed in touch with the guys from the trip. Justin and I kept our irregular running date. In the winter, I took the leap and organized a pickleball night at a local brewery with the group. The night we all planned to meet, a big snowstorm hit. Giant, wet snowflakes fell from the sky and the roads were covered in snow. But everyone showed up. They all wanted the same thing I did—a chance to connect with a chosen community, and to share our lives with each other.

———

Months later, Mary and I developed a friendship together that might have been the strangest, most surreal friendship we'd ever had. It was with a gestational carrier.

Mary met Rose through an agency that matches people with fertility problems with those who are willing to help. A gestational carrier, or surrogate, is willing to carry and give birth to a child for another family. After Mary's surgery and several additional IVF attempts, our doctors told us that surrogacy was the only chance we had at giving birth to a third child.

We discussed the pros and cons for a while, but kept coming back to the fact that we weren't ready to give up. Having a child through a surrogate might not have been conventional, but we'd given up on conventional a long time ago. We wanted a third child so badly that it felt worth it.

On a warm spring day, Rose and her husband, Sean, came over with their three kids to meet our family for the first time. The whole situation felt bizarre and magical. Both of us couldn't fathom how someone would be willing to go through pregnancy and childbirth for someone else's child. I marveled that such people even existed.

When she walked in the front door, Rose's face beamed with a smile. She had shoulder-length blond hair and a pretty voice, and immediately hugged us both. On her wrist was a tattoo in cursive lettering: *Sometimes against all odds, we hope.*

The kids scampered to the backyard to jump on the trampoline, and we sat down with Rose and Sean. She told us her story. She was a labor and delivery nurse, and Sean was a pharmacy tech. They had gone through IVF for one of their kids, so she was more in tune with fertility challenges than most. After her pregnancies had gone so smoothly, she felt called to help others who were struggling. I asked her how she came to the decision to be a surrogate.

"It's just something I thought I could do to help someone else out," she said simply.

Mary gave her a hug. We shared our own story of trying to build a family—the countless trips to the doctor, the dozens of failed pregnancy tests, the elation upon Luke and Violet's arrival, and then more failures, a surgery, and now this. Being so vulnerable so quickly with these strangers made them strangers not for long.

The kids got along, playing in the backyard, and we had an easy dinner. When it got dark, we came inside and spent more time together, walking around the house and just chatting. No one was in a hurry for them to go home.

Later that night as we were going to bed, Mary said, "I feel like we just met an angel."

Chapter 13

Bridges

T raci Tapani cut an unlikely figure as she walked up to the microphone on the factory floor. Her bright orange blazer and dress
pants were not standard attire here at Wyoming Machine, a sheet metal
fabrication company based in Stacy, Minnesota, thirty minutes north
of St. Paul. Pallets of sheet metal were stacked to either side of her, and
an American flag hung from the ceiling above.

But Traci was very much at home. For over twenty-five years, she'd
served as co-president of this family business with her sister, Lori. She
was the leader of one of the rare women-owned manufacturing businesses in the country, and her voice on business issues had gained national attention, especially since the pandemic.

Today, she was welcoming the governor and lieutenant governor,
along with a collection of other leaders from across the state.

"It has been such a pleasure to work with these individuals over the
past nine months as a member of the Governor's Council on Economic
Expansion," she said to the line of TV cameras in front of her, invited
to take part in the Formula once again.

Standing behind her, I clutched a copy of a new government
report. If there are two words that elicit more yawns than "gov-

ernment report," I'm unaware of them. Yet I could barely contain my excitement. It was a ten-year road map for economic growth in our state. My team and I had written it with a group of fifteen business and community leaders who'd joined Traci to volunteer their time and ideas. Today's announcement would launch the plan to the public and start a new conversation about where Minnesota was headed.

Ever since the pandemic, almost everything about my new life in government felt like playing defense. COVID had thrown the country into chaos. George Floyd's murder had set my new city on fire. Our community, our state, and our country felt unmoored.

Writing this new playbook for the future was refreshing. This was why I'd taken the leap from Google into government in the first place—to chase new ideas to make our new community stronger. I hoped this report might help build a bridge from the crises we'd been through to a much stronger place for my home state.

We'd assembled a diverse group of experts to create the road map. The president of the Minneapolis Fed, the head of the Minnesota Council of Nonprofits, and former CEOs of Fortune 500 companies all joined. A nonprofit executive named Paul Williams and the former CEO of Hormel Foods, Jeff Ettinger, agreed to chair the group. Everyone we asked said yes, bursting with energy to build back our community after a hard few years.

At the heart of the report was the idea that we needed big changes to our state if we were going to come out of this crisis successfully. The gaps between Black and white, urban and rural, and left and right were threatening to tear Minnesota apart. Our recommendations were designed to put it back together, covering everything from housing to education to broadband to paid family medical leave.

When the press conference was done, we did a tour of Traci's factory floor. Most of the machinists and welders we met probably hadn't voted for the governor. This was Trump country, after all. But they were kind and welcoming.

I hoped it was a sign that good things lay ahead. But a few months later, I came across another report that stopped me in my tracks.

Written thirty years earlier, when I was in grade school, the report was titled "State of Diversity," and was released under a moderate Republican governor named Arne Carlson. As I paged through it, I was stunned to see this old report highlighted the very same challenges our state was facing today, and asked the same question that ours did: "Will Minnesota be unified and prosperous, or will it be divided?" In substance, the recommendations didn't look all that different from ours.

If a thirty-year-old report that addressed some of the same challenges we faced today hadn't driven change, then would ours be any different?

I hoped so, but it was sobering to consider the history we were up against. This was exactly why people yawned at government reports. Government actions weren't the only answer to building a stronger community. If our community was going to make a comeback, a lot of different people would need to build many new bridges that hadn't been built before.

Though I didn't know it at the time, I was about to begin my final year in state government. With the punishing pace of crisis management fading behind me, the people I was about to meet would give me new faith that something special was happening here in flyover country that just might chart a new path forward for our state and our country.

————

On a cool spring Saturday morning, eleven teenagers sat in a circle of folding chairs in our living room. With paper plates in their laps, they ate sandwiches and chattered with each other. Our Silicon North Stars meetups were always boisterous affairs, but when Mary introduced our guest speaker for the day, the room fell quickly silent.

Jazz Hampton was one of the most inspiring startup founders we'd ever brought to Silicon North Stars. He commanded instant respect from the students, with a calm voice and an intense focus honed from his time as a lawyer.

Jazz grew up with a Black dad and a white mom. They sent him to a private Catholic high school called Holy Angels, just five minutes north of where his dad coached football at Richfield High School, south of Minneapolis. Over the course of his childhood, Jazz's parents would take in nine different young Black men from troubled homes to live with them.

Every morning, his brother would drive him to Holy Angels, before next dropping off the rest of the kids at Richfield High.

"When my brother dropped me off, there were more Black kids in the car with me than there were at my entire private high school," he shared. "I've always had a foot in two worlds, and I've always felt comfortable in both."

After high school, Jazz went to the University of St. Thomas in St. Paul, where he played football for a year, leaving the team after his freshman year to focus on his studies in computer science. He went on to get a law degree, the beginning of a successful career as a lawyer.

Jazz's calm and thoughtful demeanor made him good at his job, and he soon found himself on the partner track at a major law firm in Minneapolis. He got married, had kids, and bought a nice house in Southwest Minneapolis, just a few blocks from Mary and me. Life was good.

When George Floyd was murdered and Minneapolis erupted, Jazz joined peaceful protests and found himself in regular discussions about what this moment meant for his community. His biracial background, he discovered, meant people from all different walks of life trusted him in the clumsy conversations that followed. But Jazz had always identified as a Black man, and it was conversations with his Black friends that made him wonder if now was the time to do something different with his life than corporate law.

Two of those friends were Jazz's classmates from St. Thomas, Andre

"Dre" Creighton and Mychal Frelix. Both had grown up knowing the family of Philando Castile, the Black man who was shot and killed by a police officer during a routine traffic stop in a St. Paul suburb in 2016. A nutrition services supervisor at a local Montessori school, Castile had been pulled over forty-nine times in thirteen years by police, often for minor infractions. On the stop that ended his life, Castile had been in the car with his girlfriend and her four-year-old daughter. When he disclosed that he had a firearm, which he was licensed to carry, the officer quickly reacted, firing seven shots that killed Castile. Immediately afterward, his girlfriend turned on Facebook Live and within days the incident had caused an international uproar.

When the police officer was acquitted of all charges a year later, there was further uproar. It was, tragically, one of the many incidents of violence against Black people in Minnesota that built the pressure that exploded after George Floyd's murder.

As Minneapolis burned, Dre and Mychal felt they had to do something. They thought back to what might have helped Philando Castile at that traffic stop. What if a lawyer had been with him in the car, able to advise him and reduce the tension with the police officer who'd stopped him?

Their brainstorming led to TurnSignl, a mobile app that could instantly dial up a lawyer for advice during traffic stops. Without any legal background, their first call was to Jazz.

"They called and said, 'We need a lawyer,'" Jazz told the Silicon North Stars. "I gave them some advice, and then they called back a few days later and said, 'We need you to be the CEO.'"

The eyes of every student in our living room were open wide.

"This was not part of my plan," he continued. "But I kept thinking about it. I had a degree in law and computer science. I felt moved to do something to help my community. I just kept thinking, 'This makes sense.'" Jazz quit his job and joined the company.

The basic idea was simple: a one-touch system to call a lawyer on demand when you're pulled over by a police officer. With a lawyer beamed into the car via video, it would not only give the driver an opportunity to get advice on how to interact with the officer, but it could also de-escalate the situation.

"Everyone's going to be on better behavior because a lawyer is there," they reasoned.

Having been pulled over a dozen times himself, Jazz knew the feeling. He also knew that frequent traffic stops were common for Black men and that, according to research, police were seven times more likely to use force on people of color than on white people in Minneapolis.

Jazz and his cofounders started pitching their company and got dozens of lawyers to sign up. It didn't take long to prove the concept.

One early customer of TurnSignl was a middle-aged Black man who was driving with a passenger when he was pulled over by police at 2:00 a.m., for a minor traffic violation. He was instantly worried, and for good reason—he was driving with a suspended driver's license. When the police approached the car, the man opened TurnSignl and a lawyer popped up on a live stream.

When the officer asked to search his car, the man asked the lawyer if he should let them. The lawyer told him that such a search was not required by law, without probable cause.

"When was your last drink?" the officer asked next.

"Eight and a half years ago," the man said, proud of his sobriety. The lawyer listened in, his face visible to both the officer and the driver.

The cop checked the man's record and came back to the car. Rather than press him further, the officer asked him to switch seats with his passenger, who had a valid license, and drive home. The situation never escalated, and the man and his companion got home safely. It was exactly the kind of outcome that Jazz and his cofounders were hoping to see.

TurnSignl gained momentum. Within a few years, it had over three hundred lawyers on call in all fifty states, and was averaging over a hundred calls per month. Thirty percent of app downloads came from Minnesota.

Now the company just needed to figure out how to monetize this momentum. Jazz and his cofounders had a brilliant idea for how to do so: corporate partnerships. Jazz took screenshots of every Black Lives Matter social media post from corporate America that he could find, and then used them in pitch decks to the company.

"I show these executives the screenshots of their social media posts, and then say, 'I'd tell you about what a problem inequality is in our society, but I know I don't need to do that—you already know!'" Jazz shared with the students, who laughed.

It worked. Corporate packages allowed Jazz and his team to offer TurnSignl for free to anyone who made less than $40,000 a year. The students were impressed with his approach.

"If people aren't worried about their safety, they can focus on other parts of their lives," he told them.

That, he thought, was a key step in narrowing the gaps between Black and white people in Minnesota. It also helped police officers feel safer.

"The police have hard jobs, and this helps them," Jazz said. In fact, as TurnSignl grew bigger, the team created a TurnSignl Foundation that supported scholarships to police academies. The last thing Jazz wanted was to stoke division between the police and the community.

"When you started, did you know you were going to be successful?" asked one of our students.

"No. I took a risk," Jazz reflected. "Life isn't linear, you've got to pursue what you're interested in and not be worried that you have to figure it all out at once."

In the previous few weeks, a string of new national top-five lists had been released, with Minneapolis finding itself, once again, at the top of many of them. *The best city for recent college graduates. The best big city for biking. The happiest city in America.* I mentioned these accolades for our city to Jazz, and asked what he thought, given the racial wealth gaps that remained.

"Frankly, it's frustrating," he said. "Minnesota is complicated. We have the greatest gaps, but also the greatest knowledge of them. And a lot of goodwill to fix them. It's frustrating that we haven't killed the paradox yet." He saw TurnSignl as one way to make progress. But it was going to take a lot of new and different efforts to make real headway.

In the years since George Floyd's murder, the backlash to efforts focused on racial equity has been troubling, but Jazz knew change wasn't linear, and he was hopeful about progress.

"There are a lot of people pushing for change right now. It's a different conversation than it was before. Something's got to come out of that."

Jazz's skill as a bridge-builder was impressive. He'd spent his life creating connections between the Black and white communities. And now his company was building bridges between the Black community and the police, right when our state needed it most.

————

There were many other bridges that needed building. One of the biggest was a bridge for the gap between urban and rural Minnesota. That's why I was so excited when I met a fellow Minnesota boomerang named Benya Kraus.

Benya's boomerang story was different from mine. She grew up in Bangkok, Thailand, where she was born to a Minnesotan dad and a Thai mom who met doing relief work at a refugee camp on the Thailand-Myanmar border. When she went to college she chose Tufts University in Boston because it had a great international affairs program. An overachiever, she became deeply involved in campus life and even found herself appointed to the board of directors at Amnesty International before graduating summa cum laude. She imagined a future career with global reach.

But a trip home during college to see her grandparents and extended family in the southern Minnesota town of Waseca changed everything. She'd been to Minnesota before, but there was something special about this trip. She rode a four-wheeler around the farm. She fed chickens and did chores. She met the mayor and the sheriff. Everyone knew the Kraus family, which made it feel like home even though she didn't live there. Without trying to, she'd discovered something she didn't know she was looking for.

"It was a transformative experience," she told me. "I was tired of going to conferences about international affairs and hearing people talk all about 'what the local people needed to do' when none of them actually lived in those local places."

She started wondering what it would be like to move to Waseca herself. But the career office at Tufts didn't have much to offer in the way of jobs in rural America, let alone Waseca specifically. American college education didn't seem oriented to find pathways for people to rural communities.

That's when Benya heard about a few other students at East Coast universities who were trying to start an organization to change that. They called it Lead for America, and the idea was to provide funding for two-year fellowships that would send college graduates to rural American communities to work in the civic sector. Benya joined as a cofounder, and along with her new partners built the business plan and launched the effort in a matter of months.

Over 1,600 people applied in the first year alone for just fifty fellowships. They took jobs in city governments, local nonprofits, and tribal nations. In just a few years, Lead for America had placed over four hundred fellows across almost every state in the country. Over fifty of them were in Minnesota.

One of them was Celia Simpson, a native of Fairmont, a small town near the Minnesota-Iowa border. She grew up idolizing her older cousin who'd moved to New York City and envisioned a life where she lived in a different city every year. When she graduated high school, she made a beeline for the coast, enrolling in Seattle University to study forensic science.

"Leaving Fairmont was always my plan," Celia told me when I

called her to learn what brought her back home. "I think there's a feeling in my generation that it's cool to say your hometown sucks. That you need to go away to learn for yourself. I definitely felt that."

In Seattle, she met people from around the country. She made friends from Colorado, Hawaii, Guam. She studied abroad in Morocco, and began planning to enroll in the Peace Corps after graduation, inspired to do community development. Then the pandemic hit. Her campus emptied out, but Celia stayed because she'd just gotten an internship with the medical examiner's office in Seattle. That work took her around the city, where she worked in the fatal overdose surveillance program.

"Seeing people die alone in their homes of fentanyl overdoses broke the vision that I had of cities being a place where you could find your people and everyone was connected," she recalled. "I started to miss my family and my community. It was an isolating time."

When Celia discovered Lead for America, she was surprised by how appealing it seemed to her. When she discovered they had a position open in Fairmont, she instinctively applied. It reminded her what she missed about her hometown—the sense of community.

Instead of the Peace Corps, Celia chose Lead for America and returned to Minnesota. It became her own version of "America First." She was placed with a local nonprofit focused on community development. They built a mini golf course and a playground, and started a girls' robotics camp.

"My parents were like, are you sure?" she remembered when she told them about her impending move. "I had to convince them that this was really what I wanted."

After a year in the program, she got a full-time job doing community development. Today she sees a future in Fairmont because she's helped foster a new community on her own terms, and sees lots of exciting change in the town.

"The divide between urban and rural is often in people's heads," she told me. "Until you talk to somebody and find out more about what their lives are like, you don't really know." Her friends in Seattle were convinced that Minneapolis must be full of cornfields. Her friends in Fairmont thought Seattle must be riddled with crime. Neither was right. Having spent time in both places, she could help dispel the myths.

For her, being back home felt right. "I see people caring for each other here in powerful ways. When I go to the grocery store, I can't get out of there in less than thirty minutes because everyone wants to talk."

Stories like Celia's are why Benya started Lead for America. Fellows help counter misperceptions that rural and urban Americans have about each other.

Relationships were the key, Benya found. Back in Waseca, she got to know the mayor of the town, a conservative man with whom she disagreed deeply on national politics. But she was a big fan of his local leadership and offered to knock on doors to help get him reelected because "he's bringing great things to our community," she said.

Despite her passion for bridging urban-rural divides in America, Benya doesn't have rose-colored glasses about the future. She's worried the divisions that are growing in American life are taking their toll. She wondered aloud to me, "Do we still have the strong social bonds that are required to do the big things like we did in the past?"

We talked about the economic shifts that had pushed these divisions. The move toward a "bigger is better" economy and the consolidation of rural businesses had serious repercussions. Benya guessed there were around one hundred dairy farms in Waseca in the 1980s, and today there's just one big one.

"So much of the American civic spirit came from local employment," she observed. "A handful of local employers used to fund all the parks and schools in Waseca, but now most of those businesses are owned by anonymous national conglomerates that rarely give back to the community in the same way. That erodes trust."

Organizations like Lead for America may be able to help build back that trust, encouraging young people to give back to their communities and bridging the divide between urban and rural. I'd found that working in government had given me new faith in the importance of institutions. Lead for America is doing the same for its fellows.

———

American communities need people like Benya, Celia, and Jazz, focused on building bridges in our society. They're each using their talents and passions to do something new and different to stitch the country together.

As I read more from the political scientist Robert Putnam, I was struck by his definition of two different kinds of social capital: bonding social capital and bridging social capital. Bonding social capital is what you have with people who are like you, and bridging social capital is what you have with people not like you. His work makes the argument that both are important, but in a diverse and increasingly divided America, growing our bridging social capital is essential to strengthening our society.

That's exactly what these leaders I met were doing. Not only was their work building bridges among people who were different, but they were also deepening the empathy and respect that people felt for their differences. That felt a lot like adaptation. If they could help heal divisions in a state that was at the center of a global focus on inequality and division, in a state that had boasted so much progress but also had suffered so much chaos, it gave me hope that the rest of the country could do the same.

Just like in Silicon Valley, we'd need lots of new ideas and experiments if we were to find ways to avoid repeating the mistakes of the past. Which is why the bridge-builder who inspired me most was the one living under the same roof as me.

When Mary decided to start her own venture capital firm, she knew she wanted to do things differently. Venture capital is a male-dominated industry that's famously insular and focused on the coasts.

It's full of big egos, a harsh culture, and is very myopic. Over 90 percent of venture capital dollars go to companies founded by white men.

Mary and her business partner, Brett, an affable serial entrepreneur with a shaved head and a penchant for wearing sneakers and T-shirts in even the most formal settings, knew they'd need to create a different approach if they were going to get attention in flyover country. Together they struck on a unique pitch for their firm, Bread & Butter Ventures.

First, they'd focus on startups in industries that were strongest in Minnesota—medical technology, food technology, and enterprise software. Second, they'd leverage the densest Fortune 500 market in America to make introductions and connections to their startups to the likes of the Mayo Clinic, General Mills, Cargill, and beyond. And third, they'd look for startups in parts of the country that are often overlooked by coastal funds.

When I asked Mary how they were going to do all of that, she brimmed with confidence, embodying a new energy for our lives in Minnesota. "We'll pull together some kind of a network," she thought out loud. "Maybe like an innovation circle or something. We'll get all the Fortune 500s in Minnesota to join, and they can help mentor the companies we invest in. They'll probably want to invest in some of them, too, or maybe even acquire them."

Soon she and Brett had done just that. They raised nearly $75 million in two different funds, bet on over fifty startups, and had hundreds of investors from around the country—along with an innovation circle of seventeen blue-chip companies to support their startups, exactly as Mary had envisioned.

To bring it all together, Mary and Brett held a "Founder's Summit" for their startups, investors, and partners at a coworking space in the North Loop of Minneapolis. Over a hundred people descended upon Minnesota from across the country to participate. I sneaked along to watch as Mary took the stage in a bright green dress and addressed the crowd with a warm smile.

"We believe entrepreneurship can change the world," she began.

"The fact that any entrepreneur who dreams big has the potential to transform their industry, their community, and even the world is so inspiring. The companies in this room are doing just that."

Twenty percent of the companies they'd invested in were from Minnesota; just over 30 percent were from the Midwest. Almost 50 percent of the companies had female founders, and over 60 percent had founders of color. These were not your typical venture capital statistics, but Mary and Brett were convinced they were looking in places that other investors were blind to. If the coasts were going to ignore flyover country, they'd do so at their own peril.

Later that evening, I went to a happy hour they'd organized for guests. Over miniature Jucy Lucys (a Minnesota cheeseburger, where the cheese is baked on the inside of the meat instead of on top) and locally crafted cocktails, I wandered through a room buzzing with ideas. The connections that Mary was fostering among startup founders, investors, and mentors in and outside the Midwest was evident everywhere.

I talked with Senan Ebrahim, the founder of a maternal healthcare company called Delfina, based down the road in Rochester, that uses AI to help pregnant women spot challenges in their pregnancy earlier. I had a proud-husband moment as Senan told me about how important Mary was to their company.

"She just knows everyone and is willing to make any connection," he said.

Others said the same. A founder named Lindsey Hoell, who started a circular logistics platform focused on returning used goods, said the concept Mary and Brett had created was working. "There have been very few companies that we've wanted to get in front of that we haven't been able to through Mary and Brett's network," she said.

One entrepreneur used his fifteen-year journey in recovery to start a company called YourPath to help people with substance use disorders find better care. Another started a company that used technology to spot and prevent crop loss. All of them had made connections to people in Mary's "innovation circle" that had helped them grow their businesses.

The connections Mary made weren't just for the companies she invested in, however. She joined a local startup ecosystem organization called Forge North and soon became the chair. The organization connected startups to local resources and helped recruit founders from out of state to consider Minnesota. She also joined the boards of two of Minnesota's largest foundations to try to understand the role philanthropy had in our economy.

Mary was also passionate about bringing the next generation of leaders along. She hired one of our Silicon North Stars as an intern, and held online seminars for students to teach them about venture capital.

Starting her own company had unleashed a passion inside of Mary that brought momentum wherever she went. When Greater MSP, a regional economic development group, decided to create a new commercial for the Twin Cities, they asked Mary to be the face and voice of the video. Sitting behind a desk and smiling into the camera, Mary made the case for Minnesota, delivering soaring platitudes interspersed by images of robotic arms building things, white-coated scientists in laboratories, and planes flying into the Minneapolis–St. Paul airport.

"Imagine a future in which the seemingly impossible becomes reality," she read with conviction.

> What if a new generation of medical technology could solve today's unsolvable problems? What if investments in groundbreaking communities of color delivered innovation and prosperity? Together, we are writing the next chapter of our region's story. We are inventing America's next economy.

We watched the video together on our couch one night after putting the kids to bed. Mary giggled as she listened to herself delivering the platitudes, but I couldn't contain my pride. To see her go from feeling like she might want to escape this cold part of the country to starting a company that connected it with the rest of the world was a stunning evolution.

I marveled at what she'd achieved. If you'd told me two years earlier, when we were sitting in Silicon Valley on our "old-life vacation" as Mary quoted dismal sunshine statistics about Minneapolis, that she'd soon be the face of a commercial that pitched Minnesota to the rest of the world, I would have fallen out of my chair.

We closed the laptop, and I asked her how it felt.

"You know, you've just got to go all in," she reflected. "There are things I really like about Minnesota, and there's things I don't. But I love building communities like this, and I really believe in what we're doing in our company. It's exciting to start something on your own, especially when you're an underdog."

Mary was doing something she was great at, and it had caught fire in our new community. By moving to a place that others had overlooked, she was able to do what nobody else could.

Even if we weren't sure if Minnesota was our forever home, one thing was clear: the coasts were crowded. Out here, there was a lot more room to build something truly unique.

Chapter 14

On the Road

M ary and I play a game almost every time we travel to a new place. We like to imagine in great detail what our lives might be like if we lived there.

"What if we started a farm and grew our own food here?"

"What if we turned that old, abandoned post office on the corner into a brewery and a Thai restaurant?"

"What if we got a ranch and had a horse stable and campground and held an annual fall festival with pumpkins and hayrides?"

Having grown up in a small town, I'm well aware of how rose-colored these ideas sound. But I can't help myself. There's something about fantasizing another life that's uniquely comforting. Wasn't that what led us to pick up and leave Silicon Valley for Minnesota in the first place? Fantasies are the first step to reinvention. If you can see something, you can begin to imagine how to get there.

Imagining life in a small town comes with assumptions of a simpler life, of more comfort and familiarity, of a place that somehow doesn't change. It feels like an anecdote to the anxieties of modern life.

The hope of escape to a new place is a powerful desire. Sometimes we're wise to listen to it.

When we first escaped Silicon Valley and moved to Minnesota, we were motivated to come to a place in flyover country that felt more rooted in community and family. When I closed my eyes and thought about a place like that, images of a small town came to mind. But for many reasons, we chose Minneapolis, a big city. Even my hometown of Northfield, with twenty thousand people and two liberal arts colleges, wouldn't be considered small by some. It all depends on what definition of "rural" you choose.

Now my work as a government official brought me to cities and towns of all shapes and sizes in Minnesota outside the Twin Cities. It was my favorite part of the job. Every time I left Minneapolis, I learned more about the problems and possibilities that exist everywhere you go. Of course, no place is perfect. There is no idyllic life waiting in a small town where nothing ever changes. Change is everywhere.

In fact, some of the most interesting and dynamic changes happening in American life today are unfolding in rural areas. In the wake of so many crises, I wanted to see how places across my home state were trying to put themselves back together again. As I traveled Minnesota, I discovered there's no better place to see communities reinventing themselves than in rural America.

———

On a warm September day I rolled into St. Cloud, Minnesota, and immediately got lost. I was looking for a new community center that local Somali leaders had invited me to tour, but it was so new that my GPS couldn't find it.

After driving in circles for half an hour, I finally reached the state senator in the area, Aric Putnam, who guided me to a large brick building that once served as the *St. Cloud Times'* printing facility. It had been empty for years, and now local immigrant leaders wanted to turn it into a youth and family center. They referred to it as an "Islamic YMCA" to help other members of the community understand what they envisioned.

I wiped the sweat from my forehead and went inside, where I was greeted warmly by over a dozen Somali community leaders. They didn't seem annoyed that I was late. State government officials were a rare sight in this working-class city of nearly seventy thousand about an hour north of Minneapolis—or at least a rare sight within the growing Somali population here. Everyone in the group was dressed up for the occasion, causing me instant regret for having worn a flannel shirt and boots for what I thought would be a more casual affair.

"Welcome, Mr. Commissioner," said Mohayadin Mohamed, the leader of the gathering, reaching out to shake my hand. Mohayadin had been in St. Cloud since 2006, when he came to the U.S. on a lottery visa. Originally from Somalia, he met his wife in St. Cloud and together they had six kids. As the leader of the Islamic Center of St. Cloud, it was his job to galvanize support for the "Islamic YMCA."

Mohayadin and his team were still in the early stages of planning the center. Cavernous rooms that used to house gigantic printing presses still stood empty as he took me on a tour to point out the plan for each room.

Our agency would help fund the beginning stages of development, and a local foundation had pledged to contribute, too. But the center still had a long way to go. After the tour, we sat down at foldout tables and chairs for a roundtable discussion.

The leaders were passionate about growing their community here. They peppered me with questions about our agency's grant-making process, which they said was too complicated. They pressed me for new funding solutions that would help Muslim-owned small businesses, which can't take interest-bearing loans because it's forbidden under Islamic law. About halfway through, a woman in a beige burka asked for the mic.

"We want to empower ourselves," she implored. "We want to make our community the best one in the country. We've worked hard on this center. We've put all our money together to make it happen. We have to work together."

These leaders were just a few of the thousands of Somali immigrants who'd moved to St. Cloud over the last few decades. While Minnesota boasts the largest Somali population of any state in the country, not everyone who comes moves to the Twin Cities. Smaller cities like St. Cloud, abundant with manufacturing jobs, draw thousands of Somali immigrants, too. It's been part of a growing shift that has challenged the unsavory nickname this town has had for many years: "White Cloud."

In fact, in the most recent decade the percentage of residents who consider themselves non-white doubled to 32 percent, one of the highest growth rates in the state. The younger immigrant population has filled a gap left by an aging white one. The average age in St. Cloud is almost a decade lower than the rest of the state, and over 60 percent of the students in public schools are Black or brown. Thus the need for a youth and family center that Mohayadin and his group were trying to build.

"St. Cloud is more like America than any place in the Midwest," the state senator Aric Putnam told me. "It's a microcosm of the entire country."

As long-standing residents and recent immigrant arrivals have become neighbors, the city has had its growing pains, like any place going through massive change. Mosques needed to be built. Traditional African food stores cropped up. Occasionally, relationships were strained, especially in times of crisis.

In 2016, a young East African immigrant who was well liked in the community went to the local mall to buy an iPhone, but ended up on a violent rampage with two large knives, stabbing ten people before being shot and killed by an off-duty police officer. The violence shocked the community and made national news. No one could explain it. The terrorist group ISIL claimed credit for the attack, though no official connection or motive was ever found.

More violence might have ensued if it wasn't for the efforts of local leaders and officials. Chief among them was Dave Kleis, the longtime mayor who was once a registered Republican but is now an independent. Mayor Kleis had spent decades building relationships in his community. He estimates he's held nearly one thousand town halls since taking office in 2005, and holds monthly "Dinners with Strangers," where he invites people who don't know each other over to his house for homemade chili on his back deck.

Kleis is exactly the kind of person you want as your mayor. After the attack, he sprang into action. "I had the cell phone numbers of everyone I needed to call, and they all picked up the phone," he told me. "The NAACP, our community policing team, leaders in the East African community, they all came together because we'd built relationships over time."

The leaders gathered for a joint press conference in front of national media outlets like CNN and Fox, who'd descended into town expecting a riot. CNN had booked the mayor for a live interview for later that afternoon. But when the press conference with all the local leaders calmed nerves and it was clear no riot was coming, the producer called Kleis back to cancel the interview. There wasn't anything to cover anymore. Kleis was grateful to be booted.

The Somali leaders gathered in the fledgling community center told me how much Kleis's leadership mattered. "We have good leaders here."

Yet, of course, there was still backlash. A former university professor formed a group called Concerned Community Citizens (or C-Cubed) to advocate against immigration to St. Cloud. The group made claims that not only were immigrants a threat to the community but they were innately less intelligent. National media caught notice.

In 2019, the *New York Times* came to town. They profiled C-Cubed and wrote a two-thousand-word story titled "'These People Aren't Coming from Norway': Refugees in a Minnesota City Face a Backlash." To many residents here, it was the equivalent of dropping a bomb on their city.

"It infuriated a lot of people," said Kleis, who participated in the story. "They interviewed me for two and a half hours and used one bad quote."

To Kleis and the Somali leaders I met with, the article did almost irreparable damage to St. Cloud's reputation. In their eyes, it didn't represent the community, but was the words of a few extremists in C-Cubed being held up as the entire community.

The community rallied. Local leaders wrote an editorial calling the white extremists cowards. A proposed moratorium against immigrants failed at city hall. The chamber of commerce formed a DEI committee to help local businesses better recruit more immigrant workers and change perceptions.

The fact that a new community center was being built inside the hollowed-out printing facility of a newspaper that once boasted nearly fifty reporters was a poignant reminder of one of the biggest challenges rural communities like St. Cloud face: a severe lack of local news coverage. While the *New York Times* could reach millions with their takedown of "White Cloud," there were barely any reporters left in the city to tell a different story. The *St. Cloud Times* was down from fifty to only a couple of reporters. There were no local TV stations. The local radio station barely registers on people's radar.

That means that even statewide media show up primarily when something bad happens. And online platforms only amplify those stories. When I searched "St. Cloud News" on YouTube, seven of the top eight videos were about shootings or murders.

Social media has swooped in and taken the place of local media. Facebook in particular has become the hub for community news in St. Cloud, as it has in so many communities across rural America. And it's led to big challenges with misinformation.

Four years after the mall stabbing in St. Cloud and just a few weeks after George Floyd's murder, a local police officer was shot in the hand while trying to detain an eighteen-year-old suspect. The officers did not return fire. But rumors quickly spread on Facebook that an officer had killed a Black man during the arrest.

"It was a social media firestorm," Mayor Kleis told me.

Local media couldn't move quickly enough to get the real story out.

In the information vacuum, angry community members rallied and began marching toward the police station. They started throwing rocks and said they planned to take over the station. Officers had to set up barricades and use chemical irritants to stop the crowd, and four arrests were made. Luckily no one was seriously injured.

Police Chief Brian Anderson later expressed his frustration to the media.

"It is abhorrent to me that within minutes the story that went out went out," he said. "This place could have been on fire over a lie."

The next morning, Black leaders, local imams and preachers, and the mayor all called a press conference to set the record straight and praise the officer's restraint. It was a great example of the community coming together during a crisis. But the damage still felt senseless. Without the facts, community members who'd experienced decades of prejudice just assumed the worst.

But St. Cloud, like so many communities, is resilient.

"People used to call this White Cloud, but that's changed," Mohayadin told me, recalling that it used to be hard for a Muslim family to even find an apartment to rent. "People don't like change, but we're now in a stage where the younger kids who were born here are becoming local leaders. They're seen as hardworking. And local leaders have worked very hard to change perception. I think we've made a lot of progress."

Many other leaders have begun to step up. One is Eunice Adjei, a Somali immigrant who's the founder of the Jugaad Leadership Program. Her program provides training to around a dozen young leaders of color every year to help strengthen St. Cloud. It's an intensive program, where Eunice gets her participants in front of top city and state officials and gives them training to take on bigger roles in the city.

"There was a need to have representation of people in leadership roles," explained Eunice, who started the organization in 2015. She'd moved to the city to attend St. Cloud State University, and stayed because she loved it so much. Jugaad was her chance to change the shape of her new community.

"Our mission is to train and place leaders of color on local boards and commissions, by providing resources they don't have," she said.

The effort is making progress. In a recent city council election, sixteen candidates vied for three open city council seats—the largest candidate pool in over half a century. A few of them were African immigrants, and one of them, Hudda Ibrahim, ended up becoming the first Somali American city council member in city history.

The city is also making a play to expand its business sector from manufacturing into technology. When local twin brothers Rob and Ryan Weber built a software business and sold it for $25 million several years ago, they decided to use their newfound wealth to start a venture capital firm, Great North Ventures, focused specifically on St. Cloud and the surrounding region.

"We think good ideas can come from anywhere," Ryan Weber told me. "There's plenty of talent and people here, investors just aren't looking close enough."

Recently, the firm invested in a local startup modeled after VRBO called HLRBO, or Hunting Land Rentals by Owner. It's an online platform for leasing hunting land, and has quickly racked up over eighty-five thousand users. The hunting market is much larger than that, and Weber thinks the founders have leveraged their expertise into a company that can scale.

I left St. Cloud feeling hopeful that leaders were writing a new chapter for a fast-changing community. This was a place that wasn't running away from its problems. For better or worse, those problems had been exposed for all to see. But good people believed they could solve for them and build a stronger community.

After our meeting with Somali leaders, I caught up with State Senator Putnam again. I asked him about the negative press and attention that St. Cloud sometimes battled. He had a different take.

"I like that our conflicts here are public," he reflected. "That's a good sign. People are stepping up and recognizing all of our warts. We aren't saying we should go back to the way things are. That's a sign of maturity and a strong work ethic."

The idea of America—a place where people can build communities built on shared ideals rather than shared backgrounds—has not faded in St. Cloud. New immigrants bring new energy to the idea of America and remind us why our country's values are as strong today as they were at our founding. When people believe in each other and the place that they live, so much is possible.

"This is America, and America's a work in progress," State Senator Putnam said. "We're doing the work."

———

Fifty miles north of St. Cloud lies a much smaller town, on the banks of Lake Mille Lacs, called Onamia. It's home to roughly 750 people and straddles the Mille Lacs Band of Ojibwe reservation. If you're searching for insight into the very first divisions in American life, all roads lead to towns like Onamia. It's places like this where white settlers and Native Americans first collided hundreds of years ago.

I drove to Onamia out of sheer curiosity. DEED had awarded a grant to the Mille Lacs Band of Ojibwe to build a childcare center in town. The team had told me the tribe was doing something unique to build the center, and I wanted to see it for myself.

As I drove north from Minneapolis, past farm fields and small towns, I recalled the tribal-state relations training I'd taken with all the other commissioners when I started my job in state government. Professors of Native American history and tribal leaders had educated us all on the tragic story of tribes in our state.

Their treatment, like the treatment of Native peoples across the country, was the original sin of America's founding.

The Mille Lacs Band of Ojibwe migrated to central Minnesota around five hundred years ago as Europeans began settling the coasts of North America. They came to Minnesota because it was the place "where the food grows on water." Wild rice farming was a key staple of their diets and the tribe prospered in Lake Country.

But as white settlers began to move into the area, bad treaties and broken promises shrank the tribe's land and decimated their way of life. By the end of the nineteenth century, they had been almost completely driven from homes they'd lived in for generations. Even worse, Ojibwe children were stolen from their families and placed in government boarding schools for assimilation, one of the most shameful acts in U.S. government history. Generations of culture, religion, and language were nearly destroyed.

Not until the 1930s were leaders from the Mille Lacs Band able to partner with other Native leaders to establish the right to self-government. Further victories took decades to pass, with the Indian Gaming Regulatory Act coming in 1988, allowing tribes to start gaming establishments on their lands, a much-needed financial lifeline after decades of oppression.

Today, the Mille Lacs Band of Ojibwe is one of eleven sovereign tribal nations living in Minnesota. Their reservation is a fraction of the land they once roamed. The fact that they were now building a childcare center on their reservation to welcome both Ojibwe and non-Native children seemed curious to me. Why would they invest in a community governed by a country that had once tried to wipe out their people and culture?

I pulled into the parking lot and met Dustin Goslin, a Native leader who heads economic development for Mille Lacs Corporate Ventures, the business arm of the tribe.

"*Boozhoo*," Dustin greeted me, using the Ojibwe word for "welcome" as we shook hands, smiling. He wore a black dress shirt and a beautiful, beaded necklace with a blue and red star medallion hanging on his chest.

Inside the childcare center, Dustin walked me through rooms of toddlers who were playing together. The older kids in the group were running through an obstacle course the teachers had set up, weaving between colorful cones and teetering on small balance beams before throwing plastic balls into a bucket at the end of the course. Another group of kids ran a potato sack race across the room as we cheered them on.

"Around half the kids are Native, and half are white," Dustin explained. The center was open to any parent who needed care, whether they lived here in Onamia or down the road on the reservation. So far, thirty-three children were enrolled.

After the tour we went into an empty classroom and sat at a short table, squeezing into tiny chairs made for three-year-olds. I asked Dustin about their motivation to build the center.

"Building this center is part of a broader vision the tribe has for growth, which we think is very unique," Dustin started. In the 1980s, around when tribes won the right to pursue gaming on their land, the leaders of the Mille Lacs Band of Ojibwe decided to do something very different from every other tribe in Minnesota: they created a separate business development arm that operated independently from tribal politics. That allowed for much more aggressive growth strategies, right as the economic fortunes of tribes were expanding due to gaming revenue.

Led by savvy business leaders like Dustin, the tribe had built a number of profitable businesses, from hotels and casinos to housing developments and, now, a childcare center.

It took some time, but their focus on growth of the broader community won over local government partners. To Dustin and his team, it didn't matter where they invested, so long as it benefited communities the tribe engaged with.

"Locals used to throw eggs at Indian veterans during Fourth of July parades," Dustin remembered. "But now they want to partner with us. It's pretty simple—we're bringing a capital infusion to the area that wouldn't be here otherwise."

Not lost on me was that a community who, just a few generations ago, had its children kidnapped and placed in boarding schools for cultural assimilation was now creating a childcare center that would not only take care of its own children but also the children of its mostly white neighbors.

When communities let shared prosperity win over stereotypes, their differences matter less. A childcare center in a town of 750 people might not seem like a big deal. But the force behind it is a powerful example of a tribal community modeling a new kind of leadership that can strengthen not only their own fortunes but those of rural communities they engage with.

"Minnesota is a progressive state that brings tribal people to the table," Dustin said. "I feel like our state has adopted a better approach to tribal issues than others have."

The leadership of people like Dustin is a big reason why. Another was the state's lieutenant governor, Peggy Flanagan, who was the highest-ranking Native American ever elected to office when she and the governor won in 2019. With her support, one of Governor Walz's first executive orders after taking office required every state agency to hold regular consultations with all eleven tribal nations. That set the tone for expanded partnerships, like the one we'd just built with Dustin and Beth for the childcare center.

If a state that was once infamous for driving Native American tribes from their land and murdering dissenting tribal leaders in brutal fashion could, decades later, find new opportunities to partner and grow communities like Onamia together, then it's possible anywhere.

Decades of tension don't disappear overnight. But these leaders were showing that it's possible. And the kids who leave their childcare center and grow up to be the next generation of leaders will know a very different world from their parents because of it.

———

When I first heard about the "COWS Tour," I thought it was some kind of Midwestern farming expedition. But this annual road trip for the governor's cabinet wasn't named for the state's large population of dairy cattle. COWS simply stood for "Commissioners on Wheels."

Uff-da. It needed a new name.

Traditionally led by DEED, the tour had been on pause during the pandemic. Eager to use it as a comeback moment, my team tried its hand at a little government marketing. We came up with a new tagline for the state, "Build What Matters," and created a website that listed all the advantages Minnesota had to offer businesses.

For a place that had humility baked into its DNA, the effort felt uncomfortably exciting. But we leaned into it. The COWS Tour would now be known as the "Build What Matters Tour," a chance to show off Minnesota's purpose-driven economy. We printed binders with the new logo and slogan and created branded giveaways to leave behind on all the stops in our tour.

But like many things in government, it was hard to unstick tradition. People still called it the COWS Tour.

We were excited anyhow. On a cool October morning, we met at six o'clock on the steps of the state capitol for a sunrise photo. Then the thirty-five government officials and staff piled into a bus. We laughed like schoolkids as we headed for northeastern Minnesota. A few people started singing. Someone suggested we form a band. It was the lightest moment I'd felt in this job in a long time.

Our destination was Minnesota's Iron Range. Perhaps no other part of the state is a better example of how communities are supporting themselves during a period of tremendous change.

The existence of the Iron Range itself is owed to the good fortune of geology and climate, going back over 2 billion years. After large-scale erosion released iron and silica into a low-lying sea in what is today northern Minnesota, it precipitated into banded iron formations deep underground. A few million years ago, the very same glaciers that scoured the state's landscape to create its ten thousand lakes also helped expose bedrocks containing these rich bands of iron. The unique formation was discovered in the 1800s, and by the 1890s Minnesota had its first mining boom.

Immigrant families, mostly from Europe, flocked to the region for good jobs. Large businesses like U.S. Steel built massive operations, employing over forty thousand people at its peak. These workers extracted millions of tons of iron ore from the Range every year. Among other accomplishments, they provided the U.S. military with the iron it needed to help win World War II.

It was big business. In fact, everything about the Iron Range feels big.

The first stop on our tour was at a manufacturing company that made the drills, excavators, and dump trucks that haul iron out of the mines. We stepped off the bus and donned hard hats and fluorescent vests, then walked out onto a massive factory floor that housed dinosaur-sized machinery.

The dump trucks had wheels that were twice my height. An excavator had a bucket so large that twelve of us could stand inside it at the same time. A tall conveyor belt was fifty yards long and had hydraulic tubes as thick as my entire body. We all stood in awe.

"I feel like a mouse in my kid's sandbox," someone quipped.

The factory was owned by a Japanese company that had arrived ten years earlier, bringing much-needed manufacturing jobs to the region. Because of the cyclical nature of mining economies, stable employment is a constant challenge. The volatility is most felt by miners themselves, who've experienced plenty of boom-and-bust periods throughout the history of the Range.

After the initial growth of iron mining here in the first half of the twentieth century, by the 1960s high-grade iron production and its corresponding jobs had started to wane. A young artist from the area, Robert Allen Zimmerman, captured the spirit of his homeland in several of his songs, most notably the 1964 track "North Country Blues." Known now only as Bob Dylan, he sang about the struggles of iron rangers who thrived "when the red iron pits ran plenty," only to find "cardboard-filled windows and old men on the benches" when the mines dried up.

Thankfully, despite the dip in production in the 1960s, the region came roaring back when University of Minnesota professor Edward W. Davis developed a new way to extract iron from a lower-grade rock called taconite. His processing innovation—which would crush, grind, and process the taconite to produce higher-grade iron pellets—saved the Iron Range and brought production back up for a few decades.

In the 1990s, however, decline began again because of geology, competition, and technology. Less ore was available. Fewer workers were needed to extract it, given advancements in equipment like we saw at the factory. Today the Range produces 30 to 40 million tons of iron every year, significantly down from its peak.

The COWS Tour climbed back on the bus to drive to the Keetac mine, operated by U.S. Steel. Governor Walz was planning to meet us there for a special event: the company was announcing the completion of a $150 million investment in a plant that could create a new kind of iron pellet designed for electric-powered furnaces. It was the largest investment any company had made in Minnesota mining in decades.

We got off the bus and milled around with local leaders under a large white tent at the edge of the mine. When the governor's SUV arrived, he emerged with a big grin. Anytime you get to celebrate new jobs is a good day.

We shook hands and I introduced the governor to David Burritt, the president of U.S. Steel. We walked to the edge of the massive canyon created by decades of digging for iron ore. It was peak leaf season, and the horizon was ablaze with yellow, red, and orange foliage. The mine below us stretched for miles.

Burritt told us about their plans for the new plant, which was designed to produce pellets that were better for the environment. Because they could be processed into steel in electric furnaces, the production produced far fewer carbon emissions.

"The best part is, we built the plant in record time—and it created two hundred fifty construction jobs and thirty-three union jobs," Burritt boasted to the governor.

Back inside the tent, the governor took the stage behind a podium that read "Mined, Melted, and Made in America." He praised U.S. Steel for the investment, saying, "It creates jobs we need here, and it ensures our Iron Range can remain strong for generations."

But while the governor was all smiles onstage, he knew he had another stop to make afterward. Just down the road in Keewatin, workers from the United Steelworkers were protesting the event because they were in the middle of a contract battle with U.S. Steel. They stood on the corner in the middle of the small town and held signs that said *FDB*, for "Fair Deal, Burritt!" (Though I wondered if the initials stood for something else, too.)

Few leaders could pull off celebrating with big business only to walk over and credibly chat with union workers who were protesting their employer. But Governor Walz was long a friend of labor—he'd been a union member himself for twenty years as a public schoolteacher. He spoke their language.

The workers said they were excited about the new U.S. Steel facility, but needed a strong contract first. After talking with the workers, the governor addressed the local media.

"The process is working," Governor Walz said. "They're collectively bargaining for a good contract. I think certainly Dave knows that your workforce is your gold up here. And so I fully expect they'll get a good contract."

Tensions between labor and business have long been a feature of the Range. Workers have been organizing in unions here for decades. That made this part of the state a rare pocket of rural America that tilted blue. Labor had waged legendary battles against Big Steel, and the Farmer-Labor Party's success ran deep here—continuing when the party merged to create the DFL.

In fact, from 1960 to 2012, the seven counties that compose the Range gave victories to the Democratic presidential nominee by wide margins every time. While statewide Republicans were able to win on the Range from time to time, the region remained largely a rural pocket of Democratic success. My fellow Northfielder, the late Paul Wellstone, won his quixotic long-shot campaign to win a U.S. Senate seat in part because of his ability to connect with labor movements on the Range.

But today, advancements in mining technology and declining production meant just 10 percent of the workers are needed to run the mines compared with their heyday. Many communities feel hollowed out, at least to long-timers. So Donald Trump's message of "America First" and his ability to address real grievances spoke to a population that had seen their fortunes and way of life evaporate rapidly. Trump won over the union mining towns that had once been reliably Democratic, and the state legislative seats in the region almost all tipped red, too.

Though these changes had been brewing over time, the extraordinary political shift happened in just a few years. This was a community trying to find the right way to hold itself together amid a lot of economic change. When your livelihood is at risk, nothing else about community matters. And when the future seems so out of your control, someone who proclaims to have things under control—and clearly makes someone else the bad guy—is naturally an appealing voice.

Yet the future of communities like those on the Range depends not just on shifting trade policies or upgraded mining technology or manufacturing; they also need new ways to make a living not dependent on decades-old industries, held together by the tenuous relationships between labor and business in a cyclical economy.

They need to diversify altogether.

That's why the next stop on the COWS Tour of the Range was the most inspiring. And it had nothing to do with mining at all.

Mountain Iron, a town of fewer than three thousand, sits right in the middle of the Range and has staked a claim for decades as the "taconite capital of the world." But it now boasts a more modern claim: it's home to the second-largest solar panel factory in America.

Four years earlier a DEED grant helped incentivize a Canadian-based solar manufacturer called Heliene to build operations in Mountain Iron. The pitch was simple: we have a highly skilled workforce here that can help you get started. And with the mines quieting down, more of those workers were available.

Inside, we met Joanne Bath, the plant manager at Heliene. She greeted our team with a big smile and was eager to show us around. The governor arrived at the same time, trading the suit jacket he wore at U.S. Steel for his barn coat and a pair of boots.

Joanne walked our entourage down a long production line that had dozens of steps required to put just one solar panel together. A massive robotic arm swung back and forth, placing solar cells into an aluminum alloy frame. Antireflective glass was secured to the top as workers stopped to do quality checks with sophisticated sensor equipment at every step of the process.

"This is about Minnesota's clean energy future. To see our carbon-free future being built right here in Minnesota is great," the governor marveled.

We stopped along the way to talk with workers. Some of them had worked in mining before; others were recently released felons who Heliene employed in a robust second-chance worker program. All of them seemed excited to be working in an industry of the future.

Solar energy has exploded in America over the past decade. The costs of production have plummeted, the capability of energy storage has skyrocketed, and the desire for clean energy sources has led to significant public investment. Yet the Chinese own 70 percent of the global market, so plants like Heliene are an important investment in helping America gain better competitive footing.

The Mountain Iron plant employed 150 people, Joanne told us. More jobs would come soon, as expansions were planned in other parts of Minnesota.

If a small mining community could pivot to solar energy, it gave me hope that other rural communities and their economies could adapt and thrive in the future.

In the same vein, if communities like the Mille Lacs Band of Ojibwe could invest not only in their own tribal lands but in the communities around them, it gave me hope that our history didn't have to determine our future.

And if leaders in St. Cloud could find ways to rewrite the story being told about them, empowering immigrant communities to succeed at a time of major demographic change, it gave me hope that maybe we weren't as fractured as we seemed.

If America felt divided in the wake of all that we'd been through, it seemed to me that the answers to bringing it back together were sitting right in front of us—in communities where people wake up every day and find ways to make their homes better.

Maybe the small-town fantasies that Mary and I often entertained weren't so far off. When you go local, there are lots of reasons for hope.

Chapter 15

Fresh Lumber

S tanding in the middle of the backyard of Mom and Dad's house
in rural Northfield was a large cluster of massive silver maple trees.
Their branches stretched wide enough to provide shade for almost the
entire lawn. Their trunks had grown into each other over time, forming
a footprint that was at least twenty feet wide. The trees had been there
long before we moved to the farm when I was twelve.

My dad loved those trees. But the branches had started to sag. Sections of the trees were completely dead.

One day when we were all visiting, a large branch snapped off and
fell into the yard. Mom was worried that the next one would drop on
one of the grandkids. It was time to take them down.

Dad hired tree trimmers to disassemble them limb by limb as he
mourned from the ground below. When they were done, Dad pointed
to the largest sections of the tree he wanted to keep, and had the men
drop them off at the house of a friend who had a sawmill on the south
side of town. The following weekend, my brother Matt and I joined
him to help make boards out of the long, thick logs.

Matt is a talented woodworker and all-around outdoorsman. With
a curly black beard and a strong collection of Carhartt gear, he looks

like a postcard of Minnesota. He'd made dozens of pieces of wooden furniture, and even carved his own canoe paddles using a drawknife and a chisel. I'd tinkered with woodworking before, but knew I'd have to lean on him to build something once the boards dried out.

Mary and the kids and I met Matt, Mom, and Dad at the sawmill. Sawdust was already flying when we pulled up. The large horizontal blade whirred loudly as we fed logs down the rollers, ripping two inches of wood off at a time. Matt and I got into a rhythm, picking the boards up in tandem and placing them on a trailer hitched to Dad's truck.

Mom was imagining all the furniture we'd build when the boards were ready. "It'll be so nice to have something to remember the trees by," she said.

Dad nodded quietly.

The kids were getting restless, so Mary and Mom left early to take them home. Once the logs had been milled and dozens of boards laid neatly stacked in the trailer, Matt hopped into his car while Dad and I got into his truck for the twenty-minute drive back.

Maybe it was the nostalgia of turning the trees from my childhood home into boards, or maybe it was just the fact that Dad and I had a rare moment alone together, but sitting in the truck I found myself drawn to bringing up the topic of religion for the first time in a very long time. Our unwritten rule of avoiding the issue had served us well. But ever since that first Christmas after I moved back home, I'd felt a growing tug to break the silence. I wanted to broach the topic that had caused us challenges so many years ago, and see if we might heal the rift.

As Dad pulled out of the farmhouse and turned onto the two-lane highway, I searched for words.

What was it I was hoping to learn? To hear what he thought about my straying from the family religion? To check back in to see if he thought any non-Christian was heading for hell? To get a sense for what he believed now, and if it had changed? Probably all of those things.

Most important, I wondered what he thought of me.

Yet I couldn't get the words out. Instead, we made idle chatter. We talked about the kids and the family. Before I knew it, we were back home. I'd chickened out.

Later that night, I laid in bed and wondered what it would take to cross the divide on religion with Dad. I was starting to feel that before retreading old ground, I needed to tread new ground first. Maybe if I knew where I stood, I'd be better able to hear where he did.

———

Less than five minutes from our house, on the shore of Lake Harriet in Minneapolis, stands St. John's Episcopal Church. Built in 1903, its distressed granite bricks and red wooden door have a look of tradition and permanence. We'd driven by the church a hundred times since we moved to Minnesota. But one Sunday in the middle of winter, Mary and I decided to walk in.

It felt like a bigger decision for me than for Mary. She grew up going to a Catholic church, and had Thai Buddhist traditions in her home as well. She shared none of my hang-ups about religion. Since we'd moved to Minnesota, she'd been taking our family to a Buddhist temple just ten minutes from our home every once in a while. I admired her connection to that part of her family tradition, which was unencumbered by any feelings of guilt or pressure. Today, she brought that same light, open approach with her.

"Let's see what it's like," she said cheerily as we walked through the red door.

We sat in the back on wooden pews and gave the kids coloring books to stay busy. The chapel wasn't large. Stained glass windows depicting the life of Jesus lined the walls, and an ornate wooden pulpit had beautifully carved inlays on it. Around the room was a mix of people, mainly with gray hair, but some younger families, too.

The head pastor, a thin woman with curly hair and a long robe, introduced herself as Lisa. She led everyone into songs whose lyrics were projected on a screen up front. Next to many of the lyrics were pictures of people in need. A child lying in rubble in Gaza. A sickly, bald woman sitting on a hospital bed. There was even a picture of the entire planet from outer space.

Lisa paused after the singing and asked people to call out what they wanted prayers for. Congregants called out the names of people in the community who were suffering. They shared global conflicts in need of resolution. Someone just said the word "peace."

Next, a Latino preacher named Daniel Romero got up to address the crowd. He was here to commemorate Martin Luther King Jr. Day. He began telling the story of Dr. King's "Letter from Birmingham Jail," which put forward King's idea of creating a "beloved community."

"Beloved community means an inclusive, interrelated society based on love, justice, compassion, responsibility, shared power and respect for all people, places, and things," Romero shared. Paraphrasing Dr. King, he said, "When one cannot find beloved community, we are called to take the steps to create it."

As I learned more about St. John's, I discovered this was a church with a tradition of focusing on the "social gospel" over calls for personal salvation. In the 1960s, the church spoke out heavily for the civil rights movement and against the Vietnam War. It also took controversial stands in favor of women's ordination in the church, part of a national movement that changed the Episcopal Church's laws by the mid-1970s. In the 1990s, St. John's affirmed the LGBTQ+ community, allowing people of all orientations to serve in leadership.

When I was growing up, my parents' church service had a weekly feature called "Missionary Moments," in which someone would share the church's work to support missionaries who were trying to convert people to Christianity in faraway lands. This felt different. St. John's was focused on helping people right here in the community. There was no hint of proselytizing. Absent was the guilt and fear that came from the evangelists with whom I'd grown up, such as the Peters Brothers, who'd stoked the satanic panic with their screeds against rock music. The message here seemed more rooted in community and service.

Paging through the church bulletin I'd been handed on the way in, I read about opportunities to volunteer. One encouraged families with kids to help package and serve meals at a congregation in a neighborhood a few miles east of our house. When we got home, I got online and signed up.

A few weeks later, Mary and I and the kids showed up at the First Nations Kitchen in Southeast Minneapolis. With a few other families from St. John's, we walked down into the basement of an Episcopal church run by a Native American couple, Robert and Ritchie Two Bulls, who had moved here from Los Angeles to lead this church. Every Sunday for the last fifteen years, they've been packaging bags of groceries for hundreds of local families, as well as serving them meals in their church basement. The produce and meat they distribute comes from local co-ops, who give it away when it's too close to its expiration date.

"It's barrier-free, anyone can come," Ritchie told us. "We tend to draw the homeless population in the area, and recent immigrants who live nearby."

Ritchie gave us all aprons. Mary tied one each around Luke and Violet, wrapping the strings around their torsos three times before tying the bow. Luke followed Ritchie to a walk-in refrigerator and came out with an armful of large carrots.

Together, the twins helped sort through strawberries to pick out the rotten ones, grabbed clumps of spinach and pushed them into bags, and dropped potatoes into paper sacks on an assembly line for pickup. We were joined by another young family from the church, whose three boys were a little older than the twins. Another woman, probably in her seventies, was there, too, sorting vegetables and flattening cardboard boxes.

The spirit in the room was light and positive. Ritchie laughed often and showed us pictures of her new granddaughter on her phone. We stayed as long as the twins could manage, and went home feeling happy.

The church seemed promising. Mary and I agreed to go to a few more services. Each time we did, I felt a little more comfortable. The "beloved community" that Reverend Romero had spoken of seemed to be a part of the culture of St. John's. It was a church that believed helping others was a central act of showing God's love.

Building community was what we'd been trying to do ever since we moved to Minnesota. Sitting in the wooden pews of St. John's, I could feel that something had been missing. Having a spiritual community whose direct purpose was to nurture connections between people and a greater power was a different level of community. Being anchored in an institution founded on love and service, amid the often choppy seas of finding our way on this new adventure, was appealing.

For the first time in my adult life, I felt drawn to a church. After a few months, I reached out to Lisa to see if she'd meet with me to talk more about St. John's. She got back to me right away, and a few weeks later we sat down at the Turtle Bread café just around the corner from our house in Southwest Minneapolis.

On an early weekday morning with strong rain falling, I scurried inside, having forgotten to bring an umbrella, as usual. Lisa was already sitting down, drinking a cup of coffee and tapping away on her laptop.

"Hello," she sang with a smile as she flipped the computer shut and got up to give me a warm embrace. "Sorry, I'm a hugger," she laughed. Something about her demeanor put me at ease.

We sat down and I told her my story. About growing up in an evangelical household. About being turned off by religion for so many years. And about the rift it had created between my dad and me.

I was surprised when she told me her own story, which was remarkably similar. She'd grown up in a Baptist family that was fundamentalist in its views.

"Hell wasn't just a place for pagans, it was a place for Catholics and Episcopalians and anyone who didn't follow the Baptist faith," Lisa remembered. She fell away from the church in her early twenties, after a study-abroad trip to Israel put her face-to-face with a rabbi who admitted to firebombing Palestinian neighborhoods. How could a religious leader who seemed so calm and peaceful also commit such violence? she wondered.

"If there's a snake in your backyard that could bite your children, wouldn't you kill it?" the rabbi had told her. The moment pushed her to leave religion. She came back to the U.S., went to Columbia Law School, and began a career as a lawyer.

Many years later, a series of struggles in her life led her to walk into an Episcopalian church to receive communion. She didn't know quite why, but she was looking for something. And there was a feeling in the church that felt right. She began going every once in a while, then every week. This community felt different to her from her upbringing.

"I liked that you could believe what you wanted, without judgment," she said. Unfulfilled by her law career, Lisa was so moved she decided to reinvent herself. Soon, she was hosting Sunday-night services at the church, and in a few years had become ordained as a pastor.

The community and the openness drew her in. The church was Christian and it was guided by the Book of Common Prayer. But it was very open to differing views.

"A key tenent of the Episcopal Church is the use of reason to interpret scripture," she told me. "Most of us aren't literalists, and we try not to use the Bible in emotionally manipulative ways."

Lisa's husband wasn't a member of the church; he held different spiritual beliefs. She knew what it was like to blend different traditions into one family. It reminded me of Mary's family.

Theologically, I discovered there was a key difference between St. John's and the church I grew up in when Lisa told me, "We don't believe in original sin. We believe in original blessing. That people were created with good in their hearts."

That sounded very different from what my parents grew up telling me. The weight of our imperfections was everywhere in the church of my childhood. Everything felt heavy, a weight that could only be lifted by personal salvation. The path Lisa described felt paved with opportunity to go outside yourself to find purpose and meaning, rather than dwelling on fixing your own personal imperfections.

As we were wrapping up our conversation, the waitress at the café stopped by presumably to give us our check, but instead she leaned over to Lisa with a nervous smile on her face.

"I'm sorry to interrupt, but I couldn't help but overhear your conversation," she said quietly. "Where is this church you're talking about?"

Lisa smiled and told her about St. John's. The waitress introduced herself as Mitta. She appeared to be in her early twenties, and explained that she'd grown up in a family where her mom was religious and her dad was a pagan. They'd go to church on Sundays and every year they'd celebrate the summer solstice, too. But since starting college, Mitta had lost time for church.

"Lately, I've been thinking, 'Gosh, I should start going again,'" she told us.

Lisa ripped out a page of notebook paper and wrote down her cell phone number and email address and handed it to Mitta, who seemed grateful and excited.

"Text me sometime, I'd love to share more," Lisa said.

It was a heartwarming moment of serendipity. It was also surprising to see a young person who wanted to reengage in organized religion. Mitta, like me, had been part of a much larger group of Americans drifting away from church in droves for decades.

————

Religious leaders and social scientists have tracked the decline of churches in the United States with amazement. In their book, *The Great Dechurching*, authors Jim Davis, Michael Graham, and Ryan P. Burge commissioned a study revealing that 40 million Americans have stopped attending churches in the last twenty-five years—the biggest change in church attendance the country has ever seen. The authors set out to understand why, and what they found was not one reason, but many.

For decades, Americans associated our identity with being Christian. During the Cold War, it helped differentiate us from the Soviets, but afterward that association felt less urgent. At the same time, scandals over religious abuse in the Catholic Church turned generations away from its teachings, as did the movements of the religious right bringing politics into church settings. Our associations with church started to change. It became increasingly acceptable to tell friends and families (and pollsters) that you didn't associate with an organized religion.

When asked why they left the church, the authors of *The Great Dechurching* found that 68 percent of Evangelicals responded that their parents played a role in their decision. Pressure to stay in a church and believe a certain thing actually drove these followers away. That sounded familiar.

Perhaps the biggest reason for rapid American secularization is that American culture has changed. How and where we form communities has shifted, and a drive toward individualism has changed how we spend our time, with technology acting as the single biggest driving factor in that shift.

When I worked in technology, I saw that the digital world has made it far easier for people to get lost in a sea of content and connections that share some qualities of real communities like churches, but miss out on several others. The rise of social media in particular has the double-edged sword of allowing for more connections, but changing their nature and diluting their strength.

It's one thing to have the feeling that you're connected to someone because you keep up with their lives on social media, but if that replaces getting together with your neighbors or friends in person, then the deep-seated social benefits of physical community that humans have evolved to thrive with for thousands of years can quickly start to decay.

And when people replace in-person spiritual connections with going online for them, our real communities suffer. What's worse, the dynamics of the internet can sometimes make online spiritual searching unhealthy or dangerous.

I saw this firsthand when I worked at YouTube. One of the most important early features we created on the site was the "related videos" loop that our algorithm served users to keep them watching video after video. Those related videos caused people who may have come to You-Tube in search of one video to end up blinking their eyes two hours later in realization they'd just watched one hundred more.

The phenomenon is widespread in every social network. The infinite scroll—or doomscroll—is how technology companies capture attention, time, and revenue. But what happens when all those videos or posts start to take someone down a religious or political rabbit hole? When conspiracy theorists or bad actors play on the openness of the web to push extremist ideologies that start to sound more reasonable when surrounded by similar messages, it can distort a person's reality quickly.

I saw the worst versions of this when I lived in Silicon Valley. Our work at YouTube fighting disinformation online led to an invitation from the White House to join four other technology leaders on a "Sprint Team" at the State Department. Our task was to build a strategy to counter the online recruitment of young people to join the Islamic State (ISIS) in Syria and Iraq. At the time, hundreds of new recruits were being lured over the internet to join the terrorist organization, under promises of creating a new Islamic utopia. Our small team spent three weeks in Washington, D.C., working with White House and State Department leaders intensely to figure out why this was happening and make recommendations on how to stop it.

What we found was a sophisticated ISIL media machine that pumped out sleek propaganda videos and social media that spoke directly to the desire of young Muslims to find community, connection, opportunity, and purpose. Using YouTube and other platforms, they put forth a spiritual narrative of warmth and strength that drew young recruits to come join them in the battle for a new Islamic state. Almost three hundred young Americans left to join the cause, which peaked in 2014 when our small group was called to Washington to help.

At the end of our three-week sprint, our group presented our findings in the Situation Room to President Obama's chief of staff, Denis McDonough (a Minnesota native himself). Our recommendations included the creation of a new Global Engagement Center in the State Department that would employ the same modern tactics ISIL was using to counter their messaging. A few months later, the department was created by executive order, and later shifted its focus toward misinformation coming from Russia and China.

The potential of the internet to polarize and radicalize is, today, a central challenge of American life. Online religions and political radicalization are hardly limited to Islamic terrorist organizations, with white supremacist Christian extremists, antisemitic crusaders, QAnon conspiracy theorists, and persecutors of the Rohingya in Myanmar representing just some of the other groups pushing extremist and violent actions. It's no accident that the precipitous rise in religious extremism in the last few decades has closely followed the growth of the internet.

The broader shift toward online communities and away from physical churches and gathering places challenges the future of the American community. One effect of the decrease in church attendance and American community, according to Tim Carney, an editor at the conservative *Washington Examiner*, is that political movements have hijacked that same space in people's lives. In his book *Alienated America*, Carney makes the argument that political movements—Donald Trump's in particular—have surged to fill the void left by church in the lives of millions of Americans. He argues that the absence of community life was one of the biggest predictors of Trump support in his first election victory. Followers of Trump, in Carney's review of surveys and data from several sources, are more likely than others to be disconnected from their communities and believe the American dream is dying.

"In Trump country," Carney writes, "even if expressions of religiosity are high, the churches are empty."

Moving from a community of worshipping God to a community

of worshipping a candidate or a country creates a different kind of relationship to your neighbor. Rather than "Love thy neighbor," it stokes polarization and drives divisions.

The Pew Research Center recently did a study of religious "nones" in America. "Nones," according to the study, are people who describe themselves as atheist, agnostic, or "nothing in particular." Twenty-nine percent of Americans characterize themselves this way, compared with just 16 percent in 2007. The researchers found that the religious unaffiliated are on average less likely to vote or volunteer in their communities, and are less satisfied with their local communities and social lives. The gaps were biggest among those who describe their beliefs as "nothing in particular," rather than those who identify as atheists and agnostics.

"It's not whether a person identifies with a religion (or not) but whether they actively take part in a religious community that best predicts their level of civic engagement," the Pew authors wrote.

Religious organizations also support the community and those in need, with faith-inspired organizations accounting for 40 percent of social safety net spending in America. The more churches we lose, the weaker our social safety net gets.

I had a feeling rising inside of me for some time: that being involved in a real church was not only a great way for me and Mary to build community, but was an important way to hold that community together. And not simply as a social club, but as a group of people with a shared belief in God and the strength of a higher power to connect us all.

I kept going to St. John's, looking for hope. In service after service, I found that what Lisa and other church leaders preached about morality and community was something I was proud to have Violet and Luke surrounded by. Mary did, too. Yet the connection to community and emphasis on service felt just as enriching. They were slowly but surely making Minnesota feel more like home.

As for the big questions I had about what I actually believed about God and the universe, they weren't answering themselves overnight. I tried not to put too much pressure on myself to figure it all out. I knew that I believed there was a higher power. I believed Christianity had tapped into it through Jesus. I was not convinced that Christianity was the only way to access that higher power. Yet I did find many of its teachings, particularly those rooted in showing love to your neighbor, were resonating with me in ways they hadn't in the church that I left behind thirty years earlier.

Living with some uncertainty seemed okay at St. John's. And I was grateful that I didn't feel judged there. I knew that being a part of a church was more than just joining a feel-good social club. Belief mattered. And I was finding new space in my heart for it to reenter, on my own terms.

I wondered what my dad would say. With a clearer sense of where I stood than I'd had in a long time, I was more ready to bring it up with him than ever before.

But I wanted to talk with someone else first.

———

On a warm May night, just on the cusp of summer, my brother-in-law Abe and I had tickets to a Minnesota Twins game. Target Field, where the Twins play, is a gorgeous outdoor stadium encased in native limestone, designed to emulate the cliffs along the Mississippi River. The field sits just on the edge of downtown Minneapolis with beautiful views of the skyline.

We met outside the stadium, greeting each other with a big hug. We'd been close friends for twenty years, ever since he and my sister Kelly were married. When they moved to Northfield fifteen years ago with their family, that's when Abe became the pastor of my parents' church. It started a new chapter in their lives.

Without any of the baggage I had with my parents about religion, I'd always felt comfortable talking with Abe about matters of faith. He never preached to me or tried to convince me of anything.

We grabbed a couple of cheddar brats and beers and found our seats along the first-base line. It was the perfect night for a game. Under a clear sky with a warm breeze, I wore a Kirby Puckett jersey and Abe donned an old beat-up Twins cap. We reminisced about the glory days when the Twins won two World Series in 1987 and 1991.

"We're about due," Abe said, echoing a sentiment expressed every year by every Minnesota sports fan.

After a few innings, I asked him how things were going at his church.

"Pretty good," he said, sounding more upbeat than I'd heard him in a while. The past four years had taken their toll on Abe, as they had for so many pastors across the country. Divisions in his Baptist congregation over COVID protocols, the polarized political environment, and the response to George Floyd's murder had tested his congregation. Abe estimated his members were split, half liberal, half conservative. His approach to the pandemic was to manage the protocols carefully. He offered online live streams, and later presented options to sit in masked or unmasked areas of the church. Many of his conservative members chafed.

But George Floyd's murder sparked even more controversy. Soon after the uprising, Abe began preaching a series on social justice. He drew from the teachings of the biblical prophet Amos, who called out the wealthy classes of Israel for abandoning the poor. He thought this approach would help his congregation, which was largely white, understand the Minnesota Paradox better. But the morning after his first sermon in the series, one of his congregants called Abe and encouraged him to "keep your politics out of the pulpit."

Abe was shocked. He'd preached about inequality before; however, tensions were higher than they'd ever been. Other congregants weighed in, saying it was wrong to claim there was racism in Northfield. Over text chains and emails, things got more heated. Several started to openly encourage their fellow worshippers to vote for Trump. Abe was dismayed by the hypocrisy of congregants telling him to keep his politics out of the pulpit, only to turn around and launch political campaigns among the congregation.

"It brought a lot of division to the church," he told me. "We were just trying to hold it together. I'd say about fifty or sixty people ended up leaving the church. For a congregation of three hundred, that's a lot. I felt like such a failure. I joked to Kelly that I'd found my true calling: driving a church community into the ground."

But these were forces beyond his control. Abe held steady to his approach on the teachings of Jesus. And it seeded the ground for a transition he long had urged his church to make to focus on community engagement and service. He titled the church's capital campaign "Love Your Neighbor," and began opening the church for community meetings in the neighborhood.

Just across the railroad tracks that ran alongside the church stood a trailer park called Viking Terrace, home to many Hispanic families who worked in factories in the area. It wasn't new; I'd even written about it twenty years earlier when I was interning at the *Northfield News*. Recently, a new company had bought the trailer park and started instituting harsh management practices.

The church decided to open its doors to local nonprofits, who came together to help residents. When Abe and his colleagues sat in on the meetings, they were surprised by what they heard. The new management company had instituted a 10:00 p.m. curfew; banned laundry lines, lawn furniture, and certain dog breeds; and prohibited children from playing in their neighbors' yards.

"We got a bunch of pastors together and organized a letter-writing campaign to the Minnesota attorney general," Abe told me.

A few weeks later, Attorney General Keith Ellison made a trip to Northfield. The visit alone pushed the new ownership to nix the new rules to avoid a lawsuit. Abe was both relieved and proud.

"Social justice is important, and personal salvation is important," he reflected. "Both things can be true. I think that people in a church community should ask themselves, 'If the church disappeared tomorrow, who in the community would be hurt, besides the members themselves?' If the answer is no one, then maybe the church should get more involved in helping its neighbors."

Abe leading his church in a new direction during difficult times gave me hope for rebuilding on the other side of the crises of the last few years. His experience inspired optimism that communities can make it through challenges and come out stronger. Religious or not, institutions that bind people together in a common purpose to help others are exactly what make communities worth living in. Abe was leading that work every day. I admired his tenacity to stick with it, and not give up when times got hard.

"I feel like we're hitting our stride again," Abe declared.

This felt like the perfect time to tell him about my experience at St. John's. I shared some of what I'd been learning from the church and why it was resonating. Abe knew about my past disagreements with my parents over religion, and I could see his surprise at hearing I was going to church. I told him it felt good to explore, and that it felt like things were changing for me.

"You know, your dad has changed a lot over the years, too," he offered. "He's got different views of the world than he once did. And he's a real voice of wisdom in the church."

He didn't know it, but that night Abe gave me what I needed to be ready to talk with Dad. My parents' church had changed. My dad had changed. And I knew I had changed. Holding on to past grievances, or even to our implicit pact to ignore the topic of religion altogether, felt silly. It was time to stop chickening out.

As the sun set at Target Field, the overhead lights came on and Abe and I watched the Twins eke out a 4–2 win over Kansas City. On the drive home, I thought about all that Abe had shared. I wondered what my dad thought of it, and what he thought of me. I was ready to find out.

If we could make fresh lumber from old trees, maybe we could also build something new between us.

Chapter 16

On the Water

I awoke with a start, and rolled over to check the time on my phone: 3:06 a.m.

Lying next to me was Luke, fast asleep on the pullout couch at the cabin we were staying at here on the North Shore of Lake Superior. Mary and Violet were sleeping in the other room. Our family had just spent a week exploring the shoreline, hiking the trails at several state parks nestled along the water's edge.

The plan was for Mary and the kids to drive back to Minneapolis today, while I would stay here and meet up with my dad, my brother Matt, and my brother-in-law Forrest for a trip into the Boundary Waters Canoe Area. One of the crown jewels of America's nationally protected lands, the Boundary Waters is riddled with hundreds of small, interconnected lakes near the Canadian border, which visitors paddle and portage through in one of the most unique and remote outdoor experiences in the country. I'd fallen in love with the area since the first time I visited fifteen years earlier, and tried to visit as many summers as possible with my dad and brothers.

But this year I was conflicted about going. Leaving the kids with Mary alone for four days was a lot to ask. She was supportive, but taking care of young twins on your own is a lot of work. And out in the Boundary Waters, I'd be completely cut off from phone service the entire time. I was nervous to be completely separated from our young family for what felt like so long.

I tossed and turned for a few hours, snuggling against Luke in the hopes it might help me fall back asleep. But as torn as I was about saying goodbye, I knew I should stick with the plan. Having more time with my dad and brothers was one of the reasons we moved to Minnesota in the first place.

I met up with the men at Betty's Pies, a famous café on the North Shore, about twenty-five minutes outside Duluth. I gave Mary and the kids a hug goodbye, then hopped into the car with Dad and the others, heading north on Highway 61.

"The mosquitoes hatched early this year," Dad warned us. "I hope you all brought plenty of spray."

I wasn't sure that I had, but when we stopped at an outdoor-gear shop in Grand Marais, I found another solution: a mosquito shirt. It claimed to be impervious to bugs, and was clearly impervious to good fashion sense. A built-in face shield made of black netting was zipped to a large hood that covered your entire head, and the rest of the shirt was made of tightly woven khaki fabric that bugs couldn't bite through, according to the tag.

There's an old saying people use often in Minnesota: "There's no such thing as bad weather, only bad clothing." An ugly mosquito shirt seemed like the most Minnesotan thing a person could possibly own. I bought it without hesitation.

We got back in the car and drove on. As we turned off the pavement and the roads became gravel, I lost the signal on my phone. The tension about the trip subsided, replaced by my excitement to head into the woods.

There's nothing quite like the Boundary Waters in the rest of America. Tourists from around the world come to traverse the same ancient pathways the Ojibwe once forged. It is not a hiker's paradise—

canoeing is the primary way to get around. Campsites are limited, as are the number of permits issued to use them. Each site contains only an unprotected latrine and a firepit. Most are well out of view of other campers, and many are located on small islands all on their own.

When you think of Minnesota as the land of ten thousand lakes, this is the image that comes to many people's minds. Federal protections have kept mining away from the wilderness area for the last century, but rich deposits in the headwaters surrounding the area have caused many conflicts between industrialists and environmentalists over the safety of mining so close to this natural habitat. The conflict has dominated environmental politics in Minnesota, even drawing national attention over the past decades as new mining permits near the Boundary Waters have been accepted or rejected based on which party is in control of the federal or state government.

But politics was far from my mind on this trip. This was an opportunity to get time with Dad and my brothers.

———————

Out in the woods, time slows down. Glancing down occasionally at a map folded into a Ziplock bag between my feet, I focused on every paddle stroke as we looked for a place to set up camp. We focused our eyes on the shoreline of each island we passed, scanning for an opening. When we found one, we pulled the canoes ashore and pitched our tents. In no rush to get anywhere, Matt and I grabbed small foldout chairs and sat on the bank of the lake to relax.

Though Matt is nine years younger than me, I've long looked up to him. His calm demeanor and enthusiasm for the outdoors exude an earthy vibe, and he has a jovial quality that draws others to him. A high school teacher, Matt has a passion for young people that is infectious. For years, he'd volunteered with our Silicon North Stars students and connected directly with them, especially the students who struggled the most. Several times throughout his teaching career, Matt's high school seniors had voted him to be their commencement speaker at graduation. Both he and his wife, Ellen, a nonprofit executive, were deeply involved in the community outside their day jobs. I always got perspective on life when we spent time together.

As we looked out across the lake in front of us, Matt pulled out a book and handed it to me. It was written by a Minnesota author and conservationist named Sigurd F. Olson, and titled *The Singing Wilderness*.

"I was up here on a trip once, and someone traded me this book for the one I was reading," he said. "It's kind of a meditation on the Boundary Waters."

I flipped it over and read the back cover. Sigurd Olson was a famous and prolific environmentalist in the twentieth century, it said, who'd spent months at a time in the Boundary Waters. Through his writing and activism, he had been instrumental in raising awareness of the area, and of wilderness preservation nationally.

I opened the book and began reading. Right away, I was drawn in by Olson's descriptions of the Boundary Waters. Though it was published in 1956, the book read like it could have been written yesterday:

> There is a magic in the feel of a paddle and the movement
> of a canoe, a magic compounded of distance, adventure, soli-
> tude, and peace. The way of a canoe is the way of the wilderness
> and of a freedom almost forgotten. It is an antidote to insecu-
> rity, the open door to waterways of ages past, and a way of life
> with profound and abiding satisfactions.

"A freedom almost forgotten" struck something inside of me. After a few years of crisis, restrictions, and conflict, being out here away from it all felt like a reconnection to something simpler. Written in a different era, Olson's descriptions of the quiet of the wilderness compared with the freneticism of our cities struck me with a searing clarity:

More and more do we realize that quiet is important to happiness. In our cities the constant beat of strange and foreign wave lengths on our primal senses beats us into neuroticism, changes us from creatures who once knew the silences to fretful, uncertain beings immersed in a cacophony of noise which destroys sanity and equilibrium.

Gazing out at the same calm blue waters and dark green tree line Olson described, I began to feel some sense of calm that had been missing from my life for a while. There is something about being deep in the natural world that lends a perspective on humanity that is hard to find in modern life. The longer you absorb your surroundings, the stronger they pull you into them. We are, in so many ways, by-products of the places we choose to call home.

That night, we took an evening paddle to see if we could catch some fish. I paired up with Dad and got in the back of the canoe, while he sat up front. The sky had become darker and suddenly raindrops began falling around us. Thankfully the downpour was fast, leaving almost as quickly as it had arrived.

Afterward I looked above Dad's head in front of me to see a beautiful rainbow spanning the sky. Soon another one appeared right on top of it. We marveled at the bright colors and took pictures of the double rainbow with our phones, whose utility had been reduced to that of simple cameras.

We paddled on, in silence for a while. Dad and I made our way toward the opposite shore, while Matt and Forrest needled their canoe toward a fallen tree a few hundred yards away. Alone, we began talking. A few weeks earlier, I'd overheard my mom talking about some missions work their church had done recently, and decided to ask Dad about it.

"Oh that, yeah, I just joined the missions board for our church," he said, casting a line into the water. He explained that it covered aspects of the church's work in the community, from volunteering in town to supporting missionaries working abroad.

"Is it focused on converting people to Christianity?" I asked.

"Not really," he answered. "It's more about sharing your faith. That door-to-door stuff I used to do, where you ask people, 'If you died tomorrow, do you know where you're headed?' doesn't really work. It turns people off. This is more about doing good in the community and sharing your own faith."

Dad fiddled with the lure on his fishing pole as I cast a line and reeled it back in without a bite. Facing the same direction, our joint view was the rocky shore ahead of us. I waited a while longer before asking another question.

"Is the ultimate goal of the work to save people from going to hell?" I asked.

"It depends on who you ask, but I don't think so."

I was surprised to hear him say that. "What do you mean?"

Dad sighed. "My faith has evolved over the years," he shared. "I don't think things are so black and white. I've become more comfortable with gray. I don't know all the answers, and I never will. And I'm comfortable with that."

This was not the Dad who I grew up with, fighting about faith and arguing over whether or not Gandhi was in hell because he was a Hindu. I could feel a window opening, and questions came rushing out, the unspoken rule not to address religion gone.

I asked him about our fights over religion, about the Peters Brothers and the music albums he took away and the Bible study he created for me. I asked him about evangelism, about other religions, and about ideology. Every question I peppered him with, he returned with a calm and thoughtful answer. We even recalled the "intervention" that he and my grandma held with me at the café. Dad turned his head and grimaced.

"We made mistakes as parents," he offered. I instantly replied that I had, too.

"I was an angry teenager, trying to figure things out," I admitted. It felt good to say it out loud.

I asked my dad what caused his thinking to change, and he shared how his faith had evolved. One of the biggest influences was a close friend of his in the church who came out of the closet. The man's name was Ron and he'd lived his entire life building a family with his wife, despite knowing deep down he was gay.

He came out to my dad, and they spent hours talking about Ron's journey. Dad saw firsthand how dogma in the church had affected Ron, and began questioning his own views on gay marriage. By the time Ron came out to the rest of the church community, Dad's perspective on the world had shifted. When the issue had become personal, he could no longer accept that gay marriage was wrong.

When Ron fell in love and got married to another man, Dad was right there to support him.

"As I've gotten older, I've found myself far more attracted to the power of grace than the power of judgment," he reflected.

After hearing this, I knew I had to ask the question I'd been wondering about ever since I left home two decades earlier.

"Have you and Mom been worried about me going to hell?"

"No, not at all," he said immediately. "I don't even believe in hell. I can't believe in a place where a loving Creator gives eternal punishment. Plus, if only Christians go to heaven, that would mean there are more people in hell than in heaven. It just doesn't make sense."

I was stunned, not sure I'd heard him right. I didn't know how to respond. On one hand, it was an enormous relief. But on the other hand, I found myself defaulting to debate mode, like when I was an angry teenager.

"If hell doesn't exist, then what's the point of missionary work to convert others to your religion?" I prodded.

Dad didn't answer directly. Instead, he proceeded to make the case for why he believed in Christianity. "It's the only faith that's focused on your beliefs, not your works. Man could never be perfect, so why should we act like we could? That's why God had to sacrifice his son, to pay the price for those sins. All other religions believe you can work your way into heaven, but humans will always fail."

I'd heard this all before. The idea of original sin held a central place in Dad's worldview. People were imperfect, and this required a solution—which stood in contrast to Lisa's focus on original blessing at St. John's. To Dad, the solution to a world with original sin was the death and resurrection of Jesus. I pressed him on it.

"Couldn't it be that there are many religious paths that all lead to the same place?" I asked.

"Could be, I don't know," Dad said calmly as we paddled to another spot farther along the shore. "All I know is that humans have messed up this world so much, and we're still looking for answers. There has to be some chance for us to find salvation. To find something beyond this world."

We went back and forth for a while longer. I pushed him on how exclusive his faith was, and he kept answering calmly, owning his uncertainties. At some point, it hit me: I was falling right back into our conversations from when I was in high school. But Dad had different answers. He'd changed. It was me who was still hung up on the questions.

I cast my line back out and stopped talking long enough to realize that Dad had just given me a gift. He didn't think I was going to hell. He wasn't worried about me. He was just continuing on his own journey and learning what he could. For the first time in a very long time, his faith journey was an example I wanted to follow.

I knew I'd have to keep finding my own way. But now I didn't have to worry about disappointing my dad. I could do it freely.

My thoughts snapped back as I felt a nibble on my line. I jerked it and hooked a small bass, not quite big enough to keep. Dad helped me get it in a net and we took a look at its shining green and yellow scales before throwing it back in.

We put our paddles in the water and caught up with Matt and Forrest, then made our way back to camp. Soon, the sun began to set.

"Look around us," Dad said after a little while, pointing at the silhouettes of the tree line reflected on the water. "This is proof enough of creation."

The next day, more paddling, fishing, and exploring. Though it was June, the winds were cold and strong. I had three layers on underneath my mosquito shirt, yet my feet were numb in my sandals inside the canoe. We paddled into the wind, and squinted our eyes as water blew off the lake into our faces.

Dad's strokes were smooth and persistent, even though he'd had shoulder replacement surgery just a few years earlier. We powered across the lake, then portaged over an island to go even deeper into the woods. Navigating through a narrow channel, we discovered purple and white wildflowers and several beaver dams. Along the shore, breaks in the vegetation signaled pathways moose had taken to approach for a drink.

Back at camp, Dad and I played a game of chess on a small magnetic board I'd packed. Matt cooked up some chicken alfredo and Forrest got out his fly rod, sending beautiful strokes onto the surface of the water from the shore.

We almost didn't take an evening paddle, but the wind had stopped, the water turned to glass, and the sky cleared just in time for the sunset. We knew the only place to be was on the water. Paddling out just a few hundred yards from camp, we watched the sun drop over the horizon and turn the shoreline into a million shades of green across the way. A loon began calling in the distance, its haunting notes echoing off the tree line.

My brothers and I marveled at the scene, but Dad was hunched over, changing the lures on his fishing pole. Since the fish had been quiet on the trip, I figured we might as well relax and enjoy the view. But ten minutes later, after getting the right lure on his rod, Dad reeled in a three-pound bass. Fifteen minutes later, another one. Both were frying size.

We got back to camp just in time to find our headlamps before the sun went down. Matt and I filleted the two fish on a flat rock and then battered them up to cook them on the camp stove. By eleven o'clock, we had an unexpected fourth meal of the day, causing Matt to offer up the comforting cliché that someone has to offer every time you're eating a meal at a campfire.

"Food always tastes better when you cook it outside."

Dad looked happy. We poured a splash of whiskey in our coffee cups and turned off our headlamps to take in the sea of stars.

Looking up at the universe, I felt so small. But inside I could feel something getting bigger. A sense of place, and a sense of peace. These waters had brought a calm I hadn't felt in a very long time. The beauty of my home state was all around me, rich and varied. And a tension I'd carried for a long time was starting to fall away, replaced by a rising feeling of gratitude for who and where I'd come from.

We'd be heading back home in the morning. Dad remarked, "I'm sad you have to leave tomorrow." I knew how he felt. Being separated from your kids is hard. I thought back to what it must have been like for my parents when I left Minnesota for California after high school.

Their desire to hold me close, to provide guidance and certainty in a world full of chaos, was their way of showing love. I hadn't always received it that way. Now as a father myself, I understood that in ways I couldn't have back then.

Though it had been only a few days, this trip to the Boundary Waters had given me something I didn't have before. My dad had softened a space in my heart that had been clenched and unyielding previously. I understood him and myself better than before. My own journey, no matter where it led, would be different now. A freedom almost forgotten was mine again.

Coming home wasn't going backward. Coming home was creating a new way forward.

———

Back in Minneapolis, I visited a different lake, just a mile from my home. My regular runs around Lake Bde Maka Ska had become part of my new routine in our neighborhood. On this Sunday morning, there was a lot to take in.

The night before, a major storm had blown through Minneapolis and uprooted dozens of trees that now lay sideways on the boulevards and streets, along with power lines dangling from their poles. As I ran around the lake, it was comforting to see people out and about, together, when the neighborhood was in disarray. A couple on a tandem bike. A biracial couple walking hand in hand. A blind runner being guided by her companion, holding a small canvas strap between them.

I looked at my watch and picked up the pace. I had to get home in time to get to church.

Mary and I got the kids out the door just in time. Lisa was preaching today and seemed to be in a reflective mood. As I sat in the pew alongside our family, I felt like she was speaking directly to me.

> I will admit that I fear for our country and what the dominant worldview is producing—increasing political violence and hatred, blame and intolerance. But I will also say Jesus's way of love was born in just such a time. The more it was crushed, the more it grew. It grew because it does not respond to violence and hatred with more violence and hatred, but with love and the insistence that we will seek and serve Christ in all persons . . .
>
> The polarity, the duality, of today's public life is imploding under its own weight, like a black hole that is caving in on itself. But we are not of this dualistic worldview in which "we" are the good guys and "they" are all bad people . . . If we go past mere humanistic niceness toward self-sacrificial love—if we go past what is convenient and what we personally prefer in order

to live in alignment with the love of God—we can do what liberalism never will. If what we are doing here is more than a polite social club with great metaphors for ethical living, we truly can experience and convey an alternative to the increasing violence all around us.

Lisa went on to reflect on what that meant in practice. She talked about modeling behavior in the example of Jesus and reaching out to those who are different from you.

We can sacrifice self-righteousness and cultivate relationships across every kind of difference. We can offer generosity and forgiveness where it seems not to be deserved, simply because this is how Jesus operated, and because we hope others will do the same for us when we have committed wrongs . . . We can refuse to demonize anyone ever, because the light of Christ exists within every person, without exception.

As Lisa spoke, tears welled up in my eyes. I wished everyone could hear her message. We desperately needed to pull our community together after so many struggles. If we had a shot at moving beyond the division that felt so thick in the air, then simply showing love to one another was surely the first step.

All kinds of institutions can bind communities together. Churches are just one of them. But I was becoming more convinced they were uniquely powerful ones. Drawing on the wisdom of ancient texts through modern interpreters like Lisa brings a level of depth and insight to our communities that's been part of our moral tradition since the country's founding. When people join religious communities—no matter what their faith might be—it pulls them together toward a higher cause in ways that few other institutions can.

Of course, churches can just as easily use the extraordinary power of the spiritual realm to manipulate or exploit their members. When that happens, it's not only deeply harmful but also gives religion a bad name, driving people away, like what had happened to me.

But good churches with good leadership like St. John's, or the church Abe led in Northfield, call upon the better angels of our nature to connect and serve others in our community who might not be just like us. That is something that, I'm convinced, has never been more important in American life. Because people aren't just connected by geography or family or friendships or community. We're connected by our souls.

After searching for a long time, I knew now that I'd made a choice. A choice to believe. The shape of that belief would evolve over time. I'd never have all the answers. Lisa, Abe, and my dad had each shown me in their own way that that was okay. Life evolves, people and communities grow and change. By committing to believe in a higher power and joining a community to help me deepen that faith, I was putting down roots in a new way.

I still had lots of questions. But I'd started finding some answers, too.

Chapter 17

Home

Twelve days before the 2022 election that would serve as a referendum on four of the most tumultuous years in Minnesota's history, Governor Walz paid a visit to my hometown, Northfield.

He was in a great mood. We were here to celebrate a $100 million fund that we'd just secured from the federal government to support small businesses. We invited a group of local small business owners to the Reunion restaurant on Division Street, which has long been the "townie" hangout of our main street.

But first, the governor had a more important group to greet. My family was gathered out front when we arrived.

"It's great to see you again!" the governor roared to my mom, dad, Abe, and Kelly. My nieces Emily and Kate, who'd skipped school to meet the governor, beamed as they shook his hand.

"This is way better than going to school," Emily said.

"Well, you probably shouldn't skip school, but seeing your uncle in action is a pretty good excuse," the governor joked back.

We walked down Division Street and I showed him a few of the mainstays of my hometown. We walked past Hogan Brothers, a popular sandwich shop, as patrons looked out the window to smile and wave. We popped into the coffee shop I once worked at for a few months, Goodbye Blue Monday, and chatted with the staff behind the counter. I bought a coffee, and the barista joked to the governor that she was sorry they didn't have any Diet Mountain Dew on hand, his famous favorite drink.

Out on the street, a woman walking behind us sped up to stop the governor. She introduced herself as a former teacher.

"I voted for you!" she proclaimed, pointing to a red "I voted" sticker on her chest that she'd gotten from early voting. The governor smiled and took a picture with her in front of the local bank.

Walking down the streets of my small hometown with the governor of Minnesota felt a little surreal. I'd spent hundreds of hours with Walz over the last four years, but there's something about seeing the leader of your state pay attention to the small town you grew up in that made even me feel a little giddy.

At the event, we heard from the small business owners. One of them was Matt Eastvold, a furniture maker who, when my dad retired, bought his old landscaping building at the edge of town. My dad and Matt had become friends, and Matt loved telling the story of why he chose to live in Northfield.

"My wife and I were living in St. Paul, but looking for a small town to raise our kids," he told the governor. "When we found this spot in Northfield, we fell in love. But we could only make it work because it had access to high-speed internet. Without that, we couldn't market and sell our furniture to clients across the country."

His business had taken off, selling high-end furniture to major companies in New York, Los Angeles, and other urban centers. I knew my dad took pride that another family business was now using the same building he once did to support our family.

"Northfield occupies a unique niche," the governor reflected. "The vibrant storefronts on Main Street, the strong family connections. It's a joy to be here."

A week and a half later, the governor won his job back in a landslide. All the tough decisions he'd made—the ones he thought might cost him reelection—turned out to be the reason people stuck with him. The idea of "One Minnesota" may have taken a hit, but in the end more people believed in it than didn't.

In a country that often felt divided, the election showed that at least here, people didn't want it to be that way. They voted for a vision for staying together, even when it's hard.

For all of us who worked on Walz's team, the election felt like a validation. No one thought we'd gotten everything right. But after taking the criticism and strife that come with leading during a crisis, we were reassured that our neighbors believed in a place where community could win over politics.

At least, that's what I hoped. Maybe it was naive, but hope can be a powerful force.

We made plans for a second term. Not only had the governor won, but Democrats had won the House and taken back the Senate by a razor-thin margin. This so-called trifecta was rare in a state that often voted for divided government. Combined with the fact that Minnesota had an unprecedented $18 billion budget surplus coming out of the pandemic, it meant that we'd be able to get some ambitious legislation passed.

All the ideas that had been sidetracked by the crises of the last few years were suddenly very real possibilities. That playbook we'd created with the Governor's Council on Economic Expansion might not just be another government report after all. I looked ahead and could see the path forward in the governor's second term. No longer would I be duking it out with Republican legislators to land new initiatives or fix problems. Rather, I'd be negotiating with fellow Democrats. As the commissioner of an agency focused both on business and job growth, I knew I'd often be the moderate voice in the room. I'd have to learn new skills and navigate new waters in a very different environment.

Yet something was nagging at me. A few months before the election, I'd received an email from someone I'd never met before titled

"MN CEO Opportunity." It was from a local recruiting firm, and I opened it to discover it was about the opening for the publisher of the *Star Tribune* newspaper. I'd heard that the previous publisher was retiring, but hadn't thought much about it.

The email laid out the case for considering the position. The *Star Tribune* was one of the largest independently owned newspapers in the country. It reached 1.3 million people every week. It was a cultural institution in Minnesota. And it was ripe for transformation.

"We're looking for a dynamic leader who can lead a powerful digital transformation and grow the *Star Tribune*'s audience while maintaining a long-held tradition of journalistic integrity at a leading national newspaper," it read.

It sounded like a great job for someone else. I didn't have experience working on the staff of a news organization or in publishing, and certainly was no expert in newspapers. Plus, I knew from my time at Google that newspapers were among the most challenged institutions in the country, often weighed down by decades of tradition and an unwillingness to change—despite being in a digital world that had turned their business models upside down.

When I first read it, I dismissed the note almost entirely. But a few days later, I found myself reopening it and rereading the job description, my interest piqued. I forwarded it to Mary to see what she thought.

"It's always worth a conversation, if nothing more than to learn what they're up to," she advised.

I called the recruiter, who made the pitch. The paper's owner, Glen Taylor, was looking for a new direction. The billionaire owner of the pro-basketball franchises the Minnesota Timberwolves and Lynx, in addition to dozens of other highly profitable businesses, Glen was a legend in Minnesota. He'd bought the newspaper in 2014, and along with the previous publisher they'd saved it from bankruptcy and brought it into profitability. But 70 percent of the revenue still came from print. That was going away, and everyone knew it.

"They're looking for a fresh pair of eyes," the recruiter said. "They know they need big change."

I thanked him and told him I'd give it some thought. I already had a job I'd come to love, and we had a monumental legislative session coming up in the new year that I knew would define the future of our state for decades to come. It was hard to imagine walking away from that.

But the recruiter's pitch stuck with me, especially when I considered all the places I'd visited across the state where there was little to no news coverage anymore. I thought about our frustration during the pandemic in getting our message out to people in a trustworthy way. And I thought about all the misinformation and fake news that had crept into our public conversations that was tearing at the community fabric across the country. If the *Star Tribune* could become a modern digital media company and grow its impact, it would make a huge difference in the communities I'd seen face so many challenges since we moved here.

I decided to call Nick, my close friend who ran the media partnerships team at Meta. I was a little sheepish to even admit I was considering working at a local newspaper. Nick ran a global team with thousands of people who had made an enormous impact on the media landscape. In many ways, I looked at his career as the model for a version of what my life might have looked like if I'd never left Google and moved to Minnesota. The idea that I was even considering applying for a job leading a local paper was a proposition that neither of us would have even thought about five years ago. But a lot had changed for me since then. And I knew that Nick, who knew more about media than I did, would give it to me straight.

"Well, it's a fascinating challenge," he said. "To be honest I think it'll be really hard."

We talked through how to approach such a job. He gave me his take on the culture and strategy of news organizations he worked with, and said the good news was there was lots of room for improvement.

If the owner was willing to reinvest and give the next publisher time to get it right, it could be worth a swing. The more we discussed it, I could hear his excitement growing about the opportunity.

"If you could do for local news what the *New York Times* or *Wall Street Journal* has done for national news, you might build a model others could follow," Nick suggested.

Though I would have never considered this path before, the last four years in government had changed me. I'd already chosen to go local. I'd become convinced in the power of institutions to hold society together. And I'd discovered that I liked big challenges and enjoyed being in tough situations without a road map. This opportunity looked similar. I decided to apply.

The following weeks were a blur. With the election and then preparation for a second term, I spent nights and weekends putting together a plan that the board asked me to pitch for the turnaround. I also had lots of conversations with Glen, who was every bit as serious and committed as the recruiter said he would be.

By the time he asked me to take the job, I was convinced it could be an exciting next chapter. I liked the idea of running something myself, without someone else to fall back on. But imagining leaving the governor and his team after all we'd been through, right as things were about to fundamentally shift in government, was hard to consider.

And an even more difficult decision was ahead than the choice between staying in government or moving to a newspaper.

It was whether Mary and I were long for Minnesota.

With the pandemic fading, Mary and I were going on regular date nights. It was helping to bring our sanity back. Often, my parents would drive to Minneapolis and look after the twins, even in the dead of winter.

But on this cold January night, just a few days after the second inauguration of the governor, we needed more than just a few hours to get out of the house. We needed to sit down to talk more deeply about life and what decisions lay ahead. We drove just a few blocks away to a nearby French-American restaurant and settled into a cozy red vinyl booth. Snow was falling outside, of course. We smiled warmly at one another, grateful to be here together.

Over the past few years, I'd come to know well the power of having a partner to navigate life with. Someone you know will tell you the truth. Someone whose happiness is as important to you as your own. Mary had been my biggest supporter, including in this unexpected journey with the newspaper. But until this job sprung up, neither of us had fully grasped what it might mean for our future. Taking on a big new role in Minnesota would feel like recommitting to our new state. We had been settling in here, but were we ready to really stay for the long term? I wasn't sure. And neither was Mary. Making that decision in the coldest month of the year made it even more real.

We'd always considered the move to Minnesota an experiment. A chance to reinvent ourselves and try something new for our young family. But the experiment didn't have a clear conclusion yet. There were things we loved, and things we didn't. Mary had started a business she was excited about, I'd found my way in government, and we were starting to build a community. But those same feelings that had come pouring out in our trip back to California a few years earlier were still bubbling around somewhere under the surface.

Mary ordered the seafood pasta, and I got a burger. The flames from a small candle on the table flickered in her eyes. She looked beautiful, as always. We both felt reflective. We'd been through a lot together— the move to Minnesota, new careers, the crisis unfolding in our new community, and our struggle with IVF that never seemed to end. I left every one of those moments feeling closer to her. We'd somehow managed to strengthen our bond at every turn.

Looking over at her now, I was overcome with a sense of peace.

No matter what we decided about the newspaper, or about where our home might be, I knew we were going to be okay. Minnesota may have been where I grew up, but my home was with Mary.

Mary told me she was happy for me, and I knew she meant it. She also said that she was nervous, and I knew she meant that, too. I told her I only wanted to do this if we both thought it was the right call. She already knew that as well.

"I love so much about our lives," she started. "Being near family is amazing. And things with Bread and Butter are taking off. We're right in the middle of raising a big fund. I wouldn't want to leave Minnesota right now even if this hadn't come up."

Our conversation wandered toward our IVF journey with our surrogate, Rose. We wouldn't know for a few months if surrogacy would be successful. If it was, we'd have another variable to consider of raising a new child here, or taking that moment to imagine a new life back in California.

We talked about what we might be committing to if I took the new job.

"I don't know, maybe a few years? It'll probably take at least that long to see if this job is for me and if success is possible," I guessed. The truth is, I didn't know. Most newspapers across the country were failing. The odds would be long, and I didn't fully know what I was getting myself into.

But more than that, I wasn't going to get into anything that we both didn't think would work for us.

"I don't know yet if I want to be here forever," Mary admitted, tears beginning to pool in her eyes. "Minnesota feels like home. But California does, too. It always will."

We talked about the vibrancy and diversity of the Bay Area, and the culture of California that Mary had grown up in. There was a lot to love about California, just as there was a lot to love about Minnesota.

We sat quietly for a while. I imagined future reinventions in other places. Life still had many chapters. I could feel tears coming, too.

Mary broke the silence with a joke. "It's just so fucking cold here."
We both laughed and wiped tears from our faces.

We continued to discuss the pros and cons, like we did back in California when we were thinking about moving to Minnesota. Mostly, we talked about what we wanted our lives to be like. Life can be complicated, but Mary is always so good at bringing focus to things.

"It's pretty simple. I want to live in places we care about, with people we care about, doing things we care about," Mary said. "And we could probably do that in a lot of different places. But this is what's in front of us now. I think you should do it. We don't have to figure out our whole lives right now. Let's just take the next step in front of us and see how it goes."

Deep down, I knew she was right. Already our journey together had taken turns we never could have expected. Neither of us had to believe we had it all figured out. We just had to believe that the person we loved the most in the world was going to be there for us. That was home.

By the end of dinner, we'd decided I'd give it a shot.

What mattered more than what I was doing was who I was doing it with. A partner I loved, and who loved me.

———

Not long after, we drove to the fertility clinic one last time. We had one embryo left, and our angel, Rose, was ready. She'd been taking fertility shots for weeks in preparation for this moment.

When we met her in the lobby, she gave Mary a small gift bag. Inside was a wooden carving of a woman holding a small plant in her palm. Mary gave Rose a warm hug, and then we all embraced. For the rest of my life, I would never be able to fully appreciate the kindness expressed in Rose's willingness to help our family grow.

Inside the clinic, Rose put on a pink gown and we all crammed into the transfer room. Mary and I had been here dozens of times before.

It felt oddly familiar, even though the act itself was extraordinary. Up on the screen above the petri dish was a magnified embryo again, ready for transfer. We all marveled at it, and I snapped a picture, just in case.

I was trying to hold my expectations in check. But it was impossible not to hope. Hope was all we had.

When it was over, we walked out of the building together. I asked Rose how she felt.

"I feel pregnant," she joked. We all laughed, hugged again, and parted ways.

But a few weeks later, we found out that she was not. Mary called me at work to let me know. I felt the same disappointment that I heard in her voice. We'd been here many times before. Bad fertility news is always strange. It affects your entire life, yet nothing changes. It's a silent loss.

"We've tried everything," Mary said. I could sense her slowly moving on. I remembered our doctor telling us once that the challenge with a fertility journey is that there's always one more step you could take. Another fertilization, surrogacy, donor eggs, or another procedure or protocol that might work . . . For a couple lucky enough to have the means (or great health insurance), the only people who could draw the finish line was you. That made it hard to stop trying.

We decided to take some time to let everything sink in before deciding what to do next.

That Saturday, Mary went out with a few friends. I took the twins for the afternoon. It felt good to focus on them, and I was excited for some dad time.

"How about we go skiing?" I suggested.

"Yes!" said Luke.

"No!" said Violet.

"How about biking?" I tried.

"Yes!" said Violet.

"No!" said Luke.

A classic twin battle. They fought about what we'd do until they were both in a foul mood. So I did the only thing I could—I packed one bike and one pair of skis in my truck, and we headed for Lake Harriet. By the time I parked the truck and unloaded it, neither of them was interested in biking or skiing. I could feel my frustration rising.

"Let's stick with the plan," I suggested. But the kids had another idea. They wanted to play on the frozen lake. It was forty degrees outside, with giant pools of water on the surface of the thick ice at the lake's edge. We hadn't worn winter boots, and I warned them their feet would freeze if they played in the puddles.

But they were Minnesota kids; I couldn't hold them back. They ran out onto the lake and started sloshing through the pools. Luke giggled as he kicked water at Violet, and she returned the favor. Their bad mood evaporated. My feet were already freezing just standing there, but they lasted another thirty minutes goofing around on the frozen lake, delighted to prove me wrong.

Sometimes letting go of trying to direct everything opens up a new way forward.

When they finally got cold, we huddled together at the lake's edge in a tight hug. Then we got in the truck and I peeled off their socks so they could hold their feet up to the heat vent.

"That was fun," Violet said.

Luke agreed. "Take us home, Daddy."

I pulled the truck out of our parking space and headed along the lakeshore, then turned up the street toward our house. I drove slowly, looking up at the tall, firmly planted trees that towered above us along the way, feeling thankful.

———

I find no greater comfort in the world than the comfort of coming home. No matter where or who or what we call home, returning to a place we belong brings a solace and security that nothing else can match. Coming home is what grounds us. It recharges us. It reduces our world into something we can understand. It brings familiarity, re-lief and, if we're lucky, a little bit of joy.

Coming home to the place I grew up brought all of those comforts, in time. But it also gave me something entirely different. It gave me the chance to reinvent my life, and in the process learn more about myself and my community than I ever had before.

Coming home brought new adventures. I got to serve my home state at a difficult time. I got a fresh opportunity to build a new com-munity. I got to reconnect with my parents and family, to find reconcil-iation. I got to find new ways to feed my soul, and I got to strengthen my bond with my partner in life. I got a new chance to live deliberately.

Many of those things weren't comfortable at all. But they were worth it. And they gave me perspective.

Being a new person in your home state is odd. It gives you a dif-ferent lens on something that still feels familiar. That fresh perspective taught me not only about my old friend Minnesota but also about the changing shape of our communities and our country.

Maybe every generation has said that America is at a crossroads, but there is something uniquely unsettling happening now that is chipping away at the bonds that have held America together since its founding. We're losing trust in the institutions we've built and relied on to make life better: government, the judiciary, churches, the media, technology companies, businesses, and more. It is a uniquely American problem—the same decline is not happening in other developed nations.

The reasons are varied and depend on the institution. But one thing is true of all systems: when they don't improve our well-being, we have less reason to believe in them. America was founded on a big promise with high expectations: that this was a country of unlimited possibil-ity with a fair shot for everyone to succeed. But the scaffolding we've built to make that possible feels like it's teetering. Everywhere you look, inequality is growing, not shrinking. Our systems aren't working for people.

The technology industry was supposed to change that. I saw this when I worked in Silicon Valley. My colleagues were good people trying to do good things. We were filled with optimism—at times, euphoria—for the power of technology to disrupt old systems and put power in the hands of people who didn't have it before. Watching You-Tubers use citizen reporting to hold the powerful accountable was exhilarating. Building a new economy for creative people to make money on the open web felt revolutionary.

But our excitement often clouded our judgment about the downsides of new tech. We were motivated to keep pushing the boundaries because that's what great companies in competitive economies do. But some of the most basic societal norms around community, information, and connection were being upended right before our eyes. Too often we didn't see it. Or we didn't want to.

One of the problems in big technology companies is that they have to think about scale from the start. Every new product or feature has to work for a broad group of people around the world to be worth investing in. That kind of global thinking is exciting, but appealing to the masses can water down your approach—and it influences the problems you choose to solve in the first place. To succeed in big tech, you need to make assumptions about human behavior across a vast population, which can lead to unintended consequences. That can damage people's trust.

Starting local is different. I saw this at Google, when I spent time on the Google Plus team (the company's failed attempt to build a social network). One of the reasons that our competitor, Facebook, had been successful was that it started on a college campus and built features that worked for that local community, carefully expanding from there. Meanwhile we built Google Plus for the whole world, which led to all kinds of mistakes. It was unclear if we were building something people wanted, or just something Google wanted.

That's one reason why big tech today feels less like a savior and more like another institution we can't trust. The industry accrues massive wealth for founders and investors and leaves the rest of the public to grapple with the outcomes of their innovations. That doesn't help build community.

When I moved to Minnesota, I met tech entrepreneurs focused on solving problems that felt more immediate to the health of their local communities. They choose problems that matter to them and their neighbors. Sure, they dream of global scale. But seeing them stay focused on a purpose that feels immediately meaningful builds a culture I find refreshing.

By watching Mary build Bread & Butter, I've gotten to meet lots of startup founders who come from different backgrounds. They buck the trends of Silicon Valley, where the vast majority of founders are white men. Creating access to funding for founders of color and women has a huge upside to our economy and will, I'm convinced, lead to better solutions to our problems than the monoculture you often find in traditional, coastal markets.

Jazz Hampton is a great example. He doesn't come from the Silicon Valley culture. He's a smart guy trying to help a community challenged by racism feel safer. It matters to him—the choices he makes with TurnSignl are personal. Once he got it right here first, for individual use cases and for the community, then scale could happen responsibly, not recklessly.

I think more people in technology need to focus first on local communities across the country. More people need to start tech companies in places like Nashville, Madison, Detroit, or Minneapolis. A technology industry that has smart people from all backgrounds creating solutions to our problems in a variety of local communities yields much more thoughtful and trusted results than when our innovations come from just a few coastal hubs.

Moving to Minnesota taught me that that shift is happening already, but it needs to happen a lot faster for us to start feeling like technology is working with and for us, rather than rashly running ahead of us.

When I left tech to work in state government, I had the chance to see another institution that suffers from declining trust. I found many of the tired clichés about government to be wrong—my colleagues surprised me with their resilience and innovation, especially in the crises we navigated together. I enjoyed working with elected leaders from both political parties, and became a believer that divided government can lead to powerful outcomes.

But I did discover reasons why people's trust in government is sliding. Some of them are well documented, like polarization, lack of transparency, entrenched bureaucracies. There are hosts of ideas for government reform to address these challenges, but my experience highlighted two that resonated with me most.

The first is that we need to change our view of the role of government to meet modern demands. If we want our governments to keep up with the speed of change in the private sector, we have to give them the opportunity to try new things and fail. We expect that in our greatest companies. Why not create that expectation around government? Making government innovation—not just government efficiency—a public priority would create a culture of experimentation that can help our most important institutions adapt to modern life rather than stay rooted in the past.

The advice I got to never say anything you wouldn't want to end up on the front page of the newspaper was good advice, but a sad commentary on how defensive government cultures can seem to criticism and failure. We need to give our government bodies the license to try new things and to screw up, and not only when crisis demands it.

My four years in state government convinced me you can do that without taking huge risks with programs that can't fail. You can run a great unemployment insurance program that people can depend on, while changing an antiquated 1939 law to adapt it to the future. You can create innovation labs inside government bureaucracies to spark new ideas, without jeopardizing basic services.

It just requires all of us to look at government differently—not as faceless bureaucracies but as a group of our neighbors doing public service for us all. If we want our government to be modern, we have to fund innovation and tolerate a culture of experimentation, failure, and fresh approaches to solving problems old and new.

Which brings me to the second thing I learned that can help us restore faith in government bodies: more people should spend time working in, or closely with, their local governments.

I discovered that when you spend time working in local government, you gain a new appreciation for public service. And you can bring a new perspective on how to make government work better. Governments are facing new challenges at the same breakneck speed as every industry. They need new people and ideas to help solve them. Working in government is a noble act, and more people should consider giving it a try.

Programs like Benya Kraus's Lead for America that create short stints for people to spend time in government are great. We need more ideas like it that incentivize shorter tours of duty in local government so that people can take chapters of their career in public service without having to devote their whole lives to the exercise.

Joining government isn't going to be for everyone, but participating in local government can be. Attending a city council or school board meeting, sitting in on a committee hearing at the state capitol, or joining a group advocating for a change you want to see in your community—these are all ways to reinvest in local government. The outcome of working with local government is tangible and immediate and, I found, can make a place really feel like home.

More people spending time with local government can also help turn the dial down on polarization. Working at the local level gives you empathy for your neighbor, regardless of their political views. When you go local, the problems you're trying to solve aren't inherently political. Working with people who might not have voted the same way you did in the last election can help rebuild trust.

You know what else I found out about working in government? It's fun. No, really, it is. The outcomes are tangible, and the work is fascinating. Nothing beats being on a team that's trying to do something big for the community together.

The last institution that I've worked with since I found myself back in the Midwest is one that touches almost every other institution in our society: the media.

If there's one fabric that holds a community together, its quality information about what's happening in it. When we have a shared understanding of the news across all the important institutions in our community, we have the power to make them better. Study after study have shown that the presence of quality journalism has a direct correlation to an increase in voter participation and charitable giving, a decrease in polarization, and an increase in feelings of attachment to your community.

But the number of journalists and local news organizations in America is spiraling downward at a dangerous rate, and with it the trust we place in them.

My experience revealed just how pressing this crisis is for our local communities. Journalism has long been the way we share the stories that shape our lives. It's the way we give power to the people. But that power has rapidly shifted to the internet, as now anyone can share their own stories with the world directly. When I worked in tech, I thought that was democratic. But when I left tech, I began to realize that it's closer to anarchy.

I'm a strong believer in free speech and the power of technology to give everyone a voice. Yet without a trusted source to give credibility to our information ecosystem, we're just awash in noise—and the only voices we hear are the most extreme.

Here again, I think the remedy for rebuilding trust starts in community. We have to subscribe or donate to our local news organizations if we want them around. But that alone won't do it. We need new models to support the public service that journalism provides, and government must play a role in that future. There are ideas being tried in states across the country that safely direct taxpayer dollars toward local news organizations, without influencing the coverage. If we believe news organizations are a civic good, we need to fund them like one.

If you spend too much time looking at the decline in institutions in America, it's easy to get pessimistic. But I found that by going local, there's all kinds of reasons for optimism. We aren't as divided as we think we are. The institutions that bind us together aren't broken, they just need new investment and ideas. Whether its tech, government, media, or any other system we rely on, the answer to making them stronger is lying in plain sight. Get involved. Go local. Work with your neighbor on something you care about.

No matter the outcome, the simple act of going local can restore your faith in your community, and your understanding of your place in it. It did for me.

When my friends from the coasts ask me what I've learned since we moved to Minnesota, the list is long. I learned the satisfaction of investing in a physical place rather than an online community. I learned the power of spending time with people who aren't just like you. I experienced the personal growth of returning to a spiritual journey and a church. I learned how to make new friends in a new place.

I've learned a lot from those friends and neighbors about the place we've chosen to call home. I've seen what makes Minnesota truly exceptional, and what it needs to work on. I've gotten to discover what I believe makes my community special: A sense of neighborliness. A purpose-driven culture. A belief that investing in our community is a responsibility. A humility tinged with a quiet belief that we've got something pretty special here.

These are part of what makes Minnesota stand out, and what makes it anything but flyover country.

These discoveries, the by-product of my own reinvention, have helped me see my world in a new way. In the process I've found out more about myself. I've learned that I like to be part of things that are moving fast. I like to be part of teams focused on changing institutions. I enjoy being in the hot seat, even with its downsides. I've learned that I do best when I'm connected to purpose. Whether that's at work or in church or with my family, feeling a sense of calling—and finding a way to answer it—is one of the most powerful feelings in the world.

I think that's probably true for just about everyone. But you don't have to move across the country to find it. You just have to choose a place you want to be, and start listening. Hear your neighbors. Look outside your front door at what's working and isn't. Ask yourself what skills or passions you might bring to make your local community better. Or start something yourself.

No matter what, do it with someone you love.

———

A few months had passed since our latest attempt at growing our family had failed. On a cool Friday evening, Mary and I got a babysitter for the twins and bundled up for a walk around Lake Harriet.

It was early March, but unseasonably warm. The ice on the lake was almost completely gone. A pair of ducks paddled across the water, forming a long *V* behind them that shimmered in the setting sun. Aside from birds, we were the only ones at the lake.

"This is perfect," Mary said from behind her pink fleece balaclava. "I can't believe no one else is out here."

Mary and I caught up on the details of our lives. We talked about the kids. She shared the latest progress at her fund. We chatted about what we'd like to do for fun the next few months, and what we might do once summer came. We discussed all the normal, boring, wonderful things that were part of our new life.

After a lap around the lake, we tucked into a cozy restaurant in our neighborhood and sat at the dark, wooden bar. A young bartender with long black hair made us drinks, then took our orders. When he stepped away, Mary leaned her elbow against the bar and turned toward me.

"Should we have the conversation?" she asked. I knew what she meant. We could try for another round of fertility treatments, or we could end our journey and let Rose move on to another family.

It was hard to give up. But we'd been at this for five years. You can spend your whole life thinking there's something else out there. Sometimes, you have to embrace what's right in front of you and cherish it. We had two great kids. A new life we'd invented for ourselves. A new community we were building, a step at a time. It wasn't perfect. It never is. But it was full.

We didn't spend a long time talking about options.

"We've tried everything," Mary said, voicing what we both felt.

On the speakers behind the bar, a remix of Springsteen's "Dancing in the Dark" started to play. I put my drink down and looked over at Mary. We'd been through a lot, with a lot more to come. After weeks of feeling depressed about our fertility failure, I felt a surge of gratitude. Together, we could handle whatever came next.

Mary grabbed my hand, just as I'd grabbed hers in that Land Rover twelve years earlier.

"We have a good life," she said softly. "From Baghdad to Minneapolis, I never would have expected it."

I smiled. "We have each other."

Mary dropped her head on my shoulder, and I rested my cheek on top of her head.

"It feels right."

Acknowledgments

Writing a book about your life only partway through it can be a daunting exercise. For anyone of good conscience who tries, it requires you to ignore the worry that your story isn't yet worth telling. Every time that doubt crept in, I was fortunate to have people who gave me the confidence to keep going with this project. Their encouragement reminded me that we all have stories to tell, and that sharing them is how we learn from each other.

First and foremost is Mary. While this story is mine, so much of it is hers, too. No one else in the world inspires me more. Her willingness to be open and vulnerable in this project was just another example. So much of what I wrote here is stronger thanks to her advice, edits, and support.

My parents have been my longest-running source of encouragement, and this project was no different. I hope their willingness to revisit the past and strengthen our relationship comes through in these pages. They are truly extraordinary parents and grandparents. So is Mary's father, Dr. John Himinkool, who is my second dad. To my siblings and their spouses, Kelly, Abe, Matt, Ellen, Mary Beth, and

Forrest, thank you for making Minnesota, and our family, feel like home. The same to Annie, Joe, Greg, and Liesl.

This book would not be possible without Amanda Urban, the most incredible agent who had no reason to work with someone in the middle of the country she'd never heard of. I'm so grateful that she did, and that she helped me meet Stephanie Frerich, a fellow Minnesotan who was the perfect editor for this project. To the extent my book hung together I give credit to Stephanie, who has an excellent eye for story, is full of insight, and is a kind and encouraging editor. Thanks also to the rest of the amazing team at Simon & Schuster: Priscilla Painton, Sean Manning, and Jonathan Karp for taking a chance on this book.

Early encouragement and advice from Nick Grudin, a dear friend who's always there, was indispensable. The same goes for James Crabtree, Kevin Allocca, Mark Bergen, Ken Auletta, and James Fallows. There were many other mentors and community members who have been generous with their time and helped shape my thinking in this book. While it's impossible to list them all, Susan Brower, Aaron Brown, Scott Burns, Louis Johnston, Louis King, Samuel Myers, Marcus Pope, Peter Rachleff, Steven Ruggles, R. T. Rybak, Myles Shaver, Julie Tesch, Kathy Tunheim, and Paul Williams are all thoughtful and encouraging sources and advisors.

To those who allowed me to tell some of your story as a part of my own, I'm grateful. Jazz, Benya, Celia, Dustin, Mayor Kleis, Mohayadin, Pastor Lisa, Matt Eastvold, DeLonn, Eunice, Ryan, Jeff, Tawanna, Ritchie, Mary Ghebremeskal, Cole, Kevin, Justin and the 45G crew, KSG Safe Space, Rose and Sean, and Jon Slock, thank you all. Thanks also to Yashe Bros, a constant source of encouragement and inspiration, and to mentors at YouTube and Google, Mia Quagliarello, Marvin Chow, and Lorraine Twohill, who gave me such unique opportunities. The same to my two dearest friends at the company, Olivia and Ramya.

In state government, there are far too many to thank, but it all starts with Tim and Gwen Walz, who are every bit the kind and dedicated servant leaders that the country got to meet during the 2024 election. Lieutenant Governor Flanagan, just the same. I wouldn't have had the chance to serve my home state if they hadn't invited me to join their team.

Chris Schmitter, Patrick Tanis, Teddy Tschann, Kristin Beckmann, Karl Procaccini, Anne O'Connor, and Kayla Castaneda were just a few of the governor's team who helped me find my way in the administration, along with all my fellow commissioners, especially Jan Malcolm and Myron Frans. I learned so much from legislators Bobby Joe Champion, Aric Putnam, Mohamud Noor, Eric Pratt, Jason Rarick, Tim Mahoney, and many others. At DEED, Kevin McKinnon, Hamse Warfa, Darielle Dannen, Elizabeth Frosch, Blake Chaffee, Anna Peterson, Alicia Cordes-Mayo, Jim Hegman, Jake Loesch, Jen Gates, and Amy Schrempp were the best of partners through some tough but rewarding times.

Glen and Becky Taylor, and Christine Fruechte and our entire board, have been great mentors in my time so far at the *Minnesota Star Tribune*. And the *Strib*'s newsroom is the strongest source out there of insight and understanding into what's happening in the Midwest—I'm inspired by you all.

Lastly, to Luke and Violet, who are the most wonderful people I've ever met, thank you for bringing a love into my heart unlike anything I've ever felt. The simple joy of spending time with you and Mom is the truest definition of home I'll ever know.

Notes

Chapter 1: From the Valley to the Prairie

3   *Margie Koivunen, owner of the Roosevelt Bar:* Angie Riebe Mesabi, "Local Business Owners Express COVID Restriction Concerns with DEED Official," *Mesabi Tribune*, October 7, 2020, https://www.mesabitribune.com/free_press/local-business-owners -express-covid-restriction-concerns-with-deed-official/article_eb c930f6-08fb-11eb-bb44-f35bd78aaa42.html.

5   *Minnesota lost over 416,000 jobs: Minnesota: 2030 / 2023 Edition: Minnesota's Economic Performance, 2020–2023,* Minnesota Chamber of Commerce, https://www.mnchamber.com/minnesota-chamber-foun dation/minnesota-2030-2023-edition-minnesotas-economic-perfor mance-2020-2023#:~:text=Economic%20downturn%20and%20 initial%20response&text=Total%20nonfarm%20employment%20 fell%20by,30%25%20in%20the%20second%20quarter.

12   *The Bay Area has seen some of the highest out-migration:* "The Top 10 Metro Areas Homebuyers Are Moving Into and Out Of," Freddie Mac, accessed May 24, 2023, https://www.freddiemac

.com/research/insight/20230524-top-10-metro-areas-homebuy ers-are-moving-and-out.

Chapter 2: Exceptionalism

20 *An old 1973 issue of* Time *magazine*: "American Scene: Minnesota: A State That Works," *Time*, August 13, 1973, https://content .time.com/time/subscriber/article/0,33009,907665,00.html.

22 *77 percent of Bay Area voters*: Richard Florida, "Mapping How America's Metro Areas Voted," Bloomberg, December 1, 2016, https://www.bloomberg.com/news/articles/2016-12-01/map ping-how-america-s-metros-voted-in-the-2016-election.

23 *some of the longest-standing democracies*: Celestine Bohlen, "For a Road Map to Successful Democracies, Scandinavia Offers Clues," *New York Times*, October 6, 2022, https://www.nytimes .com/2022/10/06/world/europe/scandinavia-democracy.html; Jeff Desjardins, "Mapped: The World's Oldest Democracies," World Economic Forum, August 8, 2019, https://www.weforum .org/stories/2019/08/countries-are-the-worlds-oldest-democra cies/.

23 *Public service was seen as a duty*: Geoff Kabaservice, "Minnesota's Progressive Republican Tradition, with Lori Sturdevant," Niskanen Center, December 6, 2023, https://www.niskanencenter.org/min nesotas-progressive-republican-tradition-with-lori-sturdevant/.

24 *It's in the top three for volunteerism and charitable giving*: Sarah Brady, "The Most and Least Generous States," *Forbes*, October 30, 2023, https://www.forbes.com/advisor/banking/most-and -least-charitable-states/; Erin Schneider and Tim J. Marshall, "At Height of Pandemic, More Than Half of People Age 16 and Over Helped Neighbors, 23% Formally Volunteered," U.S. Census Bureau, January 25, 2023, https://www.census.gov/library/stories /2023/01/volunteering-and-civic-life-in-america.html.

24 *It has the second-highest number*: Michael Maciag, "Number of Local Governments by State," Governing, September 14, 2012,

https://www.governing.com/archive/number-of-governments-by-state.html.

24 *It regularly lands near the top*: "Best States Rankings," *U.S. News & World Report*, 2024, https://www.usnews.com/news/best-states/rankings.

24 *"Give to the Max Day"*: "Give to the Max Day," GiveMN, November 21, 2024, https://www.givemn.org/gtmd.

25 *Even the national media*: David Rogers, "In Minnesota, 'Everyman' on the Ballot," *Wall Street Journal*, October 30, 2006, https://www.wsj.com/articles/SB116216454872607291.

Chapter 3: Government Man

34 *Almost 70 percent of people*: Ana Pranger, Pia Orrenius, and Madeline Zavodny, "Texas Natives Likeliest to 'Stick' Around, Pointing to State's Economic Health," Federal Reserve Bank of Dallas, August 29, 2023, https://www.dallasfed.org/research/economics/2023/0829.

Chapter 4: Mary

49 *As I learned more*: Samuel L. Myers Jr., "The Minnesota Paradox," Hubert H. Humphrey School of Public Affairs, https://www.hhh.umn.edu/research-centers/roy-wilkins-center-human-relations-and-social-justice/minnesota-paradox.

50 *The hanging of thirty-eight Dakota men*: "Mass Killings of Native Americans," Equal Justice Initiative, September 20, 2019, https://eji.org/news/history-racial-injustice-mass-killings-of-native-americans/.

50 *Racial covenants in the early 1900s*: Greta Kaul, "With Covenants, Racism Was Written into Minneapolis Housing. The Scars Are Still Visible," MinnPost, February 22, 2019, https://www.minnpost.com/metro/2019/02/with-covenants-racism-was-written-into-minneapolis-housing-the-scars-are-still-visible/.

50 *Today, the life expectancy*: Dan Kopf and Daniel Wolfe, "What

Does Your Neighborhood's Life Expectancy Tell?," *Quartz*, December 12, 2018, https://qz.com/1462111/map-what-story-does-your-neighborhoods-life-expectancy-tell.

50 *Professor Myers coauthored*: Randy Furst and MaryJo Webster, "How Did Minn. Become One of the Most Racially Inequitable States?" *Star Tribune*, September 6, 2019, https://www.startribune.com/how-did-minnesota-become-one-of-the-most-racially-inequitable-states/547537761/.

53 *The reason the program existed*: Oriane Casale, Zina Noel, and Suzanne Pearl, "Early Care and Education: Profile of an Industry in Crisis," Department of Employment and Economic Development, September 2020, https://mn.gov/deed/newscenter/publications/trends/september-2020/early-care-education.jsp.

53 *Economists estimate that*: Gianna Melillo, "What's Behind the US's Worsening Child Care Crisis?," *The Hill*, February 12, 2023, https://thehill.com/changing-america/enrichment/education/3852987-whats-behind-the-uss-worsening-child-care-crisis/.

Chapter 5: Silicon Heartland

55 *It was the bare minimum*: "The YouTube Interview with President Obama," YouTube, February 1, 2010, https://www.youtube.com/watch?v=0pqzNJYzh7I.

57 *If you wanted to*: Peter Westwick, "Silicon Valley's Gold Rush Roots," *Asterisk*, April 2024, https://asteriskmag.com/issues/06/silicon-valleys-gold-rush-roots.

57 *Stanford became the anchor*: Gabrielle Athanasia, "The Lessons of Silicon Valley: A World-Renowned Technology Hub," Center for Strategic and International Studies, February 10, 2022, https://www.csis.org/blogs/perspectives-innovation/lessons-silicon-valley-world-renowned-technology-hub.

58 *Successful chip companies*: "Spinoff: Fairchild & the Family Tree of Silicon Valley," Computer History Museum, accessed November 2, 2023, https://computerhistory.org/stories/spinoff-fairchild/.

58   *Every year, the Valley pulls in*: Maryann Jones Thompson, "Despite VC Crash, Silicon Valley Still Leads Startup Economy," *San Francisco Standard*, April 13, 2023, https://sfstandard.com/2023/04/13/san-francisco-bay-area-still-leads-nations-wounded-startup-economy/.

61   *I knew he'd need to convince*: Ernesto Moretti, *The New Geography of Jobs* (Boston: Houghton Mifflin Harcourt, 2012).

65   *In fact, its visionary founder*: Tom Crann, "Pioneer of Internet Leaves the U of M," MPR News, April 3, 2007, https://www.mprnews.org/story/2007/04/03/gopher.

66   *They serve over 1.3 million people*: "Mayo Clinic Again Earns Top Positions in 2024–25 U.S. News Best Hospital Rankings," Mayo Clinic College of Medicine & Science, July 19, 2024, https://college.mayo.edu/about/news/news-archive/mayo-clinic-again-earns-top-positions-in-2024-25-us-news-best-hospital-rankings/.

66   *Meanwhile in Minneapolis*: Nick Williams, "University of Minnesota's Startup Pipeline Helps Drive State's Innovation Economy," *Minnesota Star Tribune*, September 14, 2022, https://www.startribune.com/university-of-minnesotas-startup-pipeline-helps-drive-states-innovation-economy/600206777.

66   *Today, Minnesota ranks first*: "How Minnesota Ranks," Minnesota—Star of the North, accessed November 17, 2023, https://mn.gov/deed/joinusmn/why-mn/rankings/.

68   *While some treated the app*: Alyson Shontell, "An App That Just Says 'Yo' Has Raised $1.5 Million at a $5–10 Million Valuation," *Business Insider*, July 18, 2014, https://www.businessinsider.com/yo-raises-15-million-at-a-5-10-million-valuation-2014-7.

68   *In recent years, tens of thousands*: Levi Sumagaysay, "The Silicon Valley 'Exodus' Has Erased Population Gains of the Past Decade," Market Watch, February 15, 2023, https://www.marketwatch.com/story/the-silicon-valley-exodus-neared-record-dot-com-bust-levels-last-year-97724e0f.

Chapter 6: Boomerang

72   *I grew up in the heart*: Alan Yuhas, "It's Time to Revisit the Satanic Panic," *New York Times*, March 31, 2021, https://www.nytimes.com/2021/03/31/us/satanic-panic.html.

73   *Geraldo Rivera*: Cyriaque Lamar, "When Geraldo Rivera Took on Satanism (and a Very Confused Ozzy Osbourne)," Gizmodo, August 9, 2011, https://gizmodo.com/when-geraldo-rivera-took-on-satanism-and-a-very-confus-5829171.

80   *For the last century*: David Brooks, "The Nuclear Family Was a Mistake," *Atlantic*, March 2020, https://www.theatlantic.com/magazine/archive/2020/03/the-nuclear-family-was-a-mistake/605536/.

82   *The number of Americans*: Kiley Hurst, "More Than Half of Americans Live within an Hour of Extended Family," Pew Research Center, May 18, 2022, https://www.pewresearch.org/short-reads/2022/05/18/more-than-half-of-americans-live-within-an-hour-of-extended-family/.

82   *College-age kids leave*: "An Analysis of Migration Trends and Patterns in Minnesota," Minnesota State Demographic Center, April 2024, https://mn.gov/admin/assets/Migration%20Report_FINAL_tcm36-620018.pdf.

82   *This phenomenon has been well documented*: Josie Gatti Schafer, "Nebraska Faces Ongoing Brain Drain According to Latest 2022 American Community Survey Data from the United States Census Bureau," Center for Public Affairs Research, University of Nebraska at Omaha, https://www.unomaha.edu/college-of-public-affairs-and-community-service/center-for-public-affairs-research/documents/brain-drain-2022-release.pdf.

83   *The national average of people staying*: Austen Macalus, "What Percentage of Minnesotans Spend Their Entire Lives Here?," *Minnesota Star Tribune*, March 15, 2019, https://www.startribune.com/what-percentage-of-minnesotans-spend-their-entire-life-here/506762921/.

84   *When Mary and I decided to move here*: "A Robust and Diverse Econ-

omy," Minnesota—Star of the North, accessed December 1, 2023, https://mn.gov/deed/joinusmn/why-mn/our-economy/#:~:text =Our%20Twin%20Cities%20ranks%201st,an%20increase %20of%20about%2042%25.

84 *His research led to a book*: J. Myles Shaver, *Headquarters Economy: Managers Mobility Migration* (Oxford University Press, 2018), https://headquarterseconomy.com.

85 *In recent years, Americans have chosen*: William H. Frey, "Americans' Local Migration Reached a Historic Low in 2022, but Long-Distance Moves Picked Up," Brookings, February 2, 2023, https:// www.brookings.edu/articles/americans-local-migration-reached -a-historic-low-in-2022-but-long-distance-moves-picked-up/.

85 *Multigenerational families in America*: D'Vera Cohn et al., "1. The Demographics of Multigenerational Households," Pew Research Center, March 24, 2022, https://www.pewresearch.org/social-trends /2022/03/24/the-demographics-of-multigenerational-households/.

Chapter 8: No Playbook

101 *The plane took off*: Nora G. Hertel, "Walz: Melrose Broadband Expansion Grant Will Help Business, Quality of Life," *St. Cloud Times*, January 27, 2020, https://www.sctimes.com/story/news /2020/01/27/walz-melrose-broadband-expansion-grant-help -business-quality-life/4586933002/.

104 *Each day the governor*: Peter Callaghan, Greta Kaul, and Walker Orenstein, "'The Scope and Scale of This Is Stunning': Chronicling the First Year of the COVID-19 Pandemic in Minnesota," MinnPost, March 5, 2021, http://www.minnpost.com/health /2021/03/the-scope-and-scale-of-this-is-stunning-one-year-of -the-covid-19-pandemic-in-minnesota/.

Chapter 9: Coming Apart

114 *Similar to the rest of rural America*: "Small Business Facts: Small Businesses in Rural Areas," Office of Advocacy, August 22, 2023,

https://advocacy.sba.gov/2023/08/22/small-businesses-in-rural
-areas/.

115 *In the 1920s, the legislature began investing*: "A Brief History of MnDOT," Minnesota Department of Transportation, accessed June 3, 2024, https://www.dot.state.mn.us/about/history.html.

115 *That helped places like Rochester*: "History of Rochester," Experience Rochester, Minnesota, accessed June 3, 2024, https://www.experi encerochestermn.com/about-us/history-of-rochester/.

116 *How this Minnesota Model*: "History Revealed: The Farmer-Labor Movement: A Minnesota Story," East Side Freedom Library video, YouTube, accessed December 8, 2022, https://www.youtube.com /watch?v=JEztDIYJF10&t=1503s.

117 *The arrival of a crisis*: Quinton Skinner, "How Times of Crisis Have Defined Minnesota," *Minnesota Monthly*, June 23, 2020, https://www.minnesotamonthly.com/lifestyle/how-times-of-crisis -have-defined-minnesota/.

118 *Purely from a math perspective*: Melissa Turtinen, "Minneapolis Pays 3 Times More Than It Receives in State Funds, New Report Says," Bring Me the News, February 25, 2021, https://bringmethenews .com/minnesota-news/minneapolis-pays-3-times-more-than-it -receives-in-state-funds-new-report-says.

118 *Minnesota's manufacturing industry*: Mary Vitcenda, "Urban vs. Rural? More like Urban and Rural Together, Study Says," University of Minnesota Extension, 2011, https://extension.umn.edu /vital-connections/urban-vs-rural-more-urban-and-rural-together -study-says.

119 *In the last twenty years, the number of journalists*: "The State of Local News 2023," Local News Initiative, accessed February 2024, https://localnewsinitiative.northwestern.edu/projects/state-of-lo cal-news/2023/.

119 *According to Ballotpedia*: "Pivot Counties in Minnesota," Ballotpedia, https://ballotpedia.org/Pivot_Counties_in_Minnesota.

121 *And so, on the same day*: Torey Van Oot, "Gov. Tim Walz Under

Fire for Letter 'Templates' Supporting Mask Mandate," *Minnesota Star Tribune*, July 25, 2020, https://www.startribune.com/gov-tim-walz-under-fire-for-letter-templates-supporting-mask-mandate/571899542.

123 *The Senate had been unhappy with her*: "Minnesota Appeals Court Upholds 'Clean Cars' Plan after Dealership Pushback," MPR News, January 2023, https://www.mprnews.org/story/2023/01/30/state-appeals-court-rejects-effort-to-block-minnesotas-clean-cars-plan.

Chapter 10: Inflamed

129 *Since 2010, eleven people*: Gordon Severson, "A History of Fatal Police Encounters in Minneapolis, 11 Cases since 2010," KARE 11, May 26, 2020, https://www.kare11.com/article/news/local/minneapolis-police-fatal-encounters/89-660b1880-fd20-4bcf-adbc-85144d9c33e4.

130 *Today, the state boasts*: Jayne Williamson-Lee, "Is Minnesota Home to the Largest Number of Somali Americans in the Country?" MinnPost, July 11, 2023, http://www.minnpost.com/fact-briefs/2023/07/is-minnesota-home-to-the-largest-number-of-somali-americans-in-the-country/.

130 *The Twin Cities has the largest*: Yuqing Liu, "How Did Minnesota Become a Hub for Hmong People?" *Sahan Journal*, September 8, 2023, http://sahanjournal.com/news-partners/minnesota-how-did-hmong-people-become-largest-asian-group-in-minnesota-curious-minnesota/.

130 *In fact, in the 2000s*: Sean O'Neil, "Minnesota's Economic Future Depends on New Americans," *Minnesota Star Tribune*, March 7, 2025, https://www.startribune.com/minnesotas-economic-future-depends-on-new-americans/601232403.

130 *Only Washington, D.C., and North Dakota*: Emma Nelson and MaryJo Webster, "Minnesotans Are Among the Least Likely to Climb the Income Ladder in the U.S.," *Star Tribune*, May 16, 2024,

https://www.startribune.com/minnesotans-least-likely-climb-in come-ladder/600364589/.

131 *When the Centers for Disease Control*: "In the Minority," *Aquatics International*, October 2005. Report retrieved from: https://web .archive.org/web/20051223221642/http://www.aquaticsintl.com /2005/oct/0510_minority.html. Charts retrieved from: https:// assets.ngin.com/attachments/document/0054/1055/Minority _Drowning.pdf.

137 *In the end we settled*: "DEED's Commitments to Racial Equity: A New Blog Series," Minnesota Department of Employment and Economic Development, March 31, 2022, https://mn.gov/deed /newscenter/social-media/deed-developments/#/detail/appId/1 /id/523507.

138 *They swept up glass*: Susan Du, "A Better Lake Street? A Daring Hope for Riot-Torn Corridor," *Minnesota Star Tribune*, May 22, 2022, https://www.startribune.com/lake-street-fights-on-minne apolis-george-floyd-riot/600174854.

138 *The governor applied for FEMA*: "Federal Government Denies Gov. Walz's Request for Funds to Rebuild after Unrest," CBS Minnesota, July 11, 2020, https://www.cbsnews.com/minnesota /news/federal-government-denies-gov-walzs-request-for-funds -to-rebuild-after-unrest/.

139 *Fortunately, almost a year*: "Budget and Economic Forecast," Min- nesota Management and Budget, February 2021, https://mn.gov /mmb-stat/000/az/forecast/2021/budget-and-economic-forecast /february-2021-forecast.pdf; "State of Minnesota Releases Feb- ruary 2021 Budget and Economic Forecast," Minnesota Man- agement and Budget, February 26, 2021, https://mn.gov/mmb /media/newsroom.jsp?id=1059-469530.

139 *A powerful Republican state senator*: Walker Orenstein, "Minnesota Lawmakers Split over Using State Money to Help Minneapolis Recover from Floyd Riots," MinnPost, January 28, 2021, http:// www.minnpost.com/state-government/2021/01/minnesota-law

makers-split-over-using-state-money-to-help-minneapolis-recov
er-from-floyd-riots/.

139 *Both the governor and the mayor*: Briana Bierschbach, "Gov. Tim
Walz Laments 'Abject Failure' of Riot Response," *Minnesota Star
Tribune*, May 30, 2020, https://www.startribune.com/gov-tim
-walz-laments-abject-failure-of-riot-response/570864092.

143 *The Main Street Economic Revitalization Program would give*:
"Minnesota Main Street Economic Revitalization Program," Minnesota Department of Employment and Economic Development,
accessed June 15, 2024, https://mn.gov/deed/business/financ
ing-business/deed-programs/emergency-programs/economic-re
vitalization/.

Chapter 11: Catching Each Other

146 *It had taken Minnesota over six months*: "Emergency Executive
Order 20-99: Implementing a Four Week Dial Back on Certain
Activities to Slow the Spread of COVID-19," Executive Department, State of Minnesota, November 18, 2020, https://mn.gov
/governor/assets/EO%2020-99%20Final%20%28003%29
_tcm1055-454294.pdf.

147 *over $200 million*: Michael J. Bologna and Stephen Joyce, "Minne-
sota Offers $216 Million in Relief to Small Businesses," Bloomberg
Tax, December 15, 2020, https://news.bloombergtax.com/daily
-tax-report-state/minnesota-offers-216-million-in-relief-to-small
-businesses.

150 *When we lost the case*: Kavita Kumar, "How Minnesota Students
Helped Win the Battle for Unemployment Benefits," *Minnesota
Star Tribune*, July 31, 2021, https://www.startribune.com/how
-students-helped-change-a-state-law-that-barred-them-from-re
ceiving-unemployment-benefits/600083600.

152 *One of the foundational*: "Truckers' Strike of 1934: Overview,"
Gale Family Library, Minnesota Historical Society, accessed April
2024, https://libguides.mnhs.org/1934strike/ov.

152 *This wasn't common*: Peter Rachleff, author interview, May 28, 2024.

158 *For over 75 percent of Americans*: "Paid Family and Medical Leave Fact Sheet," Women's Bureau, U.S. Department of Labor, June 2024, https://www.dol.gov/sites/dolgov/files/WB/paid-leave/Paid Leavefactsheet.pdf.

158 *Nationally, if women participated*: Amanda Novello, "The Cost of Inaction: How a Lack of Family Care Policies Burdens the U.S. Economy and Families," National Partnership for Women & Families, July 2021, https://www.nationalpartnership.org/our work/resources/economic-justice/other/cost-of-inaction-lack-of -family-care-burdens-families.pdf.

Chapter 12: Breaking the Bubble

168 *Experts estimate it takes more than two hundred hours*: Jeffrey A. Hall, "How Many Hours Does It Take to Make a Friend?," *Journal of Social and Personal Relationships* 36, no. 4 (2019): 1278–96, https:// journals.sagepub.com/doi/pdf/10.1177/0265407518761225.

170 *In it, the political scientist Robert Putnam*: Robert Putnam, *Bowling Alone: The Collapse and Revival of American Community* (Simon & Schuster, 2000).

170 *"To what extent"*: Lulu Garcia-Navarro, "Robert Putnam Knows Why You're Lonely," *New York Times*, July 13, 2024, https://www. nytimes.com/2024/07/13/magazine/robert-putnam-interview.html.

171 *A recent survey reported*: Daniel A. Cox, "The State of American Friendship: Change, Challenge, and Loss," Survey Center on American Life, June 8, 2021, https://www.americansurveycenter.org/re search/the-state-of-american-friendship-change-challenges-and-loss/.

171 *Men seem to be in worse shape*: Daniel A. Cox, "Men's Social Circles Are Shrinking," Survey Center on American Life, June 29, 2021, https://www.americansurveycenter.org/why-mens-social-circles -are-shrinking/.

179 *If I'd met this exact group*: Katharine Smyth, "Why Making Friends

in Midlife Is So Hard," *Atlantic*, January 12, 2022, https://www .theatlantic.com/family/archive/2022/01/how-to-make-new -friends-midlife/621231/.

Chapter 13: Bridges

186 *It was a ten-year road map*: "Minnesota's Moment: Roadmap for Equitable Economic Expansion," Minnesota Council on Economic Expansion, June 30, 2022, https://mn.gov/deed/assets/ governors-council-economic-expansion-roadmap-acc_tcm1045- 535818.pdf.

187 *Written thirty years earlier*: "State of Diversity," MN Planning, November 1993, https://www.lrl.mn.gov/docs/pre2003/other /930569.pdf.

189 *Both had grown up*: Aliyah Baker, "TurnSignl Co-Founder Jazz Hampton Knows Firsthand What It's Like to Be a Statistic," *Minnesota Star Tribune*, September 9, 2022, https://www.startribune .com/turnsignl-co-founder-jazz-hampton-knows-firsthand-what -its-like-to-be-a-statistic/600205263.

189 *A nutrition services supervisor*: Sharon LaFraniere and Mitch Smith, "Philando Castile Was Pulled Over 49 Times in 13 Years, Often for Minor Infractions," *New York Times*, July 16, 2016, https:// www.nytimes.com/2016/07/17/us/before-philando-castiles-fatal -encounter-a-costly-trail-of-minor-traffic-stops.html.

190 *He also knew*: Richard A. Oppel Jr. and Lazaro Gamio, "Minneapolis Police Use Force against Black People at 7 Times the Rate of Whites," *New York Times*, June 3, 2020, *NYTimes.com*, https:// www.nytimes.com/interactive/2020/06/03/us/minneapolis-po lice-use-of-force.html.

197 *Over 90 percent*: Vasanth Ganesan et al., "Underrepresented Start-Up Founders: The Untapped Opportunity," McKinsey, June 23, 2023, https://www.mckinsey.com/featured-insights/di versity-and-inclusion/underestimated-start-up-founders-the-un tapped-opportunity.

199 *Sitting behind a desk*: "Celebrating Collaboration & Progress—
NEXT 24," Greater MSP video, YouTube, February 6, 2024,
https://www.youtube.com/watch?v=rz17hnXB224.

Chapter 14: On the Road

204 *In fact, in the most recent decade*: Jenny Berg, "As Diversity Surges,
Is St. Cloud Still 'White Cloud'?," *Minnesota Star Tribune*,
April 3, 2022, https://www.startribune.com/diversity-surges
-st-cloud-central-minnesota-white-cloud-census/600161677.

204 *The average age in St. Cloud*: "St. Cloud Public School District,"
U.S. News & World Report, 2021, https://www.usnews.com
/education/k12/minnesota/districts/st-cloud-public-school-dis
trict-102066#:~:text=Cloud%20Public%20School%20Dis
trict%20is,Hawaiian%20or%20other%20Pacific%20Islander.

204 *In 2016, a young East African*: Joe Sterling, Max Blau, and Rosa
Flores, "Stabbing Suspect Went to Mall to Buy an iPhone, Source
Says," CNN, September 19, 2016, https://www.cnn.com/2016
/09/19/us/minnesota-mall-stabbing/index.html.

205 *In 2019, the* New York Times: Astead W. Herndon, "'These People Aren't Coming from Norway': Refugees in a Minnesota City
Face a Backlash," *New York Times*, June 20, 2019, https://www
.nytimes.com/2019/06/20/us/politics/minnesota-refugees-trump
.html.

206 *The* St. Cloud Times: John Reinan, "Deep Staff Cuts Leave *St.
Cloud Times* a 'Ghost Paper,'" *Minnesota Star Tribune*, December 9, 2022, https://www.startribune.com/deep-staff-cuts-leave-st
-cloud-times-a-ghost-paper/600234582.

206 *Four years after the mall stabbing*: Kirsti Marohn and Tim Nelson, "Social Media Rumors Fuel Protest after St. Cloud Police
Officer Shot in Hand," MPR News, June 15, 2020, https://www
.mprnews.org/story/2020/06/15/social-media-rumors-fuel-pro
test-after-st-cloud-police-officer-shot-in-hand.

208 *In a recent city council election*: Jenny Berg, "St. Cloud Sees

Largest City Council Candidate Pool in Decades," *Minnesota Star Tribune*, June 6, 2024, https://www.startribune.com/st-cloud-sees-largest-city-council-candidate-pool-in-decades/600371487.

208 *The city is also making a play*: Jenny Berg, "Barely Any Venture Capital Makes It to Greater Minnesota. Meet the Folks Trying to Change That," *Minnesota Star Tribune*, May 2, 2024, https://www.startribune.com/barely-any-venture-capital-makes-it-to-greater-minnesota-meet-the-folks-trying-to-change-that/600363234.

209 *the Mille Lacs Band*: "Welcome Page," Mille Lacs Band of Ojibwe, accessed July 22, 2024. https://millelacsband.com.

210 *Further victories took decades*: "Indian Gaming History," Mille Lacs Band of Ojibwe, accessed July 22, 2024, https://millelacsband.com/government/indian-gaming-regulation/indian-gaming-history.

211 *The center was open*: "Introducing Onamia Childcare Center: A Collaborative Community Effort," Mille Lacs Corporate Ventures, September 20, 2023, https://mlcv.com/blog-1/2023/8/22/introducing-onamia-childcare-center-a-collaborative-community-effort.

211 *In the 1980s, around when tribes won the right to pursue gaming*: "Chief's Day: Arthur (Art) Gahbow's Legacy on MLCV's Founding Story," Mille Lacs Corporate Ventures, February 19, 2024, https://mlcv.com/blog-1/2024/2/18/chiefs-day-arthur-art-grabows-legacy-on-mlcvs-founding-story.

213 *The unique formation*: "Minnesota Mining History," Minnesota Department of Natural Resources, accessed June 14, 2024, https://www.dnr.state.mn.us/education/geology/digging/history.html.

215 *Thankfully, despite the dip*: June Breneman, "How Innovation Saved the Iron Range," Natural Resources Research Institute, June 3, 2018, https://nrri.umn.edu/news/davis-taconite.

215 *It was the largest investment any company had made*: Dan Kraker, "U.S. Steel to Invest $150 Million at Minnesota Mine," MPR

News, June 28, 2022, https://www.mprnews.org/story/2022/06/28/us-steel-to-invest-150-million-at-minnesota-mine.

216 *After talking with the workers*: Jimmy Lovrien, "Tough Contract Negotiations Linger over US Steel's Keetac Celebration," *Duluth News Tribune*, October 5, 2022, https://www.duluth newstribune.com/news/local/tough-contract-negotiations-lin ger-over-us-steels-keetac-celebration.

216 *In fact, from 1960 to 2012*: Paul Kane, "20 Years after His Death, Wellstone's Beloved Iron Range Has Shifted to the Right," *Washington Post*, October 25, 2022, https://www.washingtonpost .com/politics/2022/10/25/twenty-years-after-death-wellstones-be loved-iron-range-has-shifted-right/.

217 *But it now boasts*: Reid Forgrave, "Better to Simply Not Talk Politics? Minnesota's Most Evenly Divided City Values Relationships over Winning Arguments," *Minnesota Star Tribune*, October 11, 2024, https://www.startribune.com/in-minnesotas-most-politically -evenly-divided-city-a-generational-shift/601160682.

Chapter 15: Fresh Lumber

228 *In their book,* The Great Dechurching: Jim Davis, Michael Graham, and Ryan P. Burge, *The Great Dechurching: Who's Leaving, Why Are They Going, and What Will It Take to Bring Them Back?* (Zondervan, 2023), 3.

231 *In his book* Alienated America: Timothy P. Carney, *Alienated America: Why Some Places Thrive While Others Collapse* (Harper, 2019).

232 *The Pew Research Center recently did a study*: "Modeling the Future of Religion in America," Pew Research Center, September 13, 2022, https://www.pewresearch.org/religion/2022/09/13/model ing-the-future-of-religion-in-america/.

232 *Twenty-nine percent of Americans*: Gregory A. Smith et al., "Decline of Christianity in the U.S. Has Slowed, May Have Leveled Off." *Pew Research Center*, February 26, 2025, https://www.pew

research.org/religion/2025/02/26/decline-of-christianity-in-the
-us-has-slowed-may-have-leveled-off/.

232 *Religious organizations also support*: Jeri Eckhart Queenan, Peter
Grunert, and Devin Murphy, "Elevating the Role of Faith-Inspired
Impact in the Social Sector," Bridgespan, January 28, 2021,
https://www.bridgespan.org/insights/role-of-faith-inspired-im
pact-in-the-social-sector.

Chapter 16: On the Water

240 *Sigurd Olson was a famous*: Sigurd F. Olson, *The Singing Wilderness*
(University of Minnesota Press, 1956), https://www.upress.umn
.edu/9780816629923/singing-wilderness/.

Chapter 17: Home

251 *We were here to celebrate*: Pamela Thompson, "Governor's Visit to
Northfield Highlights Small Business and Economic Expansion,"
Southernminn.com, October 28, 2022, https://www.southern
minn.com/northfield_news/news/governors-visit-to-north
field-highlights-small-business-and-economic-expansion/article
_0fe7e4e8-5628-11ed-a093-cfdba900f82e.html.

262 *We're losing trust*: "Historically Low Faith in U.S. Institutions
Continues," Gallup, July 6, 2023, https://news.gallup.com/poll
/508169/historically-low-faith-institutions-continues.aspx.

262 *It is a uniquely American problem*: "America's Trust in Its Institutions
Has Collapsed," *Economist*, April 17, 2024, https://www.econo
mist.com/united-states/2024/04/17/americas-trust-in-its-institu
tions-has-collapsed.

About the Author

S teve Grove is the CEO and publisher of the *Minnesota Star Tribune.*
Previously, he was Minnesota's commissioner of employment and
economic development. Before moving back to his home state, Grove
built a career in Silicon Valley as an executive at Google and YouTube,
most recently as the founding director of the Google News Lab and
previously as YouTube's first head of news and politics. A graduate of
Claremont McKenna College, with a master's degree from the Harvard
Kennedy School, Grove has written for several national publications
and has served as an advisor to the White House and State Department on counterterrorism strategy. Steve and his wife, Mary, are the
cofounders of Silicon North Stars, a nonprofit that helps underserved
youth find career pathways in technology. They are the proud parents
of eight-year-old twins, a yellow Lab, and two farm cats.